Bible and Theology in The Netherlands

American University Studies

Series VII
Theology and Religion

Vol. 22

PETER LANG

New York • Bern • Frankfurt am Main • Paris

Simon J. De Vries

Bible and Theology
in The Netherlands

Second Edition

PETER LANG
New York • Bern • Frankfurt am Main • Paris

Library of Congress Cataloging-in-Publication Data

De Vries, Simon John.
    Bible and theology in the Netherlands / Simon J.
De Vries.—2nd ed.
    p. cm.—(American University studies. Series VII,
Theology and religion ; vol. 22)
    Includes bibliographical references and index.
    1. Bible. O.T.—Criticism, interpretation, etc.—
Netherlands—History.   2. Reformed Church—
Netherlands—Doctrines—History.   I. Title.   II. Series:
American University studies. Series VII, Theology and
religion ; v. 22.
BS1160.D4   1989   221.6'09492—dc19   88-35055
ISBN 0-8204-1052-7   CIP
ISSN 0740-0446

CIP-Titelaufnahme der Deutschen Bibliothek

DeVries, Simon J.:
Bible and theology in the Netherlands / Simon
J. DeVries. — 2. ed. — New York; Bern; Frank-
furt am Main; Paris: Lang, 1989.
    (American University Studies; Ser. 7,
    Theology and Religion; Vol. 22)
    ISBN 0-8204-1052-7

NE: American University Studies / 07

First Edition, 1968, by H. Veenman & Zonen N.V.,
Wageningen, The Netherlands (Cahiers bij het
Nederlands Theologisch Tijdschrift, No. 3) © by Simon J. De Vries

© Peter Lang Publishing, Inc., New York 1989

Printed by Weihert-Druck GmbH, Darmstadt, West Germany

In memory of James Muilenburg

Table of Contents

viii

Preface

It was with the purpose of holding up an especially instructive historical model of the origin, progress and resolution of the Scripture problem that I first published this work in 1968. The decision to republish it seems appropriate precisely because the fundamentalistic polemic has not subsided, but has increased in virulence while gaining a measure of respectability during the two decades since that date. It is important to show, now once again, that there is no scientific respectability and no validity in an otiose ideology that simply ignores the results of the long struggle through which the church at large has passed.

To the educated and unbiased mind, the only tenable theological hermeneutic toward the end of this twentieth century is one that fully allows for the human factor and employs humanistic tools precisely with the purpose and expectation of confronting Scripture with a greater clarity and, at the same time, with a more willing responsiveness. It is ironic that biblical criticism is being vehemently denounced just at a time when a respectful but insistent criticism has achieved full theological legitimacy. One thing that one should call to special prominence in the ongoing discussion with those who continue to polemicize against biblical criticism is the gross *anachronism* in which they have placed themselves. They are fighting a battle lost a century ago; this is not a new debate but an old and familiar one. Biblical criticism no longer deserves to be tagged as the tool of unbelieving rationalism and nihilistic radicalism, for it has been embraced within all the mainline Protestant churches, by official Catholicism, and by progressive Judaism.

This book draws heavily on my Union Theological Seminary Th.D. dissertation, "One Hundred Years of Dutch Old Testament Study," yet it constitutes a fresh rewriting rather than an expansive revision of it. As published by the H. Veenman company under the auspices of a distinguished theological journal, it was no longer an academic exercise. I was now writing for scholars, theologians and church leaders, rather than for my teachers, and my book was designed at the same time as a substantial apologia for my own intellectual growth and my conversion to an essentially different religious stance. Reared in Reformed orthodoxy, I was expressing my conviction that (1) the Bible must be studied critically, with rules of interpretation derived from itself and modern science rather than from an arbitrary construct imposed from church authority or from a dogmatic tradition; and (2) that in the end, theology gains in depth, maturity and relevance precisely from the rigorous application of this method. Observing this at work among nineteenth-century Dutch biblical scholars and theologians, I was able to appropriate it fruitfully for my own career as a scholar and theologian.

There have been three special considerations in the decision to republish this book: (1) the fact that its account of the battle over Scripture in one time and place continues to be instructive for other times and other places; (2) the fact that, after twenty years, it retains its status as a standard treatment of its subject; and (3) an awareness that it failed to receive an adequate exposure to the attention of the scholarly world at large.

Regarding the first consideration enough has been said. About the second consideration it may be stated that, despite ongoing research, my book has gained acceptance inside and outside Holland as an authoritative treatment of the interaction between theological speculation and biblical interpretation in opposing camps within nineteenth- and early twentieth-century Protestant Holland. Most of the forecasts made in the concluding chapter of my book have been borne out during the past twenty years. Old-style Dutch modernism has become even more decadent. A progressive liberalism -- one that maintains Scripture in reverence and authority while embracing the methods of biblical criticism — now dominates mainline Protestant theology. The rigoristic Calvinistic party has itself grown more accepting and also more appropriating. A surprise to me has been the eruption of innovative energy within Dutch Catholicism (now, alas, undergoing official repression) which occurred soon after my book was published. However, these new developments serve as an appendix to my account. What I have written about the struggle among Dutch theologians with respect to Scripture during the period from 1850 to World War I stands as a story complete in itself, and as such this story retains its usefulness as a model of ideological controversy.

The third consideration favoring republication has been the realization that it was something of a mistake to allow my treatment of Dutch criticism and theology to be published in Holland. This seemed to make sense in 1968 because the book did deal after all with Dutch scholarship and should accordingly be of special interest to the Dutch scholars themselves. Its appearance in English was no burden because English is learned as a usable language by a large segment of the Dutch population. The regrettable fact is that the market for books published in Holland is very restricted, particularly so for a learned monograph published as a supplement to a relatively obscure journal. Review copies did go out and they produced a number of favorable reviews in scholarly journals outside Holland, but few orders for copies came from outside Holland to the publisher. In a word, a work meaning to advertise Dutch scholarship to a learned readership outside Holland has not been adequately promoted outside Holland. This has led to the present arrangement with Peter Lang Publishing, Inc., for a new edition. It should be stated that Drukkerij H. Veenman & Zonen N.V. enthusiastically approves of this arrangement. This second edition reproduces the pages of the original work. There was no need to reset the virtually flawless copy and, for the reason stated above, there has been no occasion to make revisions. In response to a request from Professor Ernest Clark, I have appended a list of Dutch professors and another of doctoral dissertations at the Dutch universities in the area of Old Testament studies for the years under consideration.

The dedication of the original book was to Professor James Muilenburg, my teacher and the recognized leader of American biblical scholarship in his time, also himself of Dutch-American origin. The new dedication is to his memory, for he is long departed to his eternal rest.

Simon J. De Vries
August 26, 1988

ABBREVIATIONS

AWCC	*Algemeen Weekblad voor Christendom en Cultuur*
BWAT	*Beiträge zur Wissenschaft vom Alten Testament*
GB	*Godgeleerde Bijdragen*
GTT	*Gereformeerde Theologisch Tijdschrift*
JQR	*Jewish Quarterly Review*
JWT	*Jaarboek voor Wetenschappelijke Theologie*
LAMMNL	*Levensberichten van Afgestorven Medeleden van de Maatschappij der Nederlandsche Letterkunde*
NJWT	*Nieuwe Jaarboeken voor Wetenschappelijke Theologie*
NTS	*Nieuwe Theologische Studiën*
NwTT	*Nieuw Theologisch Tijdschrift*
SWV	*Stemmen voor Waarheid en Vrede*
TS	*Theologische Studiën*
TT	*Theologisch Tijdschrift*
TTT	*Teyler's Theologisch Tijdschrift*
VoxTh	*Vox Theologica*
ZAW	*Zeitschrift für die alttestamentliche Wissenschaft*
ZDMG	*Zeitschrift der deutschen morgenländischen Gesellschaft*

Chapter One

The Special Interest of Dutch

Old Testament Study

THE RELATIONSHIP OF BIBLICAL INTERPRETATION TO EUROPEAN THEOLOGICAL MOVEMENTS SINCE THE REFORMATION

Throughout the history of the Christian church, theology has been constantly linked to the development of improved methods of biblical interpretation. In the early church, for example, Marcion's heresy was intimately related to his truncated canon: on the one hand, his peculiar characterization of the Christian God necessitated a repudiation of such biblical writings as were in his view tainted with Hebraism, while on the other hand he employed the Bible that remained after he had made his excisions in such a way as to substantiate his notion of God. Later, the medieval church supported both its scholastic rationalizations and its mystical speculations upon the allegorical exegesis popularized by the early fathers. The Protestant Reformation, in its time, produced a theology of grace depending on a new doctrine of Scripture, wherein it was insisted not only that the Bible rather than tradition must be the supreme religious authority, but also that the only legitimate way of interpreting the Bible must be in accordance with its literal grammatical meaning.

The revival of humanistic learning that produced the Renaissance also became a powerful influence leading to the Reformation. Inasmuch as the Renaissance simultaneously inspired the principles of historical-critical inquiry, one might have expected that the Reformation should logically have moved to widespread application of these principles to the Bible. Actually, the first stirrings toward such a method emerged within the Catholic church of the late middle ages. Its beginnings are seen in the work of the St. Victor scholars during the twelfth century, continuing in the fourteenth century writings of Nicolas of Lyra, the follower of the incomparable Rashi. The fifteenth and early sixteenth centuries produced a whole group of humanistic scholars, including Valla, Gansfort, Colet, Lefèvre, and Erasmus, each of whom contributed substantially to the development of a grammatical-historical understanding of Scripture.

This was a fruit of humanistic inquiry which was, however, allowed to bear little immediate fruit, whether in Catholic or in Protestant circles.

It is true that the new critical spirit did enable Luther, Calvin, and other Reformers to practice a remarkable degree of freedom, as judged by medieval standards, in interpreting the Bible,[1] but neither they nor their successors were in a position to carry a recognition of Scripture's historical and cultural conditioning to its logical consequences. The cause for this is not hard to find. The pressing interest of the Reformation was to use the Bible both as a weapon for purging the Catholic church of its corruption and as a bulwark for defending itself against the increasingly fiercer attacks falling upon it. The pressing interest of the Catholic Counter-Reformation was to use the Bible in a similar way and to an identical purpose: to refute the Reformation and to vindicate its own dogmatic position. Although Catholicism placed tradition alongside Scripture as a source of authority, both sides felt the imperative need for an infallible and impregnable Word of God in the Bible. Neither side felt sufficiently self-assured, at least during the Reformation period, to tolerate such humanistic impulses as might seem to threaten the absolutely divine character of Scripture. Thus, as ecclesiastical and dogmatic controversies raged between Protestants and Catholics, or between Lutherans, Calvinists, Anglicans, and Anabaptists, the nascent historical understanding of the Bible produced by the humanistic awakening came nigh to dying in its cradle.

Eventually, though, both Protestant and Catholic theology were forced to make some accommodation to humanistic interest in the study of the Bible. Its claims proved irresistible. During the sixteenth and early seventeenth centuries, natural science and geographical exploration were causing drastic revisions in the traditional notion of biblical cosmology. The tools of literary criticism that were being employed with devastating effect in respect to the classic literature were beginning to be used on the Bible. Empirical and rationalistic theories were challenging the Thomistic foundations of the theistic *Weltanschauung* assumed by Catholics and Protestants, by implication calling into question the traditional dogma of the supernatural origin of Scripture.

Because the post-Reformation churches were not immediately prepared to acknowledge the humanistic approach to Scripture, religion came to suffer serious losses. The Catholics were particular adamant, and continued longest in their opposition. They vehemently cast out historical criticism as a bastard child for the church's enemies to rear, with the result that as the child came to full growth it often waged fierce warfare

1 See, e.g., J. T. McNeill, 'The Significance of the Word of God for Calvin,' *Church History*, XXVIII (1959), 140–145; J. Pelikan, *Luther the Expositor*, St. Louis, 1959.

against the church. We see this struggle from the Catholic side in the work of the Inquisition, which burned the *Praeadamitae* of Isaac de Peyrère (1592–1676), who called the Mosaic authorship of the Pentateuch into question. Bossuet similarly consigned to the flames the *Histoire critique du Vieux Testament* of Richard Simon (1638–1712), forcing him and others like him to publish their works outside France in the more hospitable environment of Protestant Holland. Thus the Catholic church declared war on historical criticism, and historical criticism has in turn attacked the claims of Catholicism. Only in the present century has Rome learned its error, professing at long last a willingness to make room for a reverent criticism of the Bible.[2]

Early Protestantism, on its part, made few concessions to historical criticism until such a time as its dogmatic controversies began to subside and until philosophical rationalism began to influence Protestant scholars. It is significant that a gradual undermining of Protestant dogmatism went hand in hand with a freer approach to the Bible. This is to be seen in the tactics of Thomas Hooker (1553–1600) of England in opposing the biblicism of his Puritan opponents, in the development of new methods of Bible interpretation carried on by Grotius (1583–1645) and Cocceius (1609–69) as they took advantage of theological shifts in Holland, and in the work of Calixtus (1586–1656) and Spener (1635–1705) in Germany in their attacks on the foundations of Lutheran orthodoxy. Traditionalists frantically but unsuccessfully labored to refute new insights produced by biblical research, as for instance the revolutionary theories of Louis Cappel (1585–1658) regarding the medieval origin of the Masoretic vowel points in the Hebrew text. The progress of historical criticism could not be held back. For a while, orthodoxy did succeed in resisting various radical challenges to its supernaturalistic system. Accordingly, Bishop Robert Lowth's pioneer work on Hebrew poetry (1753), so important in its influence on later research, found acceptance in the more progressive Protestant circles, as did so soberly critical an analysis of the Old Testament as that of Johann Eichhorn in his *Einleitung* (1780–83), while, on the other hand, deistic treatments of the New Testament miracle-stories were found to be generally offensive and the appearance of the notorious *Wolfenbüttel Fragments* of Reimarus (1774–78) created great scandal throughout the Protestant church.

The heyday of humanistic criticism arrived during a period when

2 See J. Steinmann, *Richard Simon et les origines de l'exegese biblique*, Paris, 1959; J. Levie, *The Bible, Word of God in the Words of Men* (New York, 1964), pp. 3–199.

liberal Protestantism had all but sold itself into the hands of religion's enemies. This was during the nineteenth century, when a mechanistic view of the universe gained wide acceptance among advanced thinkers, being buttressed on the one side by materialistic scientism and on the other side by positivistic rationalism. This was a traumatic period for Christian theology. The biological theories of Darwin joined hands with the philosophies of Hegel, Comte, and Feuerbach to virtually drive God out of the universe. Before such powerful forces Protestant traditionalism crumbled. There seemed to be no viable choice except between a rigidly defensive obscurantism and complete capitulation. Thus the radical views regarding the Bible that managed to gain ascendance during this period were essentially rationalistic, inescapably and immensely destructive of the supernaturalistic view of the origin of Scripture on which the church's entire dogmatic system had been erected. The great pace-setting works in New Testament criticism, such as those written by Ferdinand C. Baur(1792–1860) and David F. Strauss (1808–74), not only challenged traditional views of literary origins but threatened the dogmas of orthodox Christology at their very roots. Meanwhile, the definitive works in Old Testament criticism, particularly those of Julius Wellhausen and his school, abolished the view that Israel's sacred books were the product of a divine revelation, explaining the origin of biblical religion purely on the basis of natural development.

In this twentieth century, the Christian churches, Protestant and Catholic, are happily approaching a creative synthesis between the claims of religion and the claims of science as applied to the Bible and theology. As in other ages, these latter two prove to go hand in hand. The positivistic claims of scientific naturalism are now breaking down, allowing an authentic theological understanding to emerge that offers the possibility of integrating scientific research into a God-centered universe. Disillusionment with the possibilities of science and the claims of reason has had much to do with this theological revival, as has also a more realistic analysis of human nature through the techniques of personality analysis, but one of its most basic preconditions has been the church's belated willingness to take historical criticism into its bosom.

Within the area of biblical criticism itself, several new methods have tended toward the opening up of this new possibility. Perhaps one of the most significant of these has been the emergence of a truly biblical theology, i.e., one in which the Bible, as understood in terms both of its historical development and theological claims, has been allowed to determine Christian teaching, taking the place of the traditional approach, in which dogma has generally forced Scripture to support it at whatever cost. In other words, the Bible has regained its rightful place of sovereignty. It is important to emphasize that the historical understanding of the Bible is the result of applying scientific criticism to it, of accepting as a friend the church's erstwhile mortal enemy. It is both ironic and heartening that this bitter foe has proven to be theology's truest friend, creating a new opportunity for the church as it seeks to confront a disillusioned world with its gospel. Historical criticism has come home to the church, whose real daughter it has proven itself to be.[1]

A SIGNIFICANT OPPORTUNITY FOR HISTORICAL INQUIRY

In the light of the preceding outline, it seems clear that theological speculation and biblical interpretation are indeed inseparable. They have never lived alone; each has constantly influenced the other for good or for ill. A problem that is particularly intriguing for the historian is the exact nature of the relationship between the two, but the theologian and the biblical critic also have a vital interest in it. Which of the twins comes first from the womb? Is it theology that shapes biblical interpretation, or interpretation that determines theology? Inasmuch as the church universally gives at least lip-service to the Scriptures as the source and norm of its theology, the answer might seem apparent. But our survey has shown that historically the problem has not been so simple. We recall that every sect and every heresy has been able to appeal to the Bible for support, managing to find proof-texts for all it has desired to teach. In actuality, the relationship is far more complex than the theory would seem to allow.

The modern period, and particularly the nineteenth century, has echoed with repeated claims of objectivity regarding methods of biblical interpretation, but if there is any point in which the present century needs to be sharply critical of the previous ones, it is precisely here. We now see that those who proclaimed the most loudly their complete scientific objectivity were actually the most blinded by their own bias. Today, as theology looks in hope to the future, it urgently needs to be aware of, to acknowledge, and to make appropriate compensation for its own pre-

---

1 Cf. G. Ebeling, 'The Significance of the Critical Historical Method for Church and Theology in Protestantism,' *Word and Faith* (Philadelphia, 1963), pp. 17–61.

conditioning, for only thus can it know what it truly is, which forces have made it what it is, and where it is headed.

It would be most instructive if we could make precise cause-and-effect calculations of the relationship between theology and biblical interpretation in a carefully defined historical context. The trouble is that we are able to find very few situations in which a simple relationship of this sort can be traced. Not only is there a constant feedback between the two factors within a given cultural environment, or even in the thinking of a particular individual, but we know that influences in one country or culture have an effect on other countries or cultures. This is, of course, particularly true where scholarship has the opportunity of easy communication, where there exists wide dissemination of ideas, as has generally been the case in western Europe since the discovery of printing. Still, barriers of language and of national prejudice have often worked to counteract these influences. While in western Europe no modern nation has succeeded in completely isolating itself, there have been certain areas where prejudice has been strong and where resistance to outside influences has enjoyed at least a degree of success.

If one were to undertake the study of the relationship between theology and biblical interpretation in a cultural environment which has been sealed off from outside influences for long periods, one might turn first to such a country as Portugal, where the monopolistic church has been rigid and monolithic, and where new religious notions have been systematically suppressed. The difficulty is, from the point of view of the problem which we have defined, that this particular combination has clearly led to a sterile traditionalism. Thus the lesson that we may learn from post-Reformation Portugal is that without the constant cross-fertilization of new ideas, intellectual activity virtually ceases. We need to look, therefore, for a situation in which there has been constant receptivity to theological influences from without but comparatively little opportunity to communicate to the outside world. Here we could expect to observe a peculiar but most instructive kind of cultural inbreeding. We could expect to see the direct effect of new ideas, originating both from within and from without, creating a ferment whose main impact would be confined within the cultural enclave because the outside world would be so little aware of it.

A situation that fits this prescription is that which is found in the interplay of theology and biblical interpretation in The Netherlands during the crucial years between ca. 1850 and the first World War. Here we may observe the kind of frenetic talking to oneself that results from the combination of intense intellectual activity and a one-way communication from the outside world. Because of their peculiar kind of isolation during this particular period, Dutch biblical scholars and theologians were forced to converse mainly one with another. But most assuredly they were talking to one another. They were constantly entertaining and creating new ideas; and while the outside world payed little attention, they at times threatened to tear one another to pieces in the vehemence of their internal controversies.[1]

HOLLAND'S CULTURAL HERITAGE

But no one can begin to comprehend the intensity of this ferment or its effect unless he first understands something of the grandeur of Holland's scholarly tradition. Always The Netherlands has been open to international culture. During the late middle ages, it established for itself the distinction of being a foremost center of humanistic learning, second only to Italy. It produced a 'reformation before the Reformation' in the work of Rudolf Agricola (1400–1470), Wessel Gansfort (1419–1489), and other scholars and religious leaders associated with the Brethren of the Common Life. Its greatest humanistic scholar – and also Europe's greatest – was Desiderius Erasmus (1466–1536), who, while remaining loyal to Rome, became a prime mover in the early intellectual revival, influencing the Protestant as much as the Catholic church.

Quickly the Reformation swept the Netherlands. As the forces of the Counter-Reformation drove Protestants and free-thinkers first from Italy and Spain, next from Belgium, the Rhineland, and central Germany, and eventually from France, this little country became an asylum not only for religious refugees but for all sorts of intellectuals. During the Eighty Years' War (1568–1648), the Dutch were hard pressed to survive in the face of Spanish Catholic power, but when at last their bitter struggle came to a victorious conclusion, the United Netherlands emerged into a golden period of religious and cultural freedom. This was the Holland that reared a distinguished succession of theologians, among them Arminius (1560–1609), Grotius, and Cocceius. Here also such advanced thinkers as Descartes (1596–1650) and Spinoza (1632–1677) found refuge. As the Inquisition suppressed free publication in the lands

1 This is a subject that has nowhere received extensive study except in the writer's unpublished doctoral dissertation, 'A Hundred Years of Dutch Old Testament Study,' Union Theological Seminary, New York, 1958.

to the south and east, Holland took its place alongside of and at times surpassing England as the print-shop of Europe, a country where free thought had at least a chance to be heard.

The establishment of Holland's leading cultural centers is associated with her fight for religious and political freedom. One of the turning-points of her struggle against Spain was the siege of Leiden in 1573. This event proved to have cultural as well as political consequences inasmuch as Prince William of Orange saw fit to reward the citizens of Leiden for their heroic resistance by offering to establish a university in their midst. Previously having been convinced of his country's need for a university of its own, he wisely chose this opportunity both for stimulating his country-men's patriotism and for laying the groundwork for Holland's future cultural progress free from foreign domination. Thus the University of Leiden was opened in 1575, and soon attracted some of Europe's most distinguished scholars, such as Joseph Scaliger (1540–1609) and Francis-cus Junius (1545–1602), to its faculty. From the time of its small be-ginnings, this university has continued to enjoy the ardent support of the citizens of The Netherlands and has risen to a place of eminence among Europe's leading schools.

Soon after Leiden founded its university, other Dutch cities followed suit by establishing academies or 'Illustrious Schools,' the most important of which were at Franeker (1585), Groningen (1614), Amsterdam (1632), Utrecht (1634), and Harderwijk (1648). Several of these schools sub-sequently developed into universities rivalling Leiden's, and have come to play an important role in the cultural development of the Dutch nation.

THE INGREDIENTS OF AN INSTRUCTIVE SITUATION

It is not our purpose to review the cultural history of The Netherlands in all of its details, but only to suggest by the above facts that this little country possesses a deeply rooted heritage of religious and cultural freedom. Intellectual activity has always been honored here. At the same time, however, the Dutch have been handicapped by their country's small size and linguistic isolation. Holland lies in a cross-current of inter-national influences, politically, commercially, and culturally. It has had no opportunity to develop into a strong and self-sufficient power, like its neighbors Britain, Germany, and France, since neither industry nor agriculture has been able to provide for its economic needs. Thus it has become largely a nation of carriers and tradesmen for the other lands of Europe. Amsterdam and particularly Rotterdam have become important transit points for all of western Europe. This has had a cultural effect. Holland has proved itself to be receptive to thoughts and movements originating in other lands, and through its universities and publishing houses has served to communicate them throughout the world. By way of this constant intellectual and spiritual stimulation, it has been kept continually fertile in producing an important share of the great ideas of modern civilization.

Nevertheless, scholarship in other lands has not always paid attention to what was being created in Holland. Part of this has been due to unvarnished chauvinism, but a major barrier has also been the relative unfamiliarity of the Dutch language, of which Netherlanders have been understandably proud and which they have employed for much of their writing, but which few Germans, French, or English have felt it worthwhile to study. By necessity, every university graduate in The Netherlands must master the leading modern languages; it is for him the mark of culture, and without it his nation cannot survive. But only a very few outside Holland can call themselves masters of the Dutch language.

So long as classical norms of scholarship continued to prevail throughout Europe, this disadvantage did not produce its full effect. That is, many of the most serious scholarly works were written in Latin, which theologians everywhere understood. Only popular-devotional books and such as were addressed to internal ecclesiastical controversies were written in Dutch. For this reason, Dutch scholars and theologians were read by all cultured men, while the former actually enjoyed the advantage of being so close to the influential Dutch publishing houses.

This all began to change during the nineteenth century, when, for reasons that will be discussed below, Latin fell into disuse and Dutch came to be employed even for the most technical subjects.[1] It may be only a coincidence that the latter half of this century was also the period of Holland's greatest productivity in applying the methods of a fully developed historical criticism to the Bible under the towering leadership of Abraham Kuenen, the great Leiden scholar. The result was that during this period of linguistic isolation, Dutch scholarship was immensely productive, but was able to communicate only a meagre portion of this

[1] After ca. 1850 doctoral dissertations began to appear in the Dutch language rather than in Latin. Most other kinds of books made the shift considerably earlier.

productivity to the outside world[1]. The situation has changed during the twentieth century, particularly since World War I, inasmuch as Dutch biblical scholars have come to write many of their most serious works in English, French, or German, but unfortunately this century has produced no biblical scholar in Holland to match Kuenen either in genius or in persuasive power.

It is from this peculiar combination of circumstances that we may hope to learn something significant concerning the complex interrelationships between theology and biblical interpretation. In The Netherlands since 1850 we can observe the effects of a powerful invasion of radical new ideas, combined in the work of the leading biblical critics with immense creativeness, but because of linguistic isolation directed mainly inward. Within the Dutch church the effect was that of an irresistible force meeting a seemingly immovable object. The Dutch Calvinists had developed a dogmatic system excelled in rigidity only by that of the Roman church; it is little wonder that when a powerful humanistic criticism fell upon it, it did not bend but was virtually shattered.

Seizing this opportunity, we intend in the following discussion to attempt three things: (1) to outline, against the background of contemporary intellectual and ecclesiastical debate, the major theological movements in The Netherlands previous to and following 1850, bringing this forward to the early years of this century; (2) to enter with considerable detail into a description and critical analysis of the development of Dutch biblical criticism during this same period, in order to provide a thoroughly grounded basis for valid conclusions regarding the relationship between theology and exegesis; (3) to show the implications of this analysis not only for Dutch scholarship in one period, but for the entire ongoing theological endeavor throughout the world.

We shall find it necessary, however, to restrict our account of biblical criticism mainly to the Old Testament and closely related fields. Ideally, this should be broadened to include the New Testament, but the necessity of providing a truly in-depth analysis, while keeping this within

1 In the bibliography to the author's dissertation (supra), over 1350 strictly scholarly books, monographs, and articles dealing with the interpretation of the Old Testament and related subjects are listed. These appeared in The Netherlands between 1850 and 1950, and signify an amazing productivity for so small a country (in 1892 the population of The Netherlands was 4,600,000). Virtually all these titles are in Dutch, and translations have been made of only a few of the very most important. How little scholarship in other lands has been aware of this work may be judged from such facts as the following: R. H. Pfeiffer's voluminous *Introduction to the Old Testament* (New York, 1948) mentions only eight Dutch scholars among approximately nine hundred cited; H. H. Rowley, ed., *The Old Testament and Modern Study* (Oxford, 1951), mentions only one Hollander for

manageable limits, demands at least such a degree of selectivity. Gener-
alizations will be of little value in the kind of study contemplated here.
As can be seen from the preceding outline, theology and exegesis do
affect each other – a readily acknowledged impression to which generalization can add little. What we need is massive detail with relevant
interpretation. This we hope to provide on the basis of extensive study
of numerous documents of various kinds within the area chosen.

In any event, it is our intention, while reviewing the development of
biblical criticism in this particular area, to keep an eye upon parallel
developments in the field of New Testament exegesis, but this must
remain incidental and secondary.

It is a point of interest that Abraham Kuenen, the great Dutch critic
mentioned above, actually began his teaching career as professor of New
Testament interpretation, and only gradually abandoned this field in
favor of his greater love, the study of the Old Testament. We may wonder
what nineteenth-century Dutch New Testament criticism might have
become had Kuenen devoted his full strength to it, influencing it to the
extent that he influenced Old Testament criticism. As we shall see,
Kuenen possessed a stature equalled by no Dutch New Testament
scholar of his time. He enjoyed an influence not only within all progressive groups in Holland, but abroad as well, in the scholarly world at
large – and this in spite of the barrier of language. By comparison, New
Testament study in Holland, even in its most fervid period, was feeble
and ineffective. While it remained sterile and traditionalistic on the
orthodox side, under modernist auspices it became radical beyond all
the realm of reason, serving mainly as a monument of misguided eru-
dition. It possessed neither the logic nor the wisdom to make any lasting
impact on Dutch theology, let alone penetrate beyond the country's
borders.[2] In a word, great leadership in the one field, and the lack of
it in the other, made a striking difference, and we shall be justified in
choosing the one over the other as our area of special attention.

every thirty names; H. J. Kraus, *Geschichte der historisch-kritischen Erforschung des Alten
Testaments von der Reformation bis zur Gegenwart* (Neukirchen, 1956), lists six Dutch
authors among a total of approximately 550.

2 As we note lack of attention to Dutch Old Testament study outside The Netherlands
(cf. n. 1), we are impressed even more by how little Dutch New Testament criticism has
come to the attention of chroniclers of this field of study. Thus, e.g., one will find not the
slightest mention of the radical Dutch New Testament school – the nineteenth century's
most noteworthy and productive – either in Albert Schweitzer, *The Quest of the Historical
Jesus* (London, 1910), or in Stephen Neill, *The Interpretation of the New Testament, 1861–
1961* (London, 1964).

Chapter Two

Church and Theology in The Netherlands

During the Nineteenth Century

THE DUTCH CHURCH BEFORE 1850

As elsewhere in Europe, the first half of the nineteenth century was a time of increasing nationalism in The Netherlands. There can be little doubt that it was this force, coupled with a growing sense of modernity, that gradually led Dutch scholars to employ their own language in their technical communications. The Dutch people generally were as disillusioned with international affairs as were many of their European neighbors, thus may have deluded themselves at this time into thinking that it did not matter very much whether foreign scholars understood what they were thinking and writing.

Eighteenth-century Holland had been a republic in name, but had been mainly ruled by a line of *stadhouders* from the family of Orange in conjunction with a bourgeois oligarchy. In 1795 the last of the *stadhouders* was compelled to flee to England while a short-lived Batavian Republic, modelled on the lines of the French Revolution, took over. Ere long this patriot administration was absorbed into the expanding Napoleonic empire. For a while Napoleon's brother, Louis, ruled as puppet king, but eventually the country was completely integrated into the French domain. Netherlanders remember this era as one of the lowest points in their history, comparable in many respects to the time of Nazi domination in World War II.

In 1813 the son of the last *stadhouder* was able to enter The Netherlands with Prussian troops, and soon assumed the title of Holland's first king, being known as William I. By temperament and circumstances, William developed a virtually autocratic rule which continued to resist democratic demands until after his abdication in 1840. William II attempted for a few years to continue his father's absolute rule, but soon came to see the wisdom of allowing a constitutional monarchy, and accepted a new constitution in 1848. Since that date, Holland has developed a prime-minister type of government, with the monarch continuing as executive

1 All the standard histories of The Netherlands give these details, e.g., Vlekke, *Evolution of the Dutch Nation* (New York, 1945), chaps. xi and xii.
2 J. H. Mackay describes the spirit within the Dutch churches immediately following the Napoleonic era (*Religious Thought in Holland During the Nineteenth Century*, London, 1911, pp. 20f): 'There was a good deal of fraternization among the churches, partly due,

aided by a cabinet of ministers. Through the gradual extension of the franchise, The Netherlands has become one of modern Europe's most progressive democracies.

It is important to point out that the period between the end of the Napoleonic wars and the middle of the century was a time of deep apathy in Holland. The nation not only submitted to paternalistic rule, but was comparatively sterile in every area of economic and cultural enterprise. Commerce, science, art, literature, theology – all alike languished. Only as the second half of the century began were there significant stirrings of a new intellectual and cultural life.[1]

One needs to understand something of the church situation in this period. It was a Calvinistic Reformation that finally triumphed in The Netherlands, and in accordance with the ideas of the time, Calvinism became the official religion of the independent Dutch state. Previous to the nineteenth century the old name Nederlandsche Gereformeerde Kerk was usually applied to this state church, but gradually a slightly different title, Nederduitsch Hervormd, came into use. Since 1816 the name has been Nederlands(ch)e Hervormde Kerk.

In the beginnings, this state church was largely subsidized by the government and was to an extent controlled by it. At the Synod of Dordt (1618–19) it came to be organized nationally upon a strictly presbyterian order, but dependence upon and control by the government were not eliminated. During the time of the Batavian Republic and French domination, the church's established status was severely threatened, but was restored, with modifications, upon the return of the house of Orange. This intimate connection with the civil rule has created peculiar problems for the Hervormde Kerk, as we shall see.

In the beginning, the state church was intolerant of other groups. The Lutherans, who preceded the Calvinists into Holland, were not molested, but the same cannot be said of the Anabaptists and Catholics. Especially after the successful completion of the Eighty-Year's War, the Catholic religion was put under the ban, and after the Synod of Dordt the Remonstrants (Arminians) were for a while similarly suppressed.

In the course of time, however, tolerance for other church groups increased so that, in the early part of the nineteenth century, there prevailed a general freedom of religion.[2] The Mennonites (Doopsgezin-

at first, to revolutionary ideas, but more so to the indefiniteness of the reigning theology. Church union was in the air. Reformed, Remonstrant, and Lutheran clergymen preached in one another's pulpits, and societies were formed outside the churches to further a variety of philanthropic objects. It was well known that in the Dutch Reformed Church the old leaven of Calvinistic doctrine was still working in the minds of a section

den) and Remonstrants exercised full rights as recognized denominations. The Jewish religion was likewise tolerated. New sects had arisen, but remained of minor importance. Even the Roman Catholic religion won a degree of freedom during the French period, although it was not fully recognized by Dutch Protestants until toward the end of the century. Meanwhile, the Hervormde Kerk continued to enjoy a privileged status in spite of these changes, retaining a vast majority of the population in its organization.[1]

As has been stated, the Hervormde Kerk had been organized according to a strict presbyterian system. At the Synod of Dordt the church reaffirmed the *Heidelberg Catechism* and the *Belgic Confession* as statements of its doctrine, together with its *Canons* against the Remonstrants. By this means it officially committed itself to a strict Calvinistic faith. It did not prove easy for it to enforce adherence to these standards, however. During the two centuries from 1619 to 1816, repeated conflicts arose as various church leaders and theologians attempted to gain freedom for a broader belief. Notwithstanding, the church generally succeeded in enforcing conformity, and only to a minor degree did anyone succeed in gaining tolerance for ideas contrary to a rigid interpretation of the decisions of Dordt.

When William I mounted the throne the old order of things, also for the church, rapidly changed. The king introduced an *Algemeene Reglement* which was a radical departure from the Dordt church order. This was to become the major source of friction and schism within the Hervormde Kerk for the next hundred years. The introduction of this *Reglement* (1816) may be attributed to three circumstances: the despotic temperament of the king, the apathy of church leaders, and the humiliating dependence of the church upon the government for its subsidies. By the time William came to power the church was badly demoralized and disorganized. Thus, when the king very abruptly promulgated his *Reglement*, with secret consultation of only a select group of advisers, the church accepted it with feeble protest.

This new church order involved, primarily, the substitution of a continuing, government-controlled hierarchy in the place of the previous presbyterian system. Neither the lay members nor the ministers were to

of the people, especially in the villages and in the farm-houses, and the watchword of the party of so-called enlightenment was to proceed cautiously... It was hoped that before very long... the sword of ecclesiastical controversy would be returned for ever to its scabbard, and in Holland's green and pleasant land, all would unite in one church in working for the common weal.'

1 Sources for the history of the Dutch denominations are J. Reitsma and J. Lindeboom,

have a voice in the management of church affairs, for the General Synod and its executive committee were to be appointed by the Crown. Church control would be placed in the hands of a bureau of the government, the Ministry of Religion.[2] This *Reglement* continued in effect without substantial changes until 1867.

One of its most disruptive features was its ambiguous doctrinal subscription. There had been no doubt of what was required of church officers in subscribing to the doctrinal formularies, so long as the decrees of Dordt continued in force. Now, however, the subscription had been framed to read as follows: 'We accept in good faith and heartily believe the doctrine, which, in agreement with the Word of God, is contained in the Formularies of Unity of the Nederlandsche Hervormde Kerk.' It was the words, 'in agreement with...', which occasioned the difficulty. The change might appear insignificant, but in fact it led to violent controversy lasting for many years. The strict orthodox, determined on enforcing sound doctrine, insisted that these words meant that the doctrine of the creeds actually was in accordance with the Word of God *(quia)*; the liberal party, and particularly those of the Groningen school, which will be described presently, argued that one was only required to subscribe to the doctrine insofar as it agreed with the Word of God *(quatenus)*. The former seemed to have the exegetical advantage, but some who had been consulted in the actual framing of the *Reglement* stoutly maintained that the reading was deliberately intended to be ambiguous so as to give room for the more liberal position.

The Synod of the Hervormde Kerk decided to defer trying to judge between these two positions 'until better times, when they should have more light.' But this equivocation satisfied neither party, with the result that in 1841 a liberal formula came to be adopted which required ministerial candidates to subscribe to church doctrine only in its essence and substance. Naturally, the rigorists were more unhappy than ever with this formula, and many of them came to believe that the only way to get purity of doctrine was to withdraw from the church. Some of the liberals, on the other hand, accepted this as a challenge to redefine Reformed doctrine in the light of modern thought.[3]

Geschiedenis van de Hervorming en de Hervormde Kerk, 4th ed., 1934 (cited as Reitsma); 5th ed., 1949; L. Knappert, *Geschiedenis der Hervormde Kerk onder de Republiek en het Koninkrijk der Nederlanden*, 2 vols., Amsterdam, 1912; *idem, Godsdienstig Nederland*, Huis ter Heide, 1928; Th. Delleman, *Kerken in Nederland*, Aalten, 1947.

2 For details cf. Reitsma, pp. 448–54.

3 For a more complete description of these controversies, see Reitsma, pp. 454ff, 477ff; also Mackay, *op. cit.*, pp. 39–42.

MAJOR THEOLOGICAL MOVEMENTS BEFORE 1850

In this time, immediately before the rise of the Dutch modernist school, public interest in religion was generally quite satisfactory, as was evidenced by the wide reading of religious literature. J. H. van der Palm's Bible translation and *Kinderbijbel* were popular, and the various religious periodicals had a good following. There were the *Godgeleerde Bijdragen*, begun in 1827; *Waarheid in Liefde*, organ of the Groningen school, begun in 1837; the *Jaarboeken voor Wetenschappelijke Theologie*, begun in 1845. *De Gids*, begun in the same year, and *De Tijdspiegel*, begun the year before, although not restricted to religious topics, were both heavily theological. Hendrik Oort, a biographer of Kuenen, writes: 'It was a churchy, good-naturedly religious period; in most circles the fear of rigid orthodoxy was surpassed by revulsion for "unbelief," that is, for whatever did insufficient justice to the trustworthiness of the biblical narratives.'[1] An indication of the temper of this period was the fact that everywhere, even in the most progressive theological circles, Strauss's *Leben Jesu* (1835) was repudiated as scandalous heresy.

There were three major movements in early nineteenth-century Dutch theology: 'old liberalism,' the Groningen school, and the *Réveil*. Each of these is of sufficient importance to require a brief description.[2]

After 1816 a group of theologians arose in Holland who adopted some of the principles of rationalism together with modern views of science, without, however, making a break with traditional theology. This was the group that has been called the 'old liberals.' They were the direct predecessors of the modernists in Holland, though far more conservative than them. Some of their leading spokesmen were H. Muntinghe, professor at Groningen (d. 1824), H. H. Donker Curtius, minister at Arnhem (d. 1828), L. Egeling, minister at Leiden (d. 1835), and P. van der Willigen, minister at Tiel (d. 1847). Sympathetic with the views of this group was van der Palm, since 1796 the younger Schultens's successor in biblical exegesis at Leiden (d. 1840). These churchmen and

---

1 'Kuenen als godgeleerde.' *De Gids*, III (1893), 513f
2 The most extensive study of these movements is the dissertation of K. H. Roessingh, *De moderne theologie in Nederland, hare voorbereiding en eerste periode*, Leiden, 1914 (cited as Roessingh); see also Roessingh, *Het modernisme in Nederland*, Haarlem, 1922; J. Lindeboom, *Geschiedenis van het vrijzinnige Protestantisme*, Assen, 1935.
3 Roessingh, pp. 27f (my translation, as elsewhere in this work unless otherwise stated).
4 *ibid.*, pp. 21ff
5 *ibid.*, pp. 18ff. Mackay, *op. cit.*, pp. 17–19, explains this point: 'Tired of the scholasticism of early Dutch theology, the endless discussions of the Voetians and Cocceians, refuge was sought in a kind of Biblical theology... The Bible was regarded... as the su-

theologians were not so much influenced by the great German philosophers of the era, i.e., Kant, Fichte, and Schelling, as they were by the mediating group represented by Morus, Döderlein, and Storr (the old Tübingen school). We find the following description of their indebtedness:

Among these theologians they found the same idea of Christian doctrine as an array of saving dogmas, the same method of proof, i.e., historical-critical reasoning for the purpose of demonstrating the trustworthiness of Scripture and of the supernatural God-concept depending upon it, the same moralism, the same moderate ardor for the new age. Only these did they follow, rejecting the rest, and because of this fact Dutch theology in the first forty years of the nineteenth century manifested an entirely different and far calmer character than did German theology, where a rationalism derived from Kant was dominant. Here it was not possible to forsake a sincerely intended supernaturalism.[3]

Despite their desire to remain biblicistic and supernaturalistic, these 'old liberals' departed from church dogma in two significant points. They developed what was in effect an Arian theory of the nature of Christ, making him a supreme religious teacher and a supernatural being, but refusing him some of the distinctions of the orthodox Christology.[4] Christian doctrine, to them, was the actual teaching of Jesus, nothing less and nothing more. In their view of Scripture, moreover, they held to the supernatural origin and authority of the Bible while believing in a form of human fallibility which hardly squared with it.[5] In any case, the 'old liberals' were quite definite in rejecting the radical criticism of Scripture recently coming out of the 'new' Tübingen school of Baur and Strauss.

In the north of the land, in the city and at the university of Groningen, a most peculiar but very vigorous theological movement was arising at this same time. This was the so-called Groningen school.[6] Its leading representatives in the formative years were Professors J. F. van Oordt (d. 1852), P. Hofstede de Groot (d. 1886), and L. G. Pareau (d. 1866), together with a number of influential ministers. The first two came to

preme authority and the essence of those revelations. It["old liberalism"] did not feel the need of taking account of the relations that exist between the revelations and the world as an organic whole. It troubled itself as little about the question how miracle is in accordance with the laws of nature as about the question how inspiration is in accordance with the laws of human understanding. Thus van der Palm... is of the opinion that the stoppage of the Jordan... may have been caused by a mass of rock falling across its bed higher up its course and temporarily damming it; while the fall of the wall of Jericho might easily have been caused by the simultaneous shout from tens of thousands of throats...'
6 Roessingh, pp. 28–43, Reitsma, pp. 479ff. Cf. P. Hofstede de Groot, *De Groninger godgeleerden in hunne eigenaardigheid*, Groningen, 1855.

Groningen in 1829, Pareau in 1831. Soon it became evident that together these theologians constituted a cohesive school of thought. They established the widely read theological journal, *Waarheid in Liefde*. Throughout most of the century these 'Groningers' enjoyed extensive influence, although the middle years of the century already saw the beginning of their eclipse in the face of modernist growth.

The Groningen theology was warmly pious, frankly heterodox, and thoroughly supernaturalistic. It borrowed inspiration from a variety of sources. One of its spiritual fathers was the Utrecht philosopher P. W. van Heusde (d. 1839), known as 'Praeceptor Hollandiae.' The Groningers took from van Heusde, a Platonist, their peculiar educational theory and dialectical method. Another important source of their ideas was the teaching of Schleiermacher, Lessing, and Kant, but it was particularly the former's notion that religion must be based on feeling that influenced them. To Schleiermacher's *sensus dependentiae* they added *sensus indigentiae* and *sensus amoris* as sources of religious feeling. These latter were derived largely from the teachings of the mystical school of Ruysbroeck (the Brethren of the Common Life), which three hundred and fifty years earlier had been transplanted to Deventer in the north of Holland by Thomas Hamerken, the author of *Imitatio Christi*, and by Wessel Gansfort. The latter was actually born in Groningen. The Groningen theologians of whom we are spreaking considered this Common Life movement, and especially the work of Erasmus, who until the age of thirteen had attended the movement's school in Deventer, as the pure fountain of their teaching. Following in the mystical spirit, they emphasized love and the Christian life, rather than intellectual orthodoxy, as the mark of true discipleship.

The Groningen view of revelation was borrowed directly from Lessing and Kant. All of nature and history were, as they saw it, one great revelatory process. A special revelation centers in Christ, but this is only the kernel of the universal revelation. Thus Christianity is not an absolute religion but only one of the highest stages of revelation. Jesus did not reveal a system of doctrine but came to make men over by his personal influence. He founded a community in which men are formed and educated in heart and will to become more God-like, revealing more perfectly the divine-human nature of himself. This community of mystical fellowship

1 Cf. *ibid.*, pp. 61f.
2 Regarding the roots of the Groningen school see further Mackay, *op. cit.*, pp. 15f.
3 Roessingh explains (p. 43): 'That they, with their Christocentric theology, their non-essential but nevertheless very strong biblicism, and the supernaturalism which sprang

is the true church, rather than any particular authoritarian institution.

Central to the Groningen theology was its subordinationistic Christology. Since Christ is the fullest revelation of God, showing who God is, and what men are and are called to become, it is necessary, they believed, to go back for an understanding of Christ to the testimony of those who were under his direct influence while he was on earth. Thus the decree of Nicea must be judged as erroneous. Christ does not have two natures, but only one, which is divine and human at the same time. He was pre-existent though not eternally existent; he was born in the world miraculously; his disciples saw in him the perfect image of God and the type of perfect humanity.[1]

The Groningers were able to gain so wide a following because they were able to capitalize on the spirit of nationalism that was rampant in Holland during the post-Napoleonic period. They attempted to represent Calvinism as a foreign import, tyrannizing over what they called the truly Dutch Protestantism of Gansfort, Ruysbroeck, and Erasmus. Similarly they denounced the *Réveil*, presently to be described, as a French-Swiss import. It was inevitable that Reformed orthodoxy, allied with the *Réveil*, should meet in the Groningen school its most determined opposition. The Groningers loudly protested under the heavy yoke of Calvinistic dogmatism and did more than any other group to break its grip upon the church.[2]

Nevertheless, it was because of the centrality of Christ in their theology that the Groningers were unable to abandon their rigid biblicism. They could not see, heterodox as they were, how they could uphold their Christology apart from the entire infallibility of the biblical account. Although they did not accept the dogma of verbal inspiration, they did believe that the writers of the New Testament worked without error to provide an authentic picture of Jesus' life and teachings. Thus they too stood staunchly against the radical views of the new Tübingen criticism, and after the rise of Dutch modernism they polemicized fiercely against its denial of the supernatural.[3] Clearly, the Groningen school was no nursery of the modernist movement in The Netherlands, as some have thought, although undoubtedly their defence of doctrinal freedom did help clear the ground for its coming.

A third influential theological movement was the religious awakening

from these two, soon would belong to the adversaries of the modernist theology, speaks for itself. For them to assemble underneath this banner would have involved a betrayal of those very principles which gave warmth and life to their system and to their labors.'

called the *Réveil*.[1] It originated in French Switzerland in the early years of the nineteenth century, where it was associated primarily with the figures of Merle d'Aubigné and Cesar Malan. Spreading to many lands, it came also to the Netherlands, where it found advocates in such prominent men as Isaac da Costa (d. 1860), William Bilderdijk (d. 1831), William de Clercq (d. 1844), Abraham Capadose (d. 1874), J. A. Wormser (d. 1862), and the political leader Mr. G. Groen van Prinsterer (d. 1876). Also Nicolas Beets (d. 1903) and Daniel Chantepie de la Saussaye (d. 1874) originally adhered to this movement. The battle-cry of the *Réveil* against the rationalistic spirit of the time was clearly sounded in 1823, when da Costa published his sensational *Bezwaren tegen de geest der eeuw*. Since 1834 the movement found a literary voice in da Costa's periodical *Nederlandsche Stemmen*, whose chief aim was the cleansing of the national church from heterodox teaching and the stimulation of a spiritual revival.

The political circumstances of the time undoubtedly had an effect on the progress of this movement. We have noted how the Dutch chafed under the Napoleonic domination. The state church and the propertied classes had lost the most, and consequently were the strongest in supporting the house of Orange at its restoration. It was out of the patrician aristocracy that many of the *Réveil* leaders came. Their attempt to repristinate the orthodoxy and piety of the past had social, political, and emotional, in addition to religious, foundations.[2]

The *Réveil* was strongly pietistic, methodistic, and individualistic, though some of its adherents worked for a strengthening of the old Reformed church polity. Circles of so-called 'Christian Friends' came together in regular meetings for mutual edification and consultation. The *Réveil* assumed the form of an *ecclesiola* within the state church. After 1854, however, the 'Christian Friends' and the *Réveil* diminished in activity and importance.

---

1 See Roessingh, pp. 43–60; Reitsma pp. 464–76. For the view that the name *Réveil* should be applied to the broader national reawakening of orthodox Reformed teaching, cf. J. van Lonkhuizen, *Hermann Friedrich Kohlbrugge en zijn prediking*, Wageningen, 1905; but cf. the opposite side defended in A. Pierson, *Oudere tijdgenooten*, 2nd ed., Amsterdam, 1904.

2 Cf. Mackay, *op.cit.*, p. 23.

3 Eldred C. Vanderlaan, *Protestant Modernism in Holland*, Oxford, 1924, pp. 17f, explains as follows: 'The *Réveil* was a reawakening of the sin-and-grace type of religion. Man's depravity and hopeless condition, the wondrous escape provided by the atonement, God's free and sovereign grace – these were the ideas which lived afresh among these pietists. In controversy with the Groningers, emphasis came to be laid upon the infallibili-

A word needs to be said about the *Réveil's* use of the Bible. It was as naively and rigidly biblicistic as were similar pietistic movements of the time. The 'old liberals' and the Groningers were biblicistic too, but with them it was possible to give up in minor details the absolute verbal authority of Scripture. Thus, e.g., they developed an 'accommodation theory' to explain Jesus' use of the Old Testament. The *Réveil*-men, however, could have nothing to do with such a theory. For them the Word of God was identical with the Bible, and Jesus' view of the Old Testament had to be literally and absolutely authoritative. They insisted that God's voice was to be heard in every word of Scripture. The *Réveil* was in this respect strongly influenced by Hengstenberg and Gaussen.[3]

For the liberal and Groningen schools, the *Réveil* was an abomination, and its adherents were despised as irresponsible obscurantists. The men of the *Réveil* fully reciprocated the antipathy. They opposed the Groningen school as the *Carthago delenda* of their time, and they spoke of the Leiden theologians (the 'old liberals') as enemies of Christ.

In this delineation it must be reiterated, finally, that in spite of their mutual differences and antipathies, these three movements had in common a basic supernaturalistic belief. Thus when Abraham Kuenen enrolled as a student at Leiden University in 1846, supernaturalism ruled unchallenged. To be sure, the theology that prevailed at the universities was not the rigid orthodoxy of da Costa and Groen van Prinsterer. It was no longer popular to emphasize the distinctive Calvinistic doctrines of predestination, providence, the trinity, the vicarious atonemenent, and the deity of Christ; yet, on the other hand, these were not generally denied.

This theological confusion and self-conscious traditionalism were unquestionably related to the backward condition of the historical criticism of the Bible prevailing in Holland during this period.[4] Much of Holland's biblical scholarship was pietistic and traditionalistic. New Testament

---

ty of the Scripture, the true deity of Christ, and reconciliation through the blood of the cross. Their religion was, to be sure, really based upon feeling, experience. But the Bible in their experience acted as a means of grace, and so it was natural to insist upon the absolute, infallible, decisive authority of Scripture. Gaussen's *Sur la Theopneustie*, written in 1840, was widely read in these circles. Furthermore, they found congenial material in the doctrinal formulae of the Reformed Church, and came, with exceptions, to regard them as a complete expression of Christian truth. Hence in church politics they fought for strict enforcement of conformity. But some of their leaders were lax in regard to the doctrine of predestination.'

4 See J. Nat, *De studie van de Oostersche talen in Nederland in de 18e en 19e eeuw*, Purmerend, 1929.

study was dominated by a sterile pedantry,[1] while Old Testament study of a serious scholarly nature had become virtually extinct. Government reorganization under William I had decreed that Old Testament exegesis was no worthy subject for scientific study, hence had omitted it from the academic roster. Training in Hebrew, demanded for ministerial candidates, was in charge of the various university Oriental scholars, none of whom showed any concern for biblical exegesis beyond maintaining the traditional views. Such were Antonie Rutgers (d. 1875) at Leiden and H. C. Millies (d. 1868) at Utrecht, both men of stringent orthodoxy. Van der Palm was the best-known exegete, but demonstrated little interest in anything but the preparation of devotional and edificatory materials for popular consumption.

However, the more progressive theologians and church leaders were far from satisfied with the country's backwardness in the field of biblical criticism. Voices began to be heard calling for improvement.[2] Thus it would appear that Holland was open to something better, to the strong impulse in biblical studies that would soon be provided by Kuenen and his modernist co-workers. By 1850 the groundwork for the acceptance of a full-fledged historical criticism had been carried out, but mainly outside The Netherlands. When it arrived fully armed, the opportunity for effective resistance was already past.

---

1 Cf. Mackay, *op. cit.*, pp. 67f: 'New Testament criticism was ably represented by W. A. van Hengel at Leiden... Van Hengel is famed for his exact scholarship. Some of his countrymen were of the opinion that he carried the virtue of *akribeia* too far... He used to ponder for days on the significance of a single particle in a text, but he found time to produce substantial work which had a European reputation.'

2 The remarks of J. van Gilse in *Jaarboeken voor Wetenschappelijke Theologie*, I (1855), 843f, are especially illuminating: 'No area of theological learning has been so sparsely cultivated among us in late years as the exegesis of the Old Testament, at any rate so far as we may judge from what has appeared in print. From time to time a single academic dissertation has appeared, as also a translation and exposition of the Minor Prophets which indeed raised the hope of something good, and also the labor of Dr. H. F. T. Fockens, always upon the standpoint of van der Palm, but without his spirit or taste or tact. An exellent help for the exposition of the Old Testament has been provided by my own highly esteemed teacher, Prof. T. Roorda, in his *Grammatica Hebraica*. His successor, Prof. P. J. Veth, applied this improved insight into the construction of the Hebrew language to an even broader area, but the employment of these tools remained sealed within the walls of the study chamber and of the academic classroom, or confined itself to a few suggestions published... in *Orientalia* (which, alas, has ceased to appear!). One

THE RISE AND DECLINE OF THE MODERNIST MOVEMENT

Shortly after the beginning of the second half of the nineteenth century, things had radically changed from the way they had been before. Suddenly a vigorous new theological movement had burst upon the scene and now threatened to sweep all before it. It produced a vast outpouring of books and scholarly articles, both in the general area of theological-philosophical speculation and in the specific area of technical biblical criticism. This was the so-called Dutch modernism, which became noticable shortly before 1850, rose to a peak around 1870, and gradually declined until its metamorphosis into other movements in the beginning years of the present century.[3]

Dutch modernism was both radically critical and radically antisupernaturalistic. It combined in intimate union a theology and a biblical interpretation that brought much light, but were doomed to ultimate failure. James Hutton Mackay has given it this apt characterization:

It is a school that passed... into the sphere of history. We can trace its beginning, its course, and its end. It has been condemned by the criticism of history – the most decisive form of criticism. It was an attempt to combine a positivist or naturalistic view of life and of the world with the Christian faith, in a wide sense of the term, and it was demonstrated, clearly and conclusively, that it could not be done. At the same time, much of the theological work that was done by the eminent scholars... has undoubtedly a permanent value, if not in the form in which it left their hands, at least as leading the way to what may be more satisfactory theories with regard to the historical origin of Christianity.[4]

periodical for biblical exegesis recently excluded the exposition of the Old Testament from its domain. The *Jaarboeken voor Wetenschappelijke Theologie* at first published a few articles relating to Hebrew antiquities, but actual exegesis of the Old Testament did not appear in them. If one is to judge concerning the present level of the exegesis of the Old Testament among us from such things as the ungrounded lauding of Dr. Fockens' Bible translation and the recommendation of Hengstenberg's and Delitzsch's mystical "Spielereien" with the contents of Canticles, appearing in the last issue of that periodical, then indeed one would have to acknowledge that we are in a woeful condition... The chair of Oriental literature at one of our national universities... has already been vacant for months! An ominous omen for the neglect of the study of the Old Testament – a study so highly important for theological activity! May the new translation of the writings of the Old Testament that is now also to be undertaken under the commission of the Synod... arouse new zeal for the exposition of the books of the Old Testament, and at the same time prove that the Hebrew language still possesses alert practitioners in the fatherland of Schultens!'

3 The name dates from the publication of D. T. Huet's book, *Wenken opzigtens de moderne theologie* (1858).

4 *op. cit.*, pp. 134f

In 1848 the first edition of J. H. Scholten's *Leer der Hervormde Kerk* began to appear.[1] This was the clarion of the new movement. By 1850 a second edition was required, and a year later C. W. Opzoomer's *Weg der wetenschap* was published in two successive editions, giving the movement a further impetus that could not be resisted. There was something strikingly different about these new writings. They contained nothing more of the ambiguity and inconsistency of the books written by the Groningers and 'old liberals'. A decisive step had been taken toward a radical break with traditionalism. Scholten still embraced some of the rudiments of supernaturalism, though he was soon to abandon it completely; Opzoomer had already adopted the principles of the extremest rationalism.

The basic philosophical presupposition of modernism was the absolute sway of natural law, unbroken by any intrusion of the supernatural into the chain of material causes. The modernists believed that this scientific modern view of the world could be reconciled with religious faith. This was to be done, they thought, by the process of identification. That is, natural causation is God's activity; all that happens has a finite cause, yet this is at the same time willed by a personal, self-conscious God, and his will is perfectly good, evil being only a temporal element in the world's evolution.[2]

In the early years, discussion based upon these premises polarized itself about the monistic determinism of Scholten and the scientific empiricism of Opzoomer. Something of the development of these two leaders and of certain figures of secondary importance is required for an adequate understanding of the movement.

Without a doubt Johannes H. Scholten was the most influential leader of the modernists. By the power of his personality and the overwhelming force of his logic he won a wide following. He came to be known as 'the old general.'[3] Born in 1811, he studied at Utrecht from 1832 to 1836, where he was strongly under the influence of his uncle, Professor van Heusde,

1 *De leer der Hervormde Kerk in hare grondbeginselen uit de bronnen voorgesteld en beoordeeld*, 2 vols., Leiden, 1848–50; 4th ed., 1861–61. This was a reinterpretation of Reformed doctrine in the light of modern thought, offered in response to the synodical decision of 1841.
2 Cf. Vanderlaan, *op. cit.*, pp. 23–25.
3 Roessingh, p. 104. Primary sources for Scholten's life and thought are his pamphlet, *Herdenking mijner vijventwintigjarige ambtsbediening*, Leiden, 1865; his *Afscheidsrede bij het nederleggen van het hoogleeraarsambt aan de Universiteit te Leiden*, Leiden, 1881; H. Kuenen, 'J. H. Scholten,' *Levensberichten van de Maatschappij van Nederlandsche Letterkundigen* (1886), pp. 3–60; cf. also Vanderlaan, *op. cit.*, pp. 26–49.
4 Cf. his dissertation, *Disquisitio de Dei erga hominem amore*, Utrecht, 1836.
5 *Oratio de vitando in Jesu Christi historia interpretanda docetisme, ad rem Christianam promovendo hodiernae theologicae munere*, The Hague, 1842.

and the Groningen movement. Forsaking the tenets of 'old liberalism', with its historical arguments for biblical supernaturalism, he embraced a kind of Arianism according to which Christ is to be understood only as the manifestation of God's love.[4] After a brief pastorate, Scholten took up a position at the Athenaeum in Franeker in 1840. In his inaugural address, he declared his independence also of the Groningen school, warning sharply of its implicit docetism.[5] He emphasized the duty of Christian theologians to defend the full humanness of Jesus. Some call this the real beginning of Dutch modernism, signalling as it did a basic shift from the defense of Jesus' divinity to a defense of his humanity.[6]

The famous school at Franeker had to be closed shortly after Scholten's coming. Following a short period of idleness, he received an appointment to the University of Leiden (1843), where he became ordinary professor in 1845. Here he continued to teach until his retirement in 1881, four years before his death.

We have noted the publication of Scholten's master work, *De Leer der Hervormde Kerk*, in 1848. This book immediately found wide acceptance and passed through several editions. Its great appeal was partly due to the fact that it demonstrated a way of reinterpreting the old Calvinistic tradition in terms of a completely rationalistic system of causation.

Scholten was consciously attempting to reshape the old doctrines. Even though he rejected such characteristic Reformed dogmas as double predestination and total depravity, he sincerely believed that he was presenting faithfully the meaning and spirit not only of Jesus' and Paul's teaching but of the teaching of the Reformed theologians as well.[7] He built his work upon the material principle of divine determinism and the formal principle of *sola scriptura*.[8]

As a pastor, he had been influenced by his parishioners' high predestinarianism. Now he modified the biblical doctrine of the divine choice into a monistic determinism, while attempting to retain the idea of a personal

6 Scholten's Christology was essentially Schleiermacherian at this time. He laid emphasis on the true but ideal humanity of Jesus. Inconsistently, he admitted the supernatural birth and pre-existence of Jesus (similarly to the Groningers). These were accepted uncritically, together with much traditional language, and were ere long to be discarded by him.

7 He believed it possible to present a viable restatement of the Reformed faith following the example of Alexander Schweizer, one of Schleiermacher's followers, in his *Glaubenslehre der Evangelisch-Reformierten Kirche* (1844–47).

8 Scholten firmly defended determinism against the objections of another modernist leader, S. Hoekstra *(infra)*; cf. Hoekstra, *Vrijheid in verband met zelfbewustheid en zonde*, Amsterdam, 1858; Scholten, *De vrije wil*, Leiden, 1859. Regarding his doctrine of Scripture, see the discussion in the following chapter.

will of God. The basic philosophical argument for this construction was his observation that inasmuch as both reason and conscience are limited in man, these must point to the infinite Cause in which the rational and moral order are grounded.

A marked development appears in a comparison of the first and the fourth editions of Scholten's book. He clung in the first edition to certain remnants of the old views. But by 1861, the date of the fourth edition, his transformation was virtually complete. Two factors were of special influence on him: the impact of Opzoomer's philosophy and his own critical studies in the New Testament. He at last saw clearly the inconsistency of trying to hold opposite principles, and his only choice could be a thorough-going and far-reaching antisupernaturalistic monism. Scholten's later works reveal even further development in this direction.

Cornelis W. Opzoomer was next in influence to Scholten.[1] He did not have a formal theological education. Ten years Scholten's junior, he studied law at Leiden and in 1846, at the age of twenty-five, accepted a position on the faculty of Scholten's alma mater, Utrecht, where he continued to teach for many years. Opzoomer's development falls into two clearly-defined phases. In his early phase he was strongly influenced by Hegel[2] and Fichte, but especially by the speculative theories of Schelling's disciple, K. C. F. Krause (d. 1832). Krause had developed a doctrine of 'panentheism', according to which God contains the universe without being exhausted in it, being an essence known through conscience rather than a person. In the year of his coming to Utrecht, Opzoomer revealed the measure of his dependence on Krause in his little book, *De leer van God bij Schelling, Hegel, en Krause*. He argued that God is not just the first link in the chain of reality, as the deists held, but constituted himself the whole chain; yet he is more than the totality of the links, since his being gives unity and identity to the whole. Departing from Krause, Opzoomer held that this God must be self-conscious since otherwise it would be impossible to account for our finite self-consciousness. Nevertheless, this God is not supernatural.

This teaching came as a severe shock to sober, conservative Holland. Here was German unbelief for the first time appearing undisguised,

---

1 See Vanderlaan, *op. cit.*, pp. 19f. 49ff.

2 Cf. his inaugural oration, *De wijsbegeerte den mensch met zichzelven verzoenende*, in which he set a new fashion by writing in Dutch instead of Latin. He showed, in Hegelian fashion, man passing through three religions phases: first, naive belief; second, its denial; third, a deeper acceptance gained through philosophical speculation.

3 *De gevoelsleer van Dr. J. J. van Oosterzee beoordeeld*, Amsterdam, 1846

4 See also *De weg der wetenschap, een handboek der logica*, Leiden-Amsterdam, 1851; *De*

dismissing the supernatural and all that went with it. Opzoomer soon came into sharp conflict on many sides. Not only did he have the hardihood to attack the highly-esteemed J. J. van Oosterzee, later to become his colleague at Utrecht,[3] but he widened his criticism to include the young Professor Scholten as well. Scholten reciprocated bitterly, calling Opzoomer a pantheist and declaring him to have stepped outside the bounds of Christianity in his thinking. Ironically, Scholten eventually came to accept a philosophical position similar to this early view of Opzoomer, while the latter moved on to a scientific empiricism in the second stage of his development.

Very soon after coming to Utrecht, Opzoomer began to come under the spell of the natural sciences. He saw that the best way to combat Scholten's speculative determinism was through an empirical rather than a speculative method. Increasingly under the influence of J. S. Mill, he and his followers came to be called the empiricist or realistic school. His views received their most mature exposition in *Het wezen der kennis, een handboek der logica* (1867).[4]

Scholten had been arguing that God was to be approached via nature as well as in the inner life, and for this reason had made much of the ontological and other theistic arguments.[5] But Opzoomer came more and more to hold that the study and contemplation of nature could never lead to God, that all man's organs of perception and powers of reason reveal to him only the material world.[6] One might have expected that upon this basis Opzoomer would have become an atheist. He did not give up on God, however. Inconsistently, he argued that there is a way of knowing God; this is the way of religious feeling. Admittedly, this is a last resort. It cannot tell us much: only that God is, that he is good, that he has personality. For a while Opzoomer argued for indeterminism on the basis of man's moral freedom, but soon gave this up in favor of the unlimited sway of natural causation. It is this natural necessity that the religious man identifies as the will of God. 'Religious faith,' then, 'is nothing else than the acknowledgment that God reigns, and that he is wisdom and love; religion is nothing else than the disposition of mind that fills man when he is deeply penetrated by that faith.'[7]

---

godsdienst, Amsterdam, 1864.

5 Cf. his *Het kritisch standpunt van Mr. C. W. Opzoomer beoordeeld*, Amsterdam, 1860.

6 This was meant to be anti-Kantian; 'The laws to which man is bound in his thinking are not laws of that thinking itself, but are laws of that world which is the object of his thinking' (Roessingh, pp. 149f).

7 *De godsdienst*, p. 27. In his early Krausean phase, Opzoomer had rejected miracles on speculative grounds, but now on the testimony of science. The New Testament was

We should mention at this point Opzoomer's most brilliant pupil, Allard Pierson. Born in 1831, Pierson was reared under strong *Réveil* influence, but at Utrecht under Opzoomer and at Leiden under Scholten he became one of the most thoroughly naturalistic thinkers among the modernists. He was a dialectician rather than a creative thinker. In 1863 he wrote his book, *Rigting en leven*, considered to be a manifesto of modernist principles, but in fact far more radical than most modernist thought. Pierson declared in this book that Protestantism's claim that it bases its teaching on the infallible Word of God is a pure hallucination, and that its dependence on faith is not really different from Catholic dependence on good works. Modernism, he declared, must turn away from both Catholicism and Protestantism in an absolute rejection of the supernatural.[1] It must follow solely the empirical method, which leads to the idea that God is love and that nothing is real but the beautiful.[2]

Pierson soon came to reject both the church and the possibility of knowing God in any way whatever. Attacking his teacher Opzoomer, he denied that religious feeling has epistemological validity.[3] He declared that the church must be dismissed as possessing any religious authority; if it were to be continued, it would have to be merely as an administrative organization for achieving social betterment. In 1865 – little wonder – Pierson actually resigned from his parish, creating a great furor among his modernist colleagues. He sought satisfaction in study abroad, and was appointed in 1870 to a position on the theological faculty at Heidelberg. But he could not endure even this tenuous tie to church authority, so that in 1877 he accepted an offer to become professor of aesthetics and modern literature at the newly-organized University of Amsterdam. Here he established a great reputation for massive learning and penetrating insight, but was never able to find the intellectual certainty he constantly sought.[4] As we shall see, Pierson played an important role in the radical criticism both of the Old and New Testaments,

for him no rule of faith, only a historical source. He did not share in the liberal error, common with Scholten and others, of interpreting Jesus as a nineteenth-century religious leader.

1 Pierson claimed that the church had outlived its vocation. Catholicism had at least justified its existence by its works of charity, but in actuality Catholicism and Protestantism neutralize each other. Only two courses are open: return to the decrepit church of Rome or give up the idea of a Protestant church. The only vision still worth dreaming is that of social humanism. (Cf. Mackay, *op. cit.*, pp. 146–52, 154f.)

2 The existence of evil is accounted for by the fact that God nowhere acts directly. Faith can be expressed only in the language of poetry. Jesus is a legend, but a legend that is beautiful and inspiring. A pastor can do nothing but preach a soft, mild, lovable Jesus.

taking a position of the extremest scepticism regarding the authenticity of the biblical writings.

A word must be said about a fourth prominent modernist leader of the early period. This was Sytse Hoekstra, since 1857 professor at the Mennonite seminary in Amsterdam, and following 1877 professor at the university in that city, where he was Pierson's colleague. Hoekstra taught that man's feeling of dependence on someone greater than himself justifies the exercise of religion. Thus he acknowledged the needs of the human soul in a way that such rigid logicians as Scholten and Opzoomer were incapable of doing, to say nothing of Pierson. Hoekstra's best-known work was *Bronnen en grondslagen van het godsdienstig geloof* (Amsterdam, 1864).

Hoekstra was essentially in agreement with Scholten and Opzoomer in rejecting external authority as a source of religious truth. He believed, however, that these men were in danger of doing violence to psychological realities. He became involved in controversy with Scholten over the question of determinism versus free will. He insisted that the clue to religious reality is to be found in man's moral personality,[5] not in speculation about God's being or in empirical investigation of the natural world. It is from man's inner religious needs that the supersensible world must be postulated, and this must be understood as supplementing the natural order rather than paralleling it, as in Opzoomer's theory.

There were other important thinkers among the early modernists, but they need not detain us here. Only Kuenen beside those mentioned was outstanding. A description of his dominant role within the modernist movement must wait until the following chapter.

In the history of Dutch modernism, the period from ca. 1850 to ca. 1870 can be roughly divided into two parts. Before 1860 the movement was largely confined to theological discussions carried on by the big leaders and their respective broods, but in the following ten years it broke

3 He held that religious feeling contradicts rather than supplements science, hence has to be dismissed as irrelevant and misleading. See his book, *Gods wondermacht en ons geestelijk leven*, Arnhem, 1867.

4 Cf. Mackay, *op. cit.*, p. 161: 'His last article in *De Gids*, in 1895, was on ethics, in which, as van Hamel puts it – who describes Pierson's life as "a tragedy of vain search" – he attempts to chase the Absolute from its last entrenchment.'

5 Hoekstra's view differed from that of Kant in that he held man's whole nature, not just the moral imperative, to be the basis of religious reality. It is our need as finite persons that drives us to God, this being a need that the empirical world cannot satisfy. At first Hoekstra believed in the miraculous and in the deity of Christ, but came eventually to abandon them like the rest of the modernists. Cf. Vanderlaan, *op. cit.*, pp. 58ff.

out, not only into the general ranks of the ministry, but into the ordinary levels of church membership as well. In this second decade many succumbed to the modernist persuasion. Once the theological foundations crumbled, the flood of modernism swept away every remnant of their resistance.

K. H. Roessingh explains briefly what happened to bring about this breakthrough. He writes:

When the Leiden and Utrecht students began to fraternize in the last years before 1860, when the Leiden historical-critical research of Kuenen furnished content to Opzoomer's methodological demands for historical certainty and probability, when Scholten's God-concept found a basis in empiricism and the very hazy God-concept of the Utrechters fortified itself upon what the Leiden dogmatics had to offer, then the factors had come together from which something new had to grow.[1]

By this time, the adherents of the movement had gained a great measure of confidence and self-consciousness. Full of fire and optimism, they set out to communicate the principles and results of their new viewpoint to the congregations. They obtained a sympathetic following especially among the intellectuals, who were generally liberally inclined. Various attempts by the modernist theologians to popularize the results of their investigations were warmly received by these members and steadily gained new converts. Among such attempts were the popular-scientific periodical *Nieuw en Oud*,[2] a series of books under the general title, *Bibliotheek voor moderne theologie*, and a multi-volumed Bible history for young people.[3]

Ere long, however, the struggle for control of the laity became exceedingly bitter and involved the modernists in a predicament that led to severe losses for them. The acceptance of modernist teaching came relatively easily in the non-Reformed churches, entering without a struggle into a position of dominance among the Remonstrants and gaining a

1 Roessingh, p. 100. Vanderlaan, *op. cit.*, p. 58, adds: 'It was not uncommon for students to begin their academical careers at Utrecht, under the fascination of Opzoomer, and then to finish their theological studies at Leiden, under the overpowering influence of Scholten.' Many of these went on to become followers of Hoekstra.
2 A comparison of the first (1856) and the last (1866) volumes of this periodical shows a definite progress toward a more radical biblical criticism.
3 H. Oort, I. Hooykaas, and A. Kuenen, *De Bijbel voor jonge lieden*, 8 vols., Harlingen, 1871–73, part of which was reprinted as H. Oort, *De laatste eeuwen van Israëls volksbestaan*, 1st ed., The Hague, 1877; 2nd ed., Leiden, 1915.
4 Cf. Reitsma, pp. 477ff, 510ff; also J. C. Rullmann, *De strijd voor kerkherstel*, Amsterdam, 1915.
5 C. Busken Huet left in 1862, Pierson in 1865. For the resultant controversy, see Pierson, *Brief aan mijn laatste gemeente*, Arnhem, 1865; A. Réville, *Nous maintiendrons*, Arnhem,

place of easy tolerance among the Mennonites and Lutherans. It was different in the Hervormde Kerk. By 1850, this church had obtained a great measure of freedom from governmental control.[4] The consistories were still entirely self-perpetuating, however, and still had control over the calling of ministers. They often employed this power to install modernists in their pulpits. These ministers were afire with enthusiasm for the new way of thinking, and did all within their power to propagandize it from the pulpit, in catechism classes, and through the press. Many modernist ministers did not find it easy, however, to win their congregations. Only a small minority of churches actually accepted the modernist teaching, and many individuals whom the modernists converted soon drifted completely away from the church, so that their support within the congregations was lost. The main mass remained orthodox. Voices began to be heard in the churches calling for the resignation of the modernists. As the movement found itself on the defensive, anti-ecclesiastical sentiment began to increase sharply among modernist leaders. The situation became so tense that a few ministers actually left their pulpits.[5] Some of these joined the Remonstrants, others led separatist groups. Ministerial students at the universities became markedly fewer, evidently out of fear of synodical harrassment.

A decisive blow to the optimism of the modernist leaders proved to be the introduction of general franchise in the Hervormde Kerk. Ironically, this was a right that they themselves had been foremost in advocating. In 1867 a new *Reglement* went into effect providing for the establishment of electoral colleges in each congregation for choosing consistories and calling ministers. When this took effect, the old consistorial monopolies were broken up, and the members themselves were at last able to exercise a degree of control over their leadership. Evidently the modernists had overestimated their power. They did not anticipate the practical results of this greater democratization, which now allowed consistorial positions

1865, and *Notre foi et notre droit*, Arnhem, 1866; Busken Huet, *Ongevraagde advies*, Haarlem, 1866; A. Kuenen, *Het goed recht der modernen*, Leiden, 1866. Mackay, *op. cit.*, pp. 157f, summarizes Kuenen's argument: 'While the...church had accepted supernaturalism, and while her confession was supernaturalistic, a belief in the miraculous was characteristic neither of Christianity nor of Protestantism. The modern view of the world leaves no place for a divine supernatural revelation. But this is the result of a historical process, and a development of this kind the church is free to follow. The church is not a society that exists for maintaining and propagating supernaturalism. When she was founded she could not express her faith in any other form. But to suppose that she must retain this form or die is to misunderstand her essential nature... The assertion that modernists are no longer Christians is groundless, and rests on the notion that the significance of Jesus is to be sought, not in what distinguished him from his contemporaries, but in what he had in common with them.'

and pulpits to be filled by opponents of modernism inasmuch as the majority of the members continued to be staunchly orthodox. Thus after 1867 the modernists began to lose control of even the big city churches, besides important posts in church administration and at the universities. Only in certain country places did modernism remain in control.[1]

The years that followed were to be a time of decline. The modernists were now forced to reappraisal and retrenchment. Their supreme confidence of having the truth entirely on their side had scarcely been shaken, but they were disillusioned in the fact that they had not been able to overwhelm their opposition.

In this new period, the modernists were to find in the Protestanten Bond, paralleling Die Protestantenverein in Germany, a valuable organ of propaganda and an effective means for maintaining their unity. This Bond was organized in 1868 by a group of modernist ministers in Friesland, and soon spread over the whole land. It was able to hold its first national convention in 1871 under the chairmanship of Opzoomer. This organization originally had the purpose of speaking for all who favored freedom of thought over against confessional authority, but soon those of evangelical opinions withdrew, leaving it entirely to the modernists. It was organized outside the churches and in many instances took their place. It published a periodical, *De Hervorming* (accompanied by a scientific supplement), and propagandized its cause by issuing tracts, sponsoring lectures, organizing rallies and the like. Its character has continued to be militantly anti-orthodox.[2]

The late sixties and the decade of the seventies saw the rise of the 'ethical modernists' under the influence of Hoekstra,[3] not to be confused with the orthodox 'ethicals' who are still to be discussed. This former group of theologians were sharply critical of the intellectualistic and metaphysical emphasis of Scholten and Opzoomer. Their general complaint was that in giving up the supernatural, modernism had also surrendered any real God concerned with human need. One of the leading spokesmen for this group was J. Cramer, who in his book *De illusie der moderne richting* (1867) attacked determinism and the identification of God with the philosophical Absolute, on the ground that this left only necessity and rendered life's deepest spiritual experiences meaningless. Cramer and

1 For further description of this struggle and its immediate effects cf. Reitsma, pp. 507ff, Oort, *op. cit.*, pp. 536–41, B. D. Eerdmans, *TT*, n.r. I (1909), 5–7.
2 Cf. Reitsma, pp. 515f; Lindeboom, *op. cit.*, III, 49ff.
3 Cf. chap. 4, 'The Ethical Moderns,' in Vanderlaan, *op. cit.*,
4 See also E. C. Jungius, 'Natuur en godsdienst.' *Nieuw en Oud*, 1869; I Hooykaas, *God in de geschiedenis*, Schiedam, 1870; I. Hooykaas, J. H. Herderschee, H. Oort, A. G. van

his associates argued that God must be sought not in nature and in history, but solely in man's religious aspirations and moral consciousness. They went somewhat beyond Hoekstra in attempting to sever religion completely from any intellectual world view.[4] The discussion waxed and waned among the modernists of various groups. Several, such as Kuenen, attacked this 'ethical' view as positivistic.[5] Generally the debate made a deep lasting impression, bringing many modernists over, not to the 'ethical' position itself, but to something close to the view of Hoekstra.[6] Toward the end of the nineteenth century, it was to become a major influence in the antinaturalistic movement called 'rechtsmodernisme', which will be described at a later point in our discussion.

CONSERVATIVE GROUPS IN OPPOSITION TO MODERNISM

It can be readily understood that opposition to modernist thought came not only from the strict orthodox but from the Groningers and many of the 'old liberals' as well. These groups could tolerate no attack on rationalistic supernaturalism as it appeared in their several systems; they were, however, able to do little more than frantically attempt to defend their bulwarks against the devastating modernist bombardments. A more successful tactic came to be developed by a group called the 'modern orthodox' or the 'orthodox ethicals', now generally spoken of simply as the 'Ethicals' or, in Dutch, the 'Ethische richting'.

This group has come to constitute The Netherlands' most significant mediating group, having to some degree succeeded in offering a constructive alternative to orthodoxy and modernism. We have seen that Hoekstra and the above-described 'ethical modernists' – from whom these Ethicals must be carefully distinguished – were not capable of producing a satisfactory solution to the glaring weaknesses they observed in the modernist system, the chief reason being that they too failed to reconcile the God of nature with the God of religious experience. The group of which we are presently speaking, the Ethicals, bridged this gap, albeit

Hamel, *Godsdienst volgens de beginselen der ethische richting onder de modernen*, s' Hertogenbosch, 1876; van Hamel, *Proeve eener kritiek van de leer der goddelijke voorzienigheid*, Groningen, 1879.
5 'De godsdienst, de wetenschap, en het leven,' *TT* 1874
6 Cf. L. W. E. Rauwenhoff, *Wijsbegeerte van den godsdienst*, Leiden, 1887, which in Kantian fashion finds the ultimate source of religious faith in man's sense of unconditional duty.

with some inconsistencies, by attempting to reconcile the concept of revelation with the results of scientific and historical inquiry.

This movement has not been altogether homogeneous. It has represented, indeed, only a party within the conservative camp rather than any cohesive school. At first it could find no viable alternative to modernism and orthodoxy, thus remained essentially biblicistic. Important early leaders were the two Utrecht professors, J. J. van Oosterzee (d. 1882) and J. I. Doedes (d. 1897). Associated with them were Professor J. J. van Toorenenbergen of Amsterdam (d. 1903) and two former members of the *Réveil* movement, Nicolas Beets (d. 1903), who joined the Utrecht faculty in 1874, and Daniel Chantepie de la Saussaye (d. 1874), a Walloon minister who became a professor at Groningen in 1872. In 1845 the first two organized the journal *Jaarboeken voor Wetenschappelijke Theologie*, with the aim of reconciling orthodox belief and scientific knowledge.[1] In 1853 the five men organized another journal, *Ernst en Vrede*. The only unifying impulse in the *Ernst en Vrede* venture was a common concern to do something about the ills troubling the church. The editors were chiefly interested in correcting what they considered dangerous tendencies in the *Réveil*. Soon differences drove the group apart, leaving de la Saussaye isolated from the others. The latter, called the Utrecht group, were the ones who remained biblicistic; they opposed modernism by a somewhat naive appeal to the simple choice for or against the miraculous and the supernatural. Saussaye, however, was ready to accept scientific data while grounding theology in a purely ethical principle. Thus he adopted modernism's methods without its presuppositions. It was he and his followers, not the Utrecht group, who came generally to be known by the title 'Ethical.'

When the split occurred, Saussaye became editor of *Ernst en Vrede*,

---

1 It was given up in 1856 due to the attacks of antisupernaturalists, to be succeeded by *Nieuwe Jaarboeken voor Wetenschappelijke Theologie* under broader editorship; this also had to be abandoned in 1863 for the same reason; see below.

2 He deplored Prinsterer's way of identifying the church with the kingdom of God, laying emphasis rather on the principle of the indwelling of the Holy Spirit as constituting the real kingdom within the church. He rejected both the *Réveil's* definition of the converted as constituting the real church and Prinsterer's notion that the church was the community of the elect. Rather, said he, the church is most truly present where its members are the most spiritually alive (cf. Mackay, *op. cit.*, pp. 115–21).

3 *ibid.*, p. 109

4 See *Beoordeeling van het werk van Scholten*, Utrecht, 1859, 2nd ed., 1884. Saussaye criticized Scholten's *Leer* as making a concession to rationalistic supernaturalism in respect to his formal principle of *sola scriptura*. He argued that the Reformation, which both he and Scholten were seeking to revive, was essentially a religious and ethical movement, and

which was to remain in publication for no more than six years. Saussaye was notorious for his labored style, which no doubt accounted to some extent for the fact that he was little known outside Holland, founded no real school, wrote no standard work, and created no theological system. Nevertheless, the basic tenets of his position need to be delineated because of his extensive influence in later years. This can best be accomplished by outlining his arguments against Groen van Prinsterer on the right and against Scholten on the left.

In the *Réveil*, represented by the former, Saussaye saw two great dangers. The first was its donatistic tendency to create an *ecclesiola in ecclesiam* based on a conversion experience as the essential of Christian communion; over against this he emphasized the role of the visible church as expressed in the sacraments.[2] The second danger was the drift toward rigid confessionalism, soon to lead to sizeable secessions from the Hervormde Kerk. Prinsterer, no theologian but a statesman and lawyer, wanted to impose strict enforcement of the doctrinal formularies, but Saussaye argued that the church was in no position to require literal assent because these no longer represented adequately the church's developing theology. He himself had signed the formularies 'not as literally expressing his faith, but as an attempt to describe the same religious life in which he participated.'[3]

Saussaye agreed with Scholten that it was necessary to go beyond the old rationalistic supernaturalism[4] and that the church must seek new ways of expressing the principles of Reformed theology.[5] But he departed from Scholten on several basic issues. The first of these was that the basis of theology is the 'ethical' life of the church rather than intellectual speculation. By this he did not mean the moral faculty – the Kantian moral imperative – but the internal spiritual life in communion with

that its doctrinal formulations and its dependence on biblical authority, which lie at the root of Protestant scholasticism, are secondary and non-essential elements; thus Scholten was giving the Bible the position it came to occupy in eighteenth-century rationalism, not the position it rightfully had in the Reformation (cf. *ibid.*, pp. 94f).

5 He not only felt himself to be Calvin's intellectual heir, but desired to be in living contact with him and the whole church. Saussaye had a deep concern for the revival of Calvinism as a spiritual rather than as an intellectual movement: 'Calvinism has undergone a baptism of suffering, and is now awakening, purified and sanctified, from its grave. Our task is to unbind the ethical Calvin from the scholastic, or rather... to develop in the Reformed Church the gift of God that was in him. The consciousness of this calling binds us with childlike love and piety to the Reformed Church – to her historical origins, her whole history, her confessions and her liturgies. We feel that we are the sons of those fathers' *(ibid.*, p. 129).

God. He called this the 'ethical-mystical principle,' insisting on both qualifications to avoid the misunderstanding that moralism is religion and the notion that religion is pure subjectivism.[1]

A second point at which Saussaye took issue with Scholten was in regard to the task of theology. Inasmuch as the basis of Christian theology is the church's ongoing spiritual life, theologians simply have the duty of explicating that life. Thus theology and church are inseparable. Theology, moreover, must always view its present position from the perspective of the historical origin and development of Christianity. To Scholten, the origin of the church and of Christian doctrine was a matter of minor concern, but not so for Saussaye, who had strong feelings for the spiritual heritage of the entire Christian tradition.

A third important issue was Saussaye's definition of revelation. As we shall see, the modernists came to abandon completely all supernaturalism in the concept of revelation, but Saussaye and the Ethicals accepted fundamentally the Reformed doctrine of revelation to the effect that the Word of God is revealed from without and from above, authoritatively and sovereignly. Although it cannot be said that the Ethicals fully succeeded in explicating the meaning of this concept, it made a decisive difference in their approach to biblical interpretation, allowing them to accept higher criticism without abandoning a transcendent understanding of God.[2]

Saussaye's viewpoint found another staunch defender in J. H. Gunning, Sr., later to become a professor at Amsterdam and at Leiden. Leading biblical scholars among the Ethicals were to be J. J. P. Valeton, Jr., professor of Old Testament at Utrecht, and Gerrit Wildeboer, professor of Old Testament at Groningen and Leiden.

The Ethical movement made important gains in the early part of the period under discussion. It was largely able to take over the theological faculties of Utrecht and Groningen and was well represented among the pastoral ministry. Even Leiden, the old stronghold of modernism, was forced to make a place for some of the Ethicals after 1890. The leading theological journal of the Ethicals following 1875 was *Studiën*, published by Saussaye's son, by Valeton, and by I. van Dyk; this was succeeded in 1882 by *Theologische Studiën* under the editorship of F. E. Daubanton and others.

1 He explained, 'This at least is what we wish to be. Mysticism is our ground. We are rooted in God... The ethical is the revelation of the life hidden in him. What might be objectionable in the single word "mystical," as if we were given over to visions and ecstacies, is removed by the corrective term "ethical," which expresses the fixed laws to which the religious life is bound' (cited in *ibid.*, 124). 2 Cf. *ibid.*, p. 221; see below.
3 The importance of this secession church (out of whose tradition the present writer has

Much of the extremest orthodoxy remained within the Hervormde Kerk, particularly after the decisive conflict with the modernists in 1867. However, two large secession movements developed within this church, giving birth to two very conservative churches which eventually became one. The first of these, the so-called Afscheiding, actually took place in the first half of the century. Although not directly connected with the *Réveil*, it derived undoubted inspiration from it. Its first leaders were two ministers, H. de Cock (d. 1842) and H. Scholte (d. 1868). In 1834 de Cock was deposed because of his inflammatory preaching. He was zealous in opposition to heterodoxy in the Hervormde Kerk. Scholte supported de Cock, and was soon joined by other ministers and a few thousand lay-members. For several years this group had to endure severe repressive measures, but eventually obtained tolerance and grew into a sizeable strictly Calvinistic denomination with the name Christelijke Gereformeerde Kerk. In 1854 it established a theological school in Kampen which became an important center of orthodox resistance to liberal theology in the succeeding years.[3]

In 1886 a new secession movement took place, giving birth to a fairly large new conservative denomination which we may conveniently call the 'Gereformeerde Kerk.' Although confessional orthodoxy had rather firmly re-entrenched itself in the Hervormde Kerk during this period, continued tolerance of the modernists within the church and liberal control of ministerial training at the governmental universities led Abraham Kuyper, a future prime-minister of Holland, to organize an independent Free University in Amsterdam in the year 1880. When Kuyper's efforts to place ministerial candidates from his school met resistance, he and his followers formed separate organizations, first within but soon outside the Hervormde Kerk. This movement received the name 'Doleantie', or 'mourning'. In 1892, these new secessionists merged with a major segment of the above-described Christelijke Gereformeerde Kerk to become 'De Gereformeerde Kerken in Nederland' (the denomination's official name). The Free University of Amsterdam has continued alongside the Theological School at Kampen as an important center of conservative theological and biblical studies.[4]

By the year 1860, modernism's progress had began to diminish, as we

originally come) for the progress of biblical studies in The Netherlands has been minor, even though Kampen has produced scholars of ability (see below). For the Afscheiding see Reitsma, pp. 464–76; J. C. Rullmann, *De Afscheiding*, Amsterdam, 1916.

4 Cf. Reitsma, pp. 524ff; Rullmann, *De Doleantie*, Amsterdam, 1917. For a sympathetic appraisal of Kuyper by a pair of liberal writers, cf. J. and A. Romein, *Erflaters van onze beschaving* (6th ed., Amsterdam, 1947), chap. 5.

have seen. This year may be considered decisive as marking the end of all attempts at understanding and co-operation between the various conservative and liberal groups. In 1867 a completely modernist periodical, *Theologisch Tijdschrift*, began to appear under the editorship of Scholten, Kuenen, and others. Meanwhile, most of the old theological journals lost ground and soon expired. *Nieuwe Jaarboeken voor Wetenschappelijke Theologie* quit in 1863, *Godgeleerde Bijdragen* quit in 1870, and an end came for *Waarheid en Liefde*, the organ of the Groningen school, in 1872.

A striking feature of the theological disputes in this troubled period was their extreme bitterness and complete lack of charity. The strict orthodox excoriated the modernists as apostles of the antichrist, while these in turn looked upon the orthodox with undisguised loathing. Chantepie de la Saussaye tried to mediate between them, but his efforts were scorned by extremists on right and left alike. Thus, as there remained little possibility for continued co-operation, each party went its own way, with such results as we have depicted in the preceding paragraphs. This is the main reason why the periodicals mentioned came to their end. D. Harting, editor of *Nieuwe Jaarboeken*, wrote these sad words concerning the decease of that journal:

Parties here stand... sharply delimited over against one another with their Yes and No. Polemic has come in the place of discussion – polemic which in the nature of the case cannot be allowed to be carried on in a scientific journal unless that cease to be precisely what it above all desires to be, an organ of scientific knowledge.[1]

The editor of *Godgeleerde Bijdragen* similarly blamed party spirit for the death of his publication. These are his revealing words:

The editors and publishers announce that the publishing of this journal must be discontinued. The attempt to retain readers for a theological periodical that is not exclusively devoted to the interests of one special party no longer receives the support that is indispensable for the continuation of this venture. While on the one side the leaders of the modernist party allow none to write but those who support its cause, on the other side a number of periodicals have come into being that feature a particular party slogan of one kind or another in an equally exclusive manner. Whether this situation can continue, only time can teach us. For the present, the day of harmonious scientific enterprise in our fatherland appears to be past. The editorship sincerely thanks its collaborators, being firmly convinced that numerous essays, critiques, and reviews have been put in print to which men will turn in later years, when party spirit and party interest no longer nourish that onesidedness which listens to nothing but one's own word and admires nothing but one's own work. May a brighter future appear in which the sickness from which theology is presently suffering in our country will be healed.[2]

1 VI (1863), x   2 XLIV (1870), 863f

Chapter Three

Biblical Interpretation in the Modernist

School, ca. 1850-1910

THE DOCTRINE OF SCRIPTURE WITHIN THE MODERNIST SCHOOL

A basic principle on which all the modernists insisted was absolute freedom in the critical investigation of the Bible. Nothing could deter them from pushing this right to its limit. Necessarily, the pursuit of this investigation presupposed a doctrine of Scripture that went beyond the traditional dogma, yet it must not be assumed that there was absolute unanimity among the modernists concerning it. Three theologians, Scholten, Kuenen, and Conrad Busken Huet, did more than others to define a modernist view of Scripture, but several entered into the debate. A few arrived at rather seriously diverging conclusions.

We have mentioned that Scholten made *sola scriptura* the formal principle of his definitive book, *De Leer der Hervormde Kerk*. Chantepie de la Saussaye was right in claiming that this work paid tribute to rationalistic supernaturalism. At any rate, this criticism holds true concerning the first edition; in it, Scholten was still quite restrained in denying the supernatural element in Scripture. But in the later editions he more and more clearly adopted a strongly antisupernaturalistic view. This change is signallized in the significant definition of Scripture that appears in the third edition: where the second edition read, 'Holy Scripture is a source of Christian truth,' this third edition has, 'Holy Scripture is a source of the Christian religion.'

Even as Scholten moved to a clearly antisupernaturalistic position, he continued to adhere to his principle of *sola scriptura*. The Bible was not to be given up. He explained that modernism should not break with the Bible because the Bible is not actually supernaturalistic in its conception. It is rather Protestant scholasticism, developing in opposition to the modern concept of a natural order and erroneously interpreting the miraculous element in the Bible in terms of a supernatural power imposing itself upon the world of nature, that has actually broken with the Bible.[1]

1 Cf. Scholten, *Supernaturalisme in verband met Bijbel, Christendom, en Protestantisme, een vraag des tijds beantwoord* (Leiden, 1867), cited in Vanderlaan, *op. cit.*, p. 48. The Bible knows only usual and unusual acts of God, not supernatural acts. It is modern rationalistic supernaturalism that has withdrawn God's activity from the world of nature and science, and for this reason makes itself unbiblical and irreligious.

In the third edition of *Leer*, Scholten emphasized the fact that Christianity and Hebraism are historical phenomena, and hence need to be examined by historical criteria and techniques. He further made a sharp distinction between Holy Scripture and the Word of God, teaching, in opposition to the *Belgic Confession*, that Scripture is merely the report of God's Word. He declared that he wanted to be rid of all slavish dependence on a despicable 'authoriteitsgeloof.' i.e., faith based on ecclesiastical dogma. Appealing to Zwingli, he argued that the testimony of the Holy Spirit, not the Bible, is the ground of faith, and that this testimony is not a direct supernatural activity of God but only the persuasion of natural reason.[1] Furthermore, he taught that this *testimonium* does not guarantee the entire Bible, but only its religious content.[2]

As we shall see, Scholten did not remain content with speculative reasoning about the place of Scripture; he took a foremost place in the critical study of the New Testament, for which he had been specifically appointed. Under his supervision, New Testament studies in The Netherlands blossomed, and Leiden soon saw a number of dissertations in this field.

One of the most effective – and most controversial – attempts to popularize the critical view of Scripture was Busken Huet's *Brieven over den Bijbel*, published in 1858. This book created a great sensation and led to the author's departure from the church in 1864 (a year before Pierson's resignation). Busken Huet,[3] a Walloon minister, was strongly under the influence of rationalistic thought, although he remained essentially a theist. In this book he gave popular expression to his conviction that the old concept of revelation could no longer be maintained in the face of scientific advance, and that the church was now plainly faced with two alternatives; either to give up the Bible entirely or to acknowledge its historical and hence relative character.[4]

1 Cf. *ibid.*, pp. 21f. Scholten originally developed this in opposition to Opzoomer, who at first rejected religious feeling as a way of knowing God (see Opzoomer, *De gevoelsleer van Dr. J. J. van Oosterzee beoordeeld*, Amsterdam, 1846). Both van Oosterzee and Scholten appealed to a *testimonium spiritu sancti*, but, as it turned out, each meant something different. The former meant an actual supernatural presence, while the latter meant the persuasion of reason. Here Scholten was unconsciously moving into Opzoomer's camp.
2 Scholten argued that historical criticism cannot undermine the religious authority of the Bible, properly understood. He strongly defended the substantial historical accuracy of the Bible, which he thought provides a clear picture of the great spirit who founded Christianity: 'The Christian religion, so harmonious and pure... is the masterpiece of a single person, who realized the religion in his own life, and from whose divine spirit have flowed the treasures of knowledge and wisdom, of faith and love, of peace and salvation, which the New Testament, on every page, discloses to the believer' (cited by Mackay, *op. cit.*, pp. 100f, from *Dogmatices Christianae Initia*, 1853–54).

This writer complained of the backward condition of Dutch theological education, especially in regard to biblical criticism. 'Those,' he said, 'who are being trained at our universities as ministers of the gospel obtain a knowledge of the Bible and of its origin which deviates the breadth of the heavens from that view which predominates even among the more advanced lay-members.'[5] He believed that it was time for someone to do something about this lack, and this book was the result. In the form of nineteen cleverly composed letters between a fictional Reinout and his equally fictional sister Machteld, Busken Huet set forth his views. Machteld wrote to her brother concerning her misgivings about the inerrancy and ethical stature of the Bible, and the latter took this opportunity to discuss various critical problems with her. The idea of revelation, the occurrence of miracles, the morality of the Bible, the fulfilment of prophecy, the criticism of the Synoptics and the Fourth Gospel, etc., came under discussion. Throughout Reinout preached the historical-critical viewpoint. He spoke, of course, for Busken Huet himself.

This book must not be thought of as destructive in intent. On the contrary, it combatted the extreme naturalistic viewpoint and sought to establish, in a historical view of the Bible, a genuine religious value of abiding authority. Busken Huet insisted that he saw God's Word in the Bible – but only in a way that clearly acknowledges the human factor alongside it.

Brieven over den Bijbel had much influence in obtaining a wide acceptance of biblical criticism. It of course encountered opposition from the strictly orthodox, but also from the Groningen school. C. P. Hofstede de Groot, son of the renowned founder of the school, and later to teach at Groningen himself, made a flambouyant attempt to counteract Busken Huet's book by publishing in the following year his own series of letters, employing the same fictional correspondents while pleading for a conservative position.[6]

3 Cf. J. and A. Romein, *op. cit.*, chap. iv, 'Conrad Busken Huet, Schrijver van Beroep en Roeping, 1826–1886'.
4 Preface, p. vii
5 p. x
6 *Brieven over den Bijbel naar aanleiding van Busken Huet's brieven over den Bijbel*, Groningen, 1859. This book introduced a third correspondent, Leonard, a traditionalistic ministerial candidate. The intensity of public interest in this exchange is reflected in the satirical poem which P. A. de Génestet wrote about it (*Leekedichtjens*, Haarlem, 1860, no. xix). The following lines are especially revealing of current sentiment; Leonard is speaking:
'...Machteld! Everything can be harmonized
For one who is pious – pious and smart –
But your senses have been bewitched;
Reinout has completely overwhelmed you
With his half-way science...'

Even more influential in its lasting effects was Abraham Kuenen's attack on supernaturalism. He of course applauded the viewpoint of Busken Huet's book, supporting him against the attacks of Hofstede de Groot. The latter he refuted in an academic lecture later published in *Godgeleerde Bijdragen*.[1] Kuenen contested de Groot's claim that only supernaturalism allows a genuine revelation of God, answering that even though Israel's religion did develop purely by natural forces, it nonetheless constituted an authentic revelation of God because all religions reveal the divine. It is not a simple choice of the one or the other. The divine is in the natural. For this reason, Kuenen declared, he could see no need for a supernatural Christ. Even as Israel's development was no departure from the ordinary course of things, so too Christianity. He believed that the 'facts' would convince supernaturalists of the error of their viewpoint, and proceeded to enumerate some of them. These were, of course, the facts of nature and history as he interpreted them on the basis of a naturalistic presupposition. Kuenen concluded with an exhortation to his students to seek ' pure truth,' without any supernaturalistic bias. His close dependence on Scholten at this point is clearly apparent.

In 1869 Kuenen again had occasion to express this point of view, now in opposition to an important work of the German *offenbarungsgläubige* school, Ludwig Diestel's *Geschichte des Alten Testaments in der christliche Kirche*.[2] Kuenen reviewed this book in the *Theologisch Tijdschrift*,[3] suggesting that those who consider themselves orthodox would do well to read it in order to bring their theological ideas to self-criticism. Diestel had distinguished three legitimate principles or methods for interpreting the Old Testament, the last of which had the highest value, in his opinion. These were, first, the 'national principle,' by which Israel's history is

Reinout – but here the gentleman
   Treads upon the devil's tail;
Suddenly leaps from the forest,
Shattering this one's precious dreams,
   Reinout himself with a Tübingen sword!

'Hold, you deceiver of the innocent!'
   Cries he, 'Tremble, you dissembler!
The authenticity of the Book of Acts
Pressing upon my Machteld!
   Confess your sin, confess it – or die!'

The flash of swords. Our candidate
   Tumbles to earth in his blood.
Reinout cries out as victor;
Machteld is worth a better lover,
   Worth even a Leiden professor!

examined on the same basis as that of other ancient peoples, and its religion is considered as the product of natural forces, though with recognition of its peculiar value; second, the 'philosophical-historical principle', by which universal laws of development are to be applied to Israel's history; and third, the 'purely religious principle,' by which God is recognized as operative in Israel's history by a special intervention, endowing it with peculiar value and significance. Kuenen claimed that only the first of these was valid. He accused Diestel of bringing strange fire on the altar of science:

By giving the 'purely religious principle' a place of first importance, by viewing the Old Testament primarily from the standpoint of divine revelation, one commits himself as it were by silent approval to give preference to one particular class of historical hypotheses, choosing by predisposition one party in a struggle that ought to be settled purely by historical arguments... To put it bluntly, I believe that we need a historical solution and cannot allow ourselves to be satisfied with any other.[4]

Similar examples from the writings of two of Kuenen's pupils may be cited as further illustrations of the modernist understanding of Scripture. The first of these is the inaugural address of Hendrik Oort at the Amsterdam Athenaeum in 1873. Reviewing the past history of the study of Hebrew antiquities, Oort argued that the conclusions of each scholar had been vitiated in some degree by religious prejudgment. There had been only one, his teacher and friend Kuenen, who completely satisfied Oort in this respect. The scholar whom he held in highest regard next to Kuenen was Heinrich Ewald, but even he, with his colossal learning and unique acumen, put too much trust in tradition, with the result that his criticism often fell short of its mark. Thus Oort issued a call for a new, completely objective criticism of the Old Testament documents – as if there could actually be such a thing – which needed to be pursued, not only

1 'Het supernaturalisme en de geschiedenis van Israël,' XXXIV (1860), 705–57. The following sentences are particularly significant (p. 712): 'It is untrue that according to the antisupernaturalistic conception Israel's religion is of human origin and therefore not of divine origin. True, it is from man – but from man created by God, and living and moving and having his being in him; from man whose powers develop under God's guidance; from man nourished and nurtured by God to his own purpose; from man in whose development God's spirit and power reveal themselves.'
2 Jena, 1869. E. G. Kraeling, *The Old Testament Since the Reformation*, London, 1955, pp. 82ff, indicates the lasting significance of this work.
3 'Het tegenwoordig standpunt van de studie des Ouden Testaments,' III, 138–64
4 Pp. 154f, 151. For similar statements cf. Kuenen's polemic against Ed. Böhl in *GB* 1864, pp. 202ff and against Graetz in *TT*, V (1874), 263–300.

for the light it might shed on Christian origins, but for its own sake as well.[1]

The second example is chosen from near the end of the nineteenth century; it is also from an inaugural oration, that of W. H. Kosters delivered at Leiden University in 1892. Kosters indicated how little the modernist theory had changed in twenty years. His subject was the religious character of Israel's historiography. By this he meant the function of individual documents within the Old Testament in terms of concrete ecclesiastical or religious situations. One might wish to comment on the farsightedness of Kosters's scholarly interest, as seen from the standpoint of current issues in biblical criticism, but what concerns us for the moment is his understanding of the Bible as a vehicle of revelation. Kosters agreed with Scholten and Kuenen. He said that Israel's historical records have no unique interest for Christian theologians. They do not contain a revelation distinct from that possessed by extra-biblical religious documents. 'The one sort as well as the other comes from the heart of man. Nevertheless, in the one sort as well as in the other we can see the revelation of God.'[2] In other words, God reveals himself in Israel's sacred literature as he reveals himself in all religious life and thought.

It will be recalled that toward the end of the nineteenth century an extreme naturalistic wing developed within the modernist movement, explicating the principles of Opzoomer and Pierson and finding its chief center in Amsterdam. Opzoomer's empiricism led to a practical denial of God's presence in the world, hence to an abandonment of the idea of revelation. Adherents of the Amsterdam group, several of whom were faculty members of the municipal University of Amsterdam founded out of the Athenaeum in 1877 (to be distinguished from Kuyper's Free University), adopted a posture of profound agnosticism. Inasmuch as the early emphasis of biblical criticism within the entire modernist movement was upon the historical factor, this difference between the Leiden and Amsterdam viewpoints did not immediately make itself noticeable in critical studies, but eventually the difference did become quite obvious and led to the organizing of the journal, *Teyler's Theologisch Tijdschrift*, in 1903, as a more extreme expression of historicism.[3] We shall have occasion to observe concrete examples of critical study appearing in this periodical, but for the present we offer one example from an earlier publication to illustrate the growing divergence of viewpoint.

1 *De tegenwoordige toestand der Israëlietische oudheidskunde*, Leiden, 1873
2 *Het godsdienstig karakter van Israëls historiographie*, Leiden, 1892, p. 4
3 Published in Haarlem from 1903 to 1911 under the editorship of J. G. Boekenoogen

The statement we have in mind is from one of Pierson's ambitious works, *Een studie over de geschriften van Israël's profeten*, published in 1877. Truly, Pierson was a man of universal interest! In this book he assayed to carry forward the line of research outlined in Kuenen's great book on the prophets, which is to be discussed below. Although Pierson paid lip-service to Kuenen, he made the severe criticism that Kuenen's book was too theological, i.e., too willing to see spiritual value in Israel's prophetism. Pierson complained: 'Even liberal theology is still theology, and theology is irreconcilable with genuine scientific inquiry.' Pierson ended with the fervent wish that all theology, including biblical study, would ere long become completely secularized.

Concluding this survey, we state that Scholten's doctrine of Scripture strongly influenced the modernist movement. Scholten and his colleagues conceived of the work of God as coterminous with the natural order and with historical process, hence with all life, and particularly with all religious life, as revealing the mind and will of God. This is the theory that Busken Huet popularized. This Kuenen and his students reaffirmed. Reduced to its basic concept, this modernist doctrine of Scripture involved an affirmation of general revelation, coupled with a denial of special revelation, based upon antisupernaturalistic and historicistic presuppositions. The Amsterdam group differed only in denying the divine, transcendent element altogether.

MODERNIST NEW TESTAMENT CRITICISM

It is now necessary to view the actual biblical criticism of the Dutch modernists in some detail in order to gain an insight into the way in which their doctrine or doctrines of Scripture actually affected their critical study, and vice versa. As has been previously stated, it is specifically the critical study of the Old Testament that we are to examine; but by way of preface, we need first to provide some information concerning the leading modernist New Testament scholars, and to sketch the main aspects of their work, as the counterpart to what is to be our major object of attention.[4]

Foremost among modernist New Testament critics was Scholten, who can rightly be said to have pioneered the historical criticism of this part of the Bible in his country. This is in spite of the fact that his greatest

et al., and continued from 1912 to 1933 as *Vw II* under the editorship of H. J. Elhorst *et al.*

4 Cf. Lindeboom, *op. cit.*, pp. 14ff, 198, for a more extensive treatment.

fame derives from his work as a systematic theologian. Scholten was
one of those remarkable scholars, rare in our time but not so rare in
his own, who are equally masters of two or more demanding specialties.
Nevertheless, we are able to note a shift in his interest over the years.
During the fifties, while he was absorbed in theological debates and while
he was revising again and again his *Leer der Hervormde Kerk,* his biblical
studies remained relatively minor and incidental. In the sixties and
seventies, however, he wrote extensively in the area of New Testament
criticism. In the decade between 1864 and 1873, he composed a number
of important books, several of which were translated into German. These
included *Het Evangelie naar Johannes* (1864), *De oudste getuigenissen aangaande de Schriften des Nieuwen Testaments historisch onderzocht* (1866), *Het
oudste Evangelie* [Matt.-Mark] (1868), *Het Paulinische Evangelie* [Luke]
(1870), *De Apostel Johannes in Klein-Azië* (1871), and *Is de derde Evangelist
de schrijver van het boek der Handelingen?* (1873). In all this, Scholten showed
himself to be abreast of the most advanced German criticism. His 1866
book on the ancient witnesses to the New Testament appears to have
made the most favorable impression abroad.

Other Dutch New Testament scholars of the modernist school, at
first strongly under Scholten's influence, tended to follow the example of
the Tübingen criticism in rejecting the historicity of the Fourth Gospel, employing the 'aftrek' method in Synoptic analysis, giving the teaching of Jesus
great historical and religious value, and accepting as genuine the chief
Pauline epistles. As has been mentioned, Kuenen labored alongside
Scholten, at first as his associate in New Testament interpretation. This
was largely in the 1850's, however, before Kuenen came to devote his full
strength to the study of the Old Testament, and before Scholten produced
his major books in New Testament criticism. In any case, Kuenen
continued to share Scholten's methodology and basic point of view as
long as they labored together at Leiden. It is interesting to observe that
a relatively large number of dissertations were written at Leiden in the
field of New Testament during the 1850's. The number declined gradually during the sixties and seventies, and dwindled to virtually nothing
during the eighties and nineties.[1]

It is worthwhile observing that several modernist scholars of this

1 At Utrecht, where about the same number of New Testament dissertations were written during this half-century, the number increased gradually to a high point in the
seventies, the heyday of Doedes and van Oosterzee, dropping off rapidly thereafter.
At Groningen, where fewer New Testament dissertations were written, the sixties and
seventies were the most active period.

2 *De bergrede en andere synoptische fragmenten,* Amsterdam, 1878

period combined critical studies in the New Testament with interest in other fields. Among such were L. S. P. Meyboom, A. Réville, F. W. B. van Bell, J. Cramer, and G. J. P. J. Bolland. We pass these and others by, however, in order to devote some attention to the only noteworthy 'school' of New Testament scholarship in addition to the 'Leiden school' of Scholten, Kuenen, and their pupils. Here we have in mind a group of radical scholars whom we may designate as the Amsterdam school. It included Allard Pierson, A. D. Loman, S. A. Naber, W. C. van Manen, and several others. The designation, 'Amsterdam school,' is appropriate not because several of these men lived in Amsterdam but because this city and its university were its base and center. More precisely, one might say that Pierson, teaching in Amsterdam after 1877, was its center, since his principle of radical empiricism was its guiding principle. In this respect, Pierson was likewise the leading spirit of the Amsterdam school of Old Testament criticism, of which we shall have more to say later.

Something must now be said about these men and their work. Of Pierson's labors in New Testament criticism – not his specialty – we need note only its extremest scepticism. He did not hesitate to go so far as to deny flatly the existence of Jesus as a historical figure.[2] Loman came to share basically this same position. A Lutheran (d. 1897), he taught in Amsterdam from 1856 to 1893. Although blind after 1874, he remained energetic in New Testament research. His point of view became increasingly radical, going beyond the once extreme, but now widely accepted Tübingen criticism. He doubted, though he did not specifically deny, the historicity of a Jesus living in first-century Palestine. Nevertheless, the Jesus of the Gospels was purely mythical, being nothing but the second-century personification of an idealized Judaism. With the other members of this school, Loman likewise came to deny the authenticity of the Pauline literature and to date the New Testament books in the second century.[3]

Naber (d. 1913), another Amsterdam professor, was a classical philologist with a special interest in the New Testament writings. In 1886 he collaborated with Pierson in denying the authenticity of all the epistles traditionally ascribed to Paul, including Romans, I and II Corinthians, and Galatians.[4]

---

3 Cf. especially Loman, *De zoogenaamde symbolische opvatting der Evangelische geschiedenis, en haar jongste bestrijding*, Amsterdam 1884; *Symbool en werkelijkheid in de evangelische geschiedenis*, Amsterdam 1884.

4 *Verisimilia Saceram conditionem Novi Testamenti exemplis illustrarunt et ab origine repetierunt*, Amsterdam, 1878

Van Manen (d. 1905) taught first at Groningen and then in Leiden. A productive scholar, he developed into an eminent but extremely one-sided critic.[1] He employed his broad learning in early Christian literature to subject the Pauline literature to a minute scrutiny, coming to the conclusion of Pierson and Naber that all of it was spurious. He also shared their conclusion that Jesus was no historical personage.

Together with a small group of followers, these scholars came to be known in Germany as 'die radikale holländische Schule.' Although outside The Netherlands no one seemed to take them very seriously, or to offer a refutation of their arguments, within the country itself they encountered vigorous opposition, the most formidable of which came from Scholten and the Leiden school.[2] Even Kuenen undertook a rebuttal of Pierson's and Naber's book *Verisimilia*.[3] The Leiden scholars, it can be fairly stated, were far less affected by historical positivism and radical empiricism than were their colleagues of the Amsterdam school, remaining generally within the mainstream of progressive criticism, perhaps making few startling and original hypotheses, but not, at any rate, falling far behind the vanguard of scientific investigation.

The radical New Testament school found a few noteworthy adherents in the closing decades of the nineteenth and the early years of the twentieth centuries, but gradually faded out completely. Among these was Daniel Völter of Amsterdam, who wrote mainly in German and published most of his work on the New Testament in Germany, so scarcely counts as a Dutch scholar. We may also mention H. U. Meyboom, a specialist in old Christian literature, who taught at Groningen from 1892 to 1913. Best known, however, was has been G. A. van den Bergh van Eysinga, a pupil of van Manen who came strongly under *religions-geschichtliche* influence. Also a specialist in early Christian literature, he taught in Utrecht since 1924 and in Amsterdam after 1935, and strove valiantly to uphold the validity of the radical theories of his predecessors in a period when there were few to listen or to care.[4]

Nothing can be more apparent, from our present point of view, than that these New Testament scholars were dominated more by their theological preconceptions than by their scientific methodology. This is true

[1] Among his better known writings were *Conjecturaal-kritiek, toegepast op den tekst van de schriften des Nieuwen Testaments* (Haarlem, 1880), *Paulus* (Leiden, 1890–96), and *Handleiding van de oudchristelijke letterkunde* (Leiden, 1900). His biographer, H. U. Meyboom, remarks that 'we have more cause to be amazed at his critical acumen than at any success he may have achieved in enriching our understanding' (cited by Roessingh, *Verzamelde werken* II, 397).

of both the Leiden and the Amsterdam scholars, and of the more conservative scholars as well. They all aimed to employ an exacting methodology and the most advanced insights, although they no doubt did this with varying degrees of skill. It was all too possible for subjectivistic and positivistic theory to serve in the place of objective data, however. Indeed, this often seemed the only way out, since the common store of scientific facts available for establishing a firm critical basis in the study of the New Testament was still altogether inadequate, and the tools of scientific research were still rough hewn.

This is a generalization that is equally true of Old Testament criticism in The Netherlands. We must leave our observations regarding Dutch New Testament criticism as a generalization, but proceed now with the detailed analysis of biblical criticism in this companion field, the main purpose of our study. In this present chapter we shall turn our attention to Abraham Kuenen and the other modernist Old Testament scholars. Alongside Kuenen, in what we may again call 'the Leiden school', we find such men as C. P. Tiele, H. Oort, M. de Goeje, and W. H. Kosters. Paralleling the radical Amsterdam New Testament school we find a radical Old Testament school with J. C. Matthes as its chief exponent. The work of each of these, and of other leading modernist scholars, calls for a detailed description, far more minute than what appears above. This will also be required, in following chapters, for the writings of Old Testament scholars in the conservative camp – most notably those of the orthodox Ethical group – as well as for the work of those liberal and conservative Old Testament scholars who set new trends in the postmodernist era beginning with our present century.

A *sine qua non* for this analysis is a thorough study of the giant of modern Dutch biblical criticism, Abraham Kuenen. As we shall see, he stood head and shoulders above all his colleagues, and somehow Old Testament criticism under his leadership succeeded where the radical Dutch New Testament criticism failed. Much as details of Kuenen's theories have had to be revised with further progress in scientific study, his work stands as a milestone that time has not been able to remove.

---

2 Cf. Scholten, *Historisch-critische bijdragen naar aanleiding van de nieuwste hypothese aangaande Jezus en den Paulus der vier hoofdbrieven* (Leiden, 1882).

3 *TT*, XX (1886), 491–536

4 See his book, *Radical Views About the New Testament* (London, 1912), also in German. Among his most notable writings were *Onderzoek naar de echtheid van de eerste Brief van Clemens* (1908) and *Voorchristelijk Christendom* (1918).

ABRAHAM KUENEN AS THEOLOGIAN AND SCHOLAR

Eloquent testimony to the vast influence of Kuenen in biblical studies is the outpouring of biographical sketches and tributes written about him immediately after his death. Within a month, his close friend A. Réville reviewed his life for the series *Mannen van beteekenis in onze dagen*, giving him a place of honor alongside Tolstoy, de Lisle, Stanley, and Newman, whose biographies appeared in the same volume.[1] Kuenen's famous colleague at Leiden, C. P. Tiele, wrote another biographical tribute early in 1892 ,as did also C. H. Toy of Harvard and Kuenen's pupil and translator, Philip H. Wicksteed.[2] All of these provide in considerable detail a view of Kuenen's life, work, and significance. T. K. Cheyne, in 1893, included Kuenen among his *Founders of Old Testament Criticism*.[3] and in the same year Hendrik Oort wrote a uniquely informative description of his teacher and colleague's life, 'Kuenen als godgeleerde,' an article appearing in *De Gids*.[4] When Karl Budde issued a selection and German translation of Kuenen's most important critical articles (1894), he did not neglect to record personal reminiscence and tribute.[5] Various other sketches appearing between 1892 and 1894 include articles by G. Wildeboer, W. C. van Manen, and J. C. Matthes.[6]

Kuenen was born in Haarlem in 1828, grew up under the influence of an 'old liberal' minister, and in 1845 entered Leiden University to embark upon a course of brilliant study in the fields of theology and Oriental languages. From its beginning, this university had been noted for its excellence in these two areas. It had already become an important center of theological studies under Drusius (d. 1616) and Junius (d. 1602). When Arminius become professor at Leiden in 1603, he made it the center of the storm in Holland's first important post-Reformation theological controversy. Other well-known Leiden theologians of this early

1 Haarlem, 1891

2 'Levensberichten, Abraham Kuenen,' *Jaarboek van de Koninklijke Akademie van Wetenschappen*, pp. 1–25; *The New World*, I, 64–88; *JQR*, IV, 571–605

3 pp. 185–94

4 See chap. 2, note 6.

5 *Gesammelte Abhandlungen zur biblischen Wissenschaft von Dr. Abraham Kuenen, weiland Professor zu Leiden. Aus den Holländischen übersetzt von K. Budde*, Freiburg i.B. und Leipzig. Cf. 'Vorwort.'

6 *TS*, X (1892), 1–8; *Protestantische Kirchenzeitung*, 1892, pp. 255ff, 284ff, 307ff; *De Gids*, XII (1894), 494–517. Cf. also W. van der Vlugt, *Levensbericht van Abraham Kuenen*, Leiden, 1893; Oort in *TT*, XXV (1892), 113–16; Tiele in *De Gids*, X (1892), 191–96; M. A. Beek in *VoxTh*, VII (1935–36), 149–52; W. B. Kristensen, *Symbool en werkelijkheid* (Arnhem, 1954), pp. 31–35.

period were Arminius's successor Episcopius, Cocceius, Ludovicus de Dieu, Salmasius, Witsius, and John Marck. It is true that theological studies had declined during the nineteenth century, at Leiden as elsewhere in the country, but Scholten, who arrived here in 1843, was already bringing excellence and fame to its theological faculty. Kuenen came very deeply under Scholten's influence, as his later writings in general, and certain *stellingen* (propositions for public debate) of his doctoral dissertation in particular, clearly testify.

In Oriental studies, Kuenen gained proficiency under the tutelage of the noted Arabist T. W. J. Juynboll. One of Leiden's most famous Arabic scholars had been Erpenius, who came here in 1613, and for whom a special chair of Hebrew had been established. Later widely-known Leiden Orientalists were Raphelengius, Joseph Scaliger, Jacob Gool, Albert Schultens, H. A. Hamaker, and, in Kuenen's generation, Juynboll, R. Dozy, and M. J. de Goeje.[7] With such resources of instruction and inspiration, Kuenen might have made a name for himself as an Orientalist worthy to rank with the greatest of his predecessors. He did, as a matter of fact, publish as his dissertation an Arabic Pentateuchal manuscript,[8] and was appointed after his graduation to serve as curator of the university's extensive collection of Arabic manuscripts.

This was not to be, however, the direction of Kuenen's life, valuable as this careful linguistic training turned out to be. Scholten saw in Kuenen the person he needed to collaborate with him in biblical studies, and succeeded in getting him appointed to the theological faculty in 1852, less than two years after his graduation, when he was but twenty-four. In 1855 he became ordinary professor. Time and circumstances were unusually favorable for this gifted young man. In Tiele's opinion, Kuenen was completely ripe, ready for the responsibility and challenge of his position, ready to begin a career of constant productivity and of seldom-paralleled brilliance.[9]

---

7 Cf. A. Wensinck, 'Leiden als centrum van oostersche wetenschap,' *Leidsch Universiteitsblad*, I, 4f; Nat, *op. cit.*; B. D. Eerdmans, *Het verband tusschen de beoefening van het Oude Testament en de Semietische studiën in het algemeen*, Leiden, 1898. One of the foremost Arabists of the present century has been the Leiden scholar, C. Snouck Hurgronje.

8 *Specimin theologicum continens Geneseos libri capita xxxiv priora* (etc.), Leiden, 1851

9 'Levensbericht,' p. 7. Tiele explained: 'The life of Kuenen was not a hard one. I have called it a march of triumph. Indeed, it furnished him abundant opportunity to develop the rich talents with which he had been entrusted and make them bear fruit. He did not know agonized struggles. The misunderstanding, the working at cross-purposes, and the slightings which embitter or at least discourage so many, were spared him. The yoke of a task not suited to his aptitudes, so deadening for many, was not imposed upon his shoulders.'

It may seem strange that Kuenen was initially appointed to teach New Testament exegesis. This was because the royal decree of 1815, still in effect, had eliminated the exegesis of the Old Testament from the theological curriculum. In his first years Kuenen produced a few writings in the field of New Testament, but, as we have seen, gradually his interest turned to the other part of the Bible. He began to write and lecture on the exegesis and criticism of the Old Testament. Belatedly, in 1877, the government set up a special chair of Old Testament criticism within the theological faculty in recognition of his growing eminence in this area of study, officially adding this to his responsibilities.[1]

The wide esteem in which Kuenen came to be held, both in The Netherlands and abroad, is witnessed to by the many academic and professional honors that came to him. Soon after his inauguration in the theological faculty at Leiden he was awarded an honorary doctorate by the literary faculty. He served as officer in such professional organizations as the Teyler Stichting, the Haagsche Genootschap tot Verdediging van den Godsdienst, and the Koninklijke Akademie van Wetenschap. A supreme honor came in 1882, when he was invited to deliver the Hibbert Lectures at Oxford. He was president of the International Congress of Orientalists meeting in Leiden in 1884, and an honorary member of the American Society of Biblical Literature and Exegesis. Biographers recall how grateful the citizens of Leiden were for the fame Kuenen brought to their town and university, how they would look after him with awe and admiration as he passed them on the street.

Kuenen was heart and soul part of the modernist movement from its beginning. He joined in its repudiation of orthodox dogmatics and the supernatural authority of the Scriptures, as we have seen. In lectures and sermons he did much to popularize its cause. He took a leading part in the editing of *Theologisch Tijdschrift*, making frequent contributions to it. He belonged to the Protestanten Bond and the Vergadering van Moderne Theologen. As a natural leader, he was often burdened with duties of administration in such organizations, but even when he did not preside, his influence was often dominant.[2] But his greatest contribution to the advance of Dutch modernism was his monumental labor in Old Testament criticism. By destroying belief in the supernatural character of the Old Testament, he did more than anyone in his country to advance

1 Reitsma, pp. 521f, gives details of this law's further effects.
2 In *Het goed recht der Modernen* (cf. p. 37, n. 5), Kuenen defended the modernists' right in the church. He led in commemorating modernism's first twenty-five years; cf. his address, *Gedachtenisrede in de Vergadering van Moderne Theologen*, Leiden, 1891.
3 *op. cit.*, p. 15

modernism's cause. The presence of this eminent biblical critic in their ranks give the other leaders of the movement a supreme confidence that Truth was with them in their assault on traditionalism.

Kuenen had a sincere religiosity, which kept him from clinging to sterile traditionalism but also kept him from abandoning himself to a scoffing scepticism or an enervating agnosticism. Thus he seemed radical to some and conservative to others. He was indeed conservative in the sense of being restrained, judicious, and fair. As Tiele said, 'He was eminently thoughtful, an enemy of wild hypotheses and propositions.' Tiele preferred to call him simply 'critical,' in the sense that he clung to nothing, once he saw that it was untrue, and was constantly probing further for better understanding.[3]

To be sure, one may observe a gradual development in Kuenen's theology. Already in his student days he had become an adherent of the rising modernist movement, but at that time not even Scholten had developed to the logical outworking of the position he had taken. As with Scholten, so with Kuenen, there were still remnants of supernaturalistic and biblicistic tradition. Thus, for instance, Kuenen still adhered to belief in Jesus' resurrection as late as 1855. His biblical criticism was also still relatively conservative. Early in 1853, in his inaugural oration, he upheld a traditional position over against what he called the 'ravings' of Vatke, von Bohlen, and others of their school.[4] M. A. Beek, a Dutch scholar of the present generation, explains Kuenen's cautious attitude as follows:

By nature no fighter, conservative, and inclined to retain the old as long as possible, he departed from his old theological home out of compulsion from scientific insights. He came to results that were unpleasant to him, but the love of truth drove him to accept them.[5]

A sober and painstaking method is followed in all Kuenen's compositions. Oort has characterized his style as 'dry as cork but clear as glass,' going on to say that Kuenen was a teacher from whom one could hardly help but learn:

Kuenen is the dissector. He takes his pupil along with him and allows him to see clearly the book about whose origin and composition he wants to learn. That is, he teaches him how he must conceive of the contents, both in general lines and in particular details; he lets him observe the concepts that led the writer, as well

4 *Oratio de accuratio antiquitatis Hebraicae studio theologo Christiano magnopere commendato*, Leiden, 1853. Later, when he had arrived at essentially the standpoint that Vatke had defended, he came to apologize for his harsh criticism.
5 *op. cit.*, p. 150.

as the real and seeming contradictions appearing in the contents, pointing to the data by which these must be judged; he teaches him to assemble and arrange facts, neglecting not the slightest detail that might shed light upon them, but avoiding the distortion of depending on anything insignificant while forgetting that he is dealing with the work of living people who aimed at exerting an influence in a community where men were thinking, believing, loving, and hating. This describes the inexhaustible patience with which he goes before his readers.[1]

One of Kuenen's conscious aims as a biblical scholar was to develop the methodology of his renowned fellow-countryman Grotius, who had pioneered in the precritical era in which he lived with his claim that the Old Testament is to be interpreted in terms of its own cultural situation, rather than as a prophecy of Christ.[2] In 1880, at the peak of his career, Kuenen published a full and frank account of the way in which he worked, commending it to all students of the Bible. This is an article with the title, 'Critical Method,' appearing in *The Modern Review*.[3] Karl Budde translated it for his *Gesammelte Abhandlungen*. H.-J. Kraus has recently considered it to be still of sufficient importance to be summarized in his definitive history of Old Testament research.[4] It undoubtedly had a wide influence in demonstrating in many lands the reasonableness and necessity of biblical criticism. It is important for the purpose of the present study to gain an idea of its contents. We shall summarize it therefore in some detail.

Kuenen begins this article by describing a *jeu d'esprit* on criticism in the case of Napoleon. The writer of 'Comme quoi Napoléon n'a jamais existé,' a satirical piece appearing in the first volume of *Musée Philipon*, showed how the history of Napoleon could be entirely explained away as having arisen from myths. This was very cleverly done; its point, of course, was to ridicule the biblical critics who were doing something similar with Moses and Abraham. Kuenen thinks this satire to be quite irrelevant, though admitting that a few biblical scholars might have gone to extremes of fanciful reconstruction.

Kuenen lays bare the reasons for traditionalism's bitter polemic against modern criticism. Actually, he says, the scientific criticism of the Bible ought to enjoy the same high praise in the church that research in other fields receives, yet it has been opposed because it challenges orthodox notions and because of its supposed caprice and unreasonableness. In answer, Kuenen undertakes to justify criticism by showing its necessity, its simplicity, and its common sense.

First, he defines the goal of criticism, which is simply to reconstruct

1 'Kuenen als godgeleerde,' pp. 534f
2 Cf. Kuenen, 'Hugo de Groot als uitlegger van het Oude Verbond,' *Verslagen en mede-*

a true picture of history. History, in turn, is nothing other than a faithful and meaningful representation of reality. Thus, says Kuenen, the critic is the ally of the historian, and furnishes him with the materials he must use in his work. But whence comes the knowledge desired by critic and historian? In one word, replies Kuenen, from the documents. Documents are of two kinds: facts and accounts. Facts constitute *prima facie* evidence; accounts must be evaluated for their credibility. Although in many cases these two slide insensibly into each other, they must be carefully distinguished. As an example of facts one may mention the Assyrian inscriptions, of accounts, the narratives recorded in these inscriptions. Biblical documents must be similarly criticized:

Quite independently of their value as witnesses to the times with which they deal, they must be considered as products of the times in which they were composed, and for the history of which they contribute more or less valuable materials... In other and shorter words, all documents without distinction are subjected to literary criticism, while narratives or accounts are further subjected to historical criticism in the proper or narrow sense.

The next question is how to proceed with literary and historical criticism. Kuenen takes up this question by repeating the rules given by von Sybel for fields where materials are abundant. The historian must begin with literary criticism, examining authorship, authenticity, and composition. Next, historical criticism must be applied, but this varies as to whether the author is known or unknown. In the former case, all must be governed by what is known of the character, ideas, and situation of the author. In the latter case, contiguous facts will have to serve as a criterion of credibility. In any case, this procedure implies continuity: 'The assumption with which all certainty of knowledge stands or falls is that the development of all earthly things follows absolute laws, and that they constitute together one connected whole.' Without this law, no historical investigation would be possible.

But this describes the normal procedure, says Kuenen; it can be followed only where documents are abundant. Bible critics must follow a somewhat abnormal procedure because their controlling documents are relatively scarce. Properly speaking, literary questions such as authorship should come first, but it is an exceptional case in which such a question can be solved in dealing with the Old Testament without the help of historical criticism. This means that literary and historical criticism must

deelingen der Koninklijke Akademie van Wetenschappen, Afdeeling Letterkunde, Amsterdam, 1883. 3 I, 461–88, 685–713   4 *op. cit.*, pp. 230–35

be combined. The biblical critic is often left with conflicting possibilities, with certainty quite impossible.

The next very important question for the critic is that of miracles. Do they or do they not happen? These are abundantly reported outside the Bible, yet all reject such reports. Why then should the miracles of the Bible warrant an exception? They can be maintained only on the basis of a biblicistic prejudgment. Historical investigation alone ought to be allowed to decide the question. Miracles may be theoretically possible, but are they probable? Kuenen thinks this question should decide for the truly unbiased person where the truth lies.[1]

Next Kuenen compares the method of biblical criticism with that of sound legal procedure. A good judge goes through five carefully defined steps. First he makes a thorough investigation of all pertinent facts; then he assembles and cross-examines all available witnesses; next he constructs a working-hypothesis and tests it by the evidence; then he rechecks his hypothesis; at last he is ready to pronounce judgment. So it must be with the criticism of the Bible. Kuenen's definition of the historical criticism of the Bible is accordingly as follows: it is 'the attempt to find an hypothesis that accounts for the documents, and, if several such hypotheses present themselves, the selection of the one which appears on comparison to have the greatest probability in its favor.' It must meet the conditions of (1) accounting for the form and substance of the document in question and (2) conforming to known, established facts.

Kuenen refutes some of the common complaints made against this sort of criticism. Such are (1) that criticism substitutes theories for facts; (2) that it is destructive; (3) that it is negative; (4) that its results are variable, uncertain, and often contradictory. Kuenen considers the first of these scarcely deserving of reply because of its patent falsehood. As for the second, he remarks that criticism is destructive only of unjustified and outworn traditions; 'but now can this be considered a reproach by Protestants, who do not believe in an infallible church, and still less, we may presume, in an infallible synagogue?' As to the third charge, he answers that criticism is negative only in order to be positive. And, while admitting the relative truth in the fourth objection, he emphasizes that criticism's erratic progress has at any rate been *progress*.

Here we have a clear and full statement of the method Kuenen believed should be followed in studying the Bible. We may be grateful for the

1 Although Kuenen claimed that he always kept an open mind regarding the possibility of miracles, it was clear that this was purely theoretical; cf. B. D. Eerdmans, *TT*, n.r. I (1910), 171ff.

candor with which he set forth its philosophical and scientific presuppositions. It is apparent that Kuenen assumed the continuity of all reality. His axioms of historical judgment are generally sound, but are marred by the foreshortened perspective of the period in which he labored and by a willingness to give greater weight to an *a priori* theory of development than to the concrete evidence of the text itself.

THE CRITICAL STUDIES OF KUENEN AND THE MODERNIST OLD TESTAMENT SCHOLARS

It is now our interest to observe in detail how a man of Kuenen's genius worked out the critical exegesis of the Bible on the basis of the scientific methodology just described. Although it is not our purpose to offer a complete literary biography of either him or his associates, it will be necessary to review his and their major accomplishments and to illustrate from their writings the interaction of their philosophical-theological principles and their scientific methods.

It must be already apparent to the reader that Kuenen was a tireless scholar and a prolific writer. Besides a not insignificant number of popular pieces, written to educate the church public in the principles of modernist thought, he composed numerous long and weighty articles and monographs for a variety of publications, chiefly *Godgeleerde Bijdragen* and *Theologisch Tijdschrift*. To these he likewise contributed many lengthy critical reviews. He wrote five major books, all of world renown, including the first (1861–65) and second (1887–92) editions of an extensive work on Old Testament introduction, a two-volume history of Israel (1869–70), a lengthy book on prophecy (1877), and the 1882 Hibbert Lectures.[2]

Early straws in the wind indicating the direction of Kuenen's thought were his previously mentioned inaugural and a short series of critical appraisals appearing in *Godgeleerde Bijdragen*. The inaugural oration, a recommendation of the critical study of the Old Testament to Christian scholars, signalized the young New Testament professor's predilection for the Old Testament. The first two appraisals, criticisms of van Oosterzee's and Schwartz's 'Christologies of the Old Testament,' took these scholars to task for too dogmatic an approach to the biblical text. The third appraisal was the criticism of the younger Hofstede de Groot, in defense

2 For titles, see below. An exhaustive bibliography prepared by van Manen appears in *JQR*, IV, 471–89, and in Budde, *op. cit.*, pp. 501–11.

of Busken Huet, mentioned above, attacking supernaturalism.[1]

Only ten years after his graduation, in 1861, Kuenen began to publish a three-volume introduction to the Old Testament called *Historisch-kritisch onderzoek naar het ontstaan en de verzameling van de boeken des Ouden Verbonds*. Although it presented little that was new, it summarized the best current research in a remarkably clear and systematic manner, thus offering itself to the public as a reliable guide to the critical issues of the day. It constitutes an admirable exhibition of the scientific method which Kuenen later described in the aforementioned article.[2]

One of the most crucial problems of this period for biblical scholars was the analysis of the Pentateuch. Here were located the basic issues affecting the criticism of the entire Old Testament and the history of Israel. In this first edition of his large book on introduction, Kuenen took still a relatively conservative position respecting the Pentateuch, though this was far in advance of the traditional view to the effect that Moses wrote the entire first five books of the Bible.[3] Kuenen held that Moses did indeed compose the Decalogue and certain other laws, but declared the Book of the Covenant (Exodus 20:22ff) to be from David's time and the priestly legislation, found in Exodus to Numbers, to have originated over an extended period between Solomon's reign and the exile. Kuenen agreed with Ewald and contemporary critics that this priestly legislation constituted part of a *Grundschrift* or Book of Origins to which all the other elements in the Pentateuch came to be added, including the work of the Yahwist (J), the Elohist (E), and Deuteronomy (D). According to Kuenen, the entire Pentateuch was essentially in its present form by the beginning of the exile.

It is remarkable to observe that Kuenen saw this as the historical picture at this early period in his career, before the theory of rigid evolutionism (Vatke) had extensively affected him. Symptomatic was his judgment

1 XXX (1856), 25–67, 128–74; XXII (1858), 177–211; XXXIV (1860), 705–57 (see G. W. Stemler's very courteous and capable reply on pp. 977–84).
2 This work was widely praised and was quickly translated into English and French.
3 For a detailed presentation of this most important area of Kuenen's research, see S. J. De Vries, 'The Hexateuchal Criticism of Abraham Kuenen,' *Journal of Biblical Literature*, LXXXII (1963), 31–57.
4 'De jongste onderzoekingen omtrent de samenstelling van den Pentateuch,' XXXVI, 355–83 (against Knobel and Nicolas); 'Opmerkingen over de voor-Mozaische godsdienst,' XXXVII, 587–622 (against Pleyte); 'Verklaring van twaalf Messiaansche Psalmen', XXXVIII, 202–37 (against Böhl).
5 R. Dozy, *De Israëlieten te Mekka*, Haarlem, 1863; Kuenen, 'De Baäldienst onder Israël, *GB*, XXXVIII, 449–91, 'Simeonieten en Ismaëlieten,' XL, 449–515. Kuenen accused Dozy of *Tendenzkritik;* he carefully examined the passages in question and concluded that,

that J's deep concern for sin and intense character delineations are to be taken as indications of a date later than that of the *Grundschrift*. Kuenen believed in the law of development, but this had not yet assumed for him a rigid form.

From 1862 to 1866 Kuenen continued to use *Godgeleerde Bijdragen* for reviewing a number of important works. Among his articles were a severe criticism of the fanciful constructions of W. Pleyte, who identified the patriarch Seth in Genesis with the Egyptian god of a similar name. Kuenen also criticized severely Ed. Böhl's attempt to find Christ in the Psalms.[4] He was quite caustic with the wild hypotheses of his Leiden colleague, the Arabist Dozy, who wrote a book to the effect that the biblical tribe of Simeon became the ancestors of the Moslems in Mecca; Dozy's claim that the Genesis writers had deliberately falsified the patriarchal history stirred Kuenen to a vigorous defense of Mosaic Yahwism and of the relative trustworthiness of the patriarchal tradition.[5]

In 1866 Kuenen presented to the Koninklijke Akademie van Wetenschap in Amsterdam the first of several extensive and richly informative monographs on subjects of general interest to biblical scholars. This first monograph was concerned with the historical problem of the composition of the Jewish sanhedrin. Included among the others were the previously mentioned study of Grotius as a biblical interpreter, a refutation of the cherished notion that Ezra's 'Great Synagogue' had compiled the Old Testament canon, and a judicious history of the Masoretic Text. All were pieces of considerable weight and lasting value.[6]

It was at this particular time that Kuenen was coming to a dramatic change in his views concerning Israel's religious and literary development. A number of scholars, among them Dozy, J. Colenso, J. Popper, and K. H. Graf, brought him to see that the so-called *Grundschrift* could not be the earliest of the Pentateuchal documents, as he and others had

---

although they are not literally historical, they are nonetheless intended as bona fide accounts. Even so, Dozy's boldness soon proved to be a catalyst in forcing Kuenen to move on to a more radical criticism (see below).

6 'Over de samenstelling van het Sanhedrin,' *Verslagen en Mededeelingen der Koninklijke Akademie van Wetenschappen, Afdeeling Letterkunde*, 1866, pp. 131–68; 'Over F. Chabas, Les pasteurs en Egypte,' *idem*, 1868, pp. 22–28; 'De stamboom van den Masoretischen text des Ouden Testaments,' *idem*, 1873, pp. 289–339; 'Over de mannen der groote Synagogue,' *idem*, 1876, pp. 207–48; 'Hugo de Groot als uitlegger van het Ouden Verbond,' *idem*, 1883, pp. 301–32; 'De Melecheth des Hemels,' *idem*, 1888, pp. 157–89; 'De chronologie van het Perzische tijdvak,' *idem*, 1890, pp. 273–322. Budde translated all six for his *Gesammelte Abhandlungen*. The study on the Masoretic Text has been translated into French.

supposed, but must actually be the latest.[1] Graf was particularly influential in this matter. He argued in a book published in 1865 that the laws contained in the *Grundschrift* are later than Deuteronomy, which dates from Josiah's time; hence the *Grundschrift* laws are postexilic.[2] Kuenen accepted this conclusion, but wrote to Graf to the effect that the *Grundschrift* narratives had to remain attached to the laws, and that accordingly the whole document is postexilic. In 1869, shortly before his death, Graf published an article embodying Kuenen's proposal but neglecting to mention his indebtedness,[3] thus creating the impression that it was entirely his own original theory. Ultimately, Julius Wellhausen came to be remembered in connection with it, while the names of both Graf and Kuenen receded into the background.

As a matter of fact, this Kuenen-Graf theory followed the essential lines of Wilhelm Vatke's earlier hypothesis (1835), which on Hegelian presuppositions had similarly proposed that the priestly document must be the latest in the Pentateuch. Now the Kuenen who had been so severe with Vatke admitted that he must accept Vatke's theory, not on the basis of speculation but on the basis of an empirical investigation of the text. The redating of the *Grundschrift* was, of course, the key to this radically new construction of Israel's history, in which the writings of 'Moses' were seen as a very late accretion to the prophetic corpus, rather than as its foundation.

The transition from the early moderate stage to the later more radical stage of Kuenen's critical development was signalized decisively in 1869-70 by the appearance of a massive two-volume work, *De godsdienst van Israël*.[4] Here for the first time was a thoroughly naturalistic presentation of Israel's religious history, offering full-blown what came to be known as the Wellhau-

1 See Kuenen's 'literary autobiography' in *TT*, IV (1870), 391–426, 487–526, and in his introduction to Wicksteed's English translation (1885) of the second edition of his *Historisch-critisch onderzoek* (1887–93).

2 *Die geschichtlichen Bücher des Alten Testaments: zwei historisch-kritischen Untersuchungen*, Leipzig, 1865.

3 *Archiv für die wissenschaftliche Erforschung des Alten Testaments*, I, 466–77. Notice must here be taken of the objections of S. Külling, *Zur Datierung der 'Genesis- P-Stücke'* (Kampen: J. H. Kok, 1964), pp. 13–16, to this writer's statement in his article on Kuenen (see p. 64) claiming priority for Kuenen over Graf in respect to the dating of the entire priestly code after the exile. Külling emphasizes that Graf was also influenced by Riehm and Nöldeke – which is certainly true – and argues that in his reply to Kuenen (12 Nov. 1866), as well as in a later letter to his teacher Edouard Reuss, Graf expressed only *hypothetical* approval of Kuenen's proposal. In the light of Külling's objection, it is clear that greater care in choice of words would have been in order. I wrote: 'Graf appears to have been convinced at once: Kuenen published a letter... plainly expressing his agreement' (p. 44); 'Graf expressed his approval of Kuenen's suggestion in a letter to Reuss...' (n. 38). Graf does use the conditional verb in both instances; yet, at the very minimum, he was

sen theory. It gained wide dissemination by way of an English translation.

Kuenen showed in this book how completely he had succumbed to a rigid system of evolutionistic development. He began by stating flatly that Israel had not been the object of a special election or the recipient of a particular revelation, but that the key to an understanding of its history is purely natural development. All that was needed for unfolding this history was a fixed point from which this could be traced forward and backward. Such a point, Kuenen declared, was the preaching of Amos and Hosea, who were the very first to proclaim the purity, holiness, and omniscience of Yahweh – in other words, a high monotheism. The ordinary Hebrews meanwhile were serving Yahweh only in a purely sensual manner, as one god among many. Thus all Hebrew religion previous to the eighth century was polytheistic or at best henotheistic. Kuenen abandoned his former defence of the patriarchal narratives, now describing them as legends or sagas without historical foundation. Yahweh he described as a fire or sun god, given an ethical character by Moses, who attempted to get him acknowledged not as the only God but solely as the chief of the Hebrews' gods.

In his former book Kuenen had dated Deuteronomy ca. 700 B.C. With Graf, he now brought it down to Josiah's time (621), dubbing it a pious fraud of the reforming party. Another earlier opinion now receiving revision was his view of Ezekiel's relationship to the Pentateuch. Kuenen had declared that the prophet knew the complete Pentateuch, but now he argued that the only laws known to this prophet were those contained in the Book of the Covenant and in Deuteronomy. Thus the *Grundschrift* must be later than Ezekiel; as a matter of fact, it came into its present form at or later than the time of Ezra.

expressing provisional approval. This, at any rate, seems to be how Kuenen himself understood the matter, as Külling recognizes (p. 14). As a matter of fact, in his 1870 *TT* article Kuenen plainly states that he had been expounding essentially this view (the post-exilic date of the priestly code) in his lecture-room before the appearance of Graf's book. Moreover, although it is true that Kuenen did not fully expound his view in print until the second volume of his *Godsdienst van Israël* appeared in 1870, he mentions in *TT*, II, 452 (fall of 1868), that he had sent the first part of this work to the printer. His first reference to Graf's *Archiv* article appears in *TT*, IV (1870), 423.

My purpose in presenting this matter in the 'Kuenen' article was not to rob Graf of his proper credit. It is true that he did not become Kuenen's disciple. On the other hand, the evidence seems clear enough that Kuenen *did* influence Graf – and that was all I was trying to prove – just as, admittedly, Graf influenced Kuenen. We have Kuenen's own word for this, if nothing else (but see the striking statement by W. van der Vlugt in the 'Kuenen' article, n. 64!). Kuenen seemed very modest about his relationship to Graf – perhaps too modest. It is our duty, if we can, to assign him his proper place.

4 *De godsdienst van Israël tot den ondergang van den Joodschen staat;* English translation: *The Religion of Israel to the Fall of the Jewish State*, by A. H. May, 3 vols., London, 1874–75.

So dramatic and breath-taking are the changes that one can hardly believe the author of these sentiments to be the same Kuenen who had only ten years earlier composed the mildly critical *Historisch-kritisch onderzoek*. As Kuenen himself later looked back upon his earlier work, he explained:

The concessions I made were inevitable – but wholly inadequate. From my present position I regard them on the one hand as a tribute extorted by the power of the truth, but on the other hand as a humiliating proof of the tyranny which the opinions we have once accepted often exercise over us. When we are really called upon boldly to quit our ground and choose a new site for our edifice we too often attempt to stave off the necessity by timid and minute modifications in the plan to which we are already committed.[1]

During the years immediately preceding and following the publication of *Godsdienst van Israël*, Kuenen wrote a number of extensive articles and monographs on various phases of the literary and historical problems dealt with in this book, the book on the one hand and the articles and monographs on the other being commentaries on one another. All of these were published in *Theologisch Tijdschrift*, the new journal of modernism, ten of them under the general title, 'Critische bijdragen tot de geschiedenis van den Israëlietischen godsdienst.' In 'De integriteit van Exodus 13:11–16,' Kuenen employed the canons of judicious literary analysis to undermine the claim of Geiger, Dozy, Oort, and Hoekstra that the early Hebrews practiced child sacrifice,[2] a position he continued to defend in the two following articles, 'Kanaän en de Israëlieten' and 'Jahveh en Molech.'[3] In 'De eerste dag van het feest der ongezuurde brooden,' he undermined the textual support for J. C. Diehl's claim that Passover was celebrated on 15 Nisan, leaving the problem of contradictions in Gospel chronology unresolved.[4] In 'Zadok en de Zadokieten,' Kuenen painstakingly demonstrated that Ezekiel had been the first to call the Jerusalem priests 'Zadokites,' thus supporting his claim that the *Grundschrift* is later than the exile.[5] In a lengthy article entitled 'De

1 Introduction to Wicksteed's translation, p. xiv

2 I (1867), 53–72

3 idem, 690–706; II (1868), 559–98

4 III (1869), 167–86

5 idem, 463–509

6 IV, 391–426, 487–526 (the so called 'literary autobiography')

7 VII (1873), 492–542

8 X (1875), 512–36. Of great interest are also 'De stamvaders van het Israëlietische volk,' V (1871), 255ff, 'De stam Levi,' VI (1872), 628ff, and 'Overlevering of historische ontwikkeling?', X (1876), 549ff.

9 It is reported that Muir's brother tried to burn every copy in England; cf. Cheyne's

priesterlijke bestanddeelen van Pentateuch en Jozua,' appearing in 1870, Kuenen reviewed the influences that brought about the drastic change in his thinking concerning the date of the *Grundschrift*, then went on to establish this document's relative unity, independent status, and precise place in Israel's history.[6] In a study called 'Job en de lijdende knecht van Jahveh' he counteracted Hoekstra's claim that Job and the suffering servant of Isaiah are the same person.[7] In 'Nog eens de priesterlijke bestanddeelen van Pentateuch en Jozua' he reviewed the work of Riehm, Kosters, Duhm, Kayser, and Nöldeke, maintaining his view that the *Grundschrift* was the youngest document in the Hexateuch.[8]

As Kuenen's reputation grew, John Muir, a Scottish Sanskrit scholar, requested him to write a book to combat the notion that Israelite prophecy was a supernatural phenomenon, authentically predicting future events. Kuenen's book, *De profeten en de profetie onder Israël*, appearing in English under the title, *The Prophets and Prophecy in Israel* (1877), was the answer to this request. Kuenen tried to show that there is no fulfilment of prophecy in the traditional sense, that its value lay not in the predictive element but in the ethical monotheism that it established. The treatment was scholarly but far more polemical than is usual in Kuenen's writings. In many circles this book gained a favorable reception, but in the British Isles, for which it was chiefly intended, it stirred up a great volume of opposition.[9]

A splendid example of Kuenen's sweeping logic is found in an English composition entitled 'Yahweh and the "Other Gods,"' printed in the 1876 *Theological Review*.[10] It must be frankly stated that Kuenen appears in this article in less glory than usually, with the tendentiousness of his argumentation clear for all to behold. He claimed, against Ewald and Schultz, to be able to prove from the biblical texts that Israel gradually rose from henotheism to monotheism, the latter appearing for the first time only in the eighth-century prophets (the keystone of his argument in *Godsdienst*). Kuenen examined various passages which appear to imply

notice in *The Independent*, 18 Dec. 1891. Kuenen's viewpoint is summarized in these words: 'Truly, the Israelite prophet is a unique phenomenon in history. It does not disown its human origin; that is born witness to, both by its gradual ripening and by many imperfections which cleave to it. Every attempt to derive it directly and immediately from God must therefore fail, but yet if we view it as one of the many revelations of man's spiritual life – and surely life as a whole points back to God and testifies of Him – then we cannot estimate it highly enough, and we are right in calling it unique' (English translation, p. 591).

10 XIII, 329–68. Cf. H. Ewald, *Die Lehre der Bibel von Gott oder Theologie des Alten und Neuen Bundes*, 1873; H. Schultz, *Alttestamentliche Theologie*, 1869 (the second edition of Schultz's book (1878) moves toward Kuenen's position).

monotheism, in every instance arriving at the conclusion that these are
either inconclusive or late. Very generally his proof for lateness depended simply on the implied theology of a given passage – an *argumentum in
circulo*. In a final paragraph, Kuenen tried to show why, on avowedly critical principles, Schultz had come to opposite results from his own. It was
because of Schultz' admission of a supernatural revelation to Abraham
and Moses. 'It stands to reason,' concluded Kuenen, 'that a man who
accepts such a point of departure must find in the later literature something which does not appear to us to be there.' Kuenen apparently did
not see how much his own judgment depended on his anti-supernatu-
ralism, which in this article was plainly determinative, in spite of its
claim to critical objectivity.

We must now mention a series of ten long articles appearing in
Theologisch Tijdschrift between 1877 and 1884. These constitute an
imposing demonstration of Kuenen's analysis of the Hexateuch. The
series is called 'Bijdragen tot de critiek van Pentateuch en Jozua.' These
studies constitute the brick and mortar of Kuenen's criticism, yet all but
two appearing in Budde's anthology have remained untranslated. They
deal with particular passages in minute detail, building upon and
explicating the theory of the relative lateness of the so-called *Grundschrift*.

The first article, 'De aanwijzing der vrijsteden in Joz. 20,' argued for
the conclusion that not only the passages referring to the cities of refuge,
but the very tradition and institution itself, is of postexilic origin. In
the next article, 'De stam Manasse,' Kuenen tried to show that the claim
of Manasseh to part of Transjordan is the late and tendential invention
of the postexilic priestly school. 'De uitzending der verspieders in Nu. 13,
14,' argued for the postexilic origin of the story of the twelve spies. In 'De
opstand van Korach, Dathan, en Abiram,' Kuenen demonstrated the
weaving-together of three literary sources in the narrative of Numbers 16–17, the last of them, the Korah source, being of postexilic date. The
article, 'De godsdienstige vergadering bij Ebal en Gerizim,' analyzed the
passages containing the Ebal-Gerizim tradition, dividing them among

1 XI (1877), 465–78; 478–96; 545–66; XII (1878), 139–62; 297–324; XIV (1880), 257–
81; 281–302; XV (1881), 164–223; XVIII (1884), 121–71; 497–540. For further details concerning the content of these important articles, see De Vries, 'Hexateuchal
Criticism of Kuenen,' pp. 48–51.
2 Trans. P. H. Wicksteed, London, 1882; Dutch ed., Leiden, 1882; also German and
French translations, 1883
3 Cf. Tiele, 'Levensbericht,' p. 19; Oort, 'Kuenen als godgeleerde,' p. 588. A reviewer in
The Nonconformist and Independent of 26 Oct., 1882, representing conservative reaction,

four different sources, the earliest being the original Deuteronomist and the latest being a postexilic redactor. 'Dina en Sichem' divided Genesis 34 into a J and a priestly source; here for the first time Kuenen began to use the symbol 'P' for the erstwhile *Grundschrift*, a practice which all critical scholars came to adopt. 'Manna en kwakkelen' was a defense of the literary unity of Exodus 16 over against Kayser and Wellhausen, which Kuenen at the same time judged to be postexilic in origin on account of its highly supernaturalistic viewpoint. 'Israël bij den Sinai,' by far the longest of the series, developed a progressive analysis of the Sinai pericope (Exodus 19–34) in which Kuenen argued for an old Book of the Covenant unknown to the Deuteronomist and the insertion of numerous fragments from various sources into a basic E source. 'De geboortegeschiedenis van Gen. 1–11' was a refutation of Budde's complex scheme of three J sources in the early chapters of Genesis. The final article, with the simple title 'Bileam,' argued against Wellhausen for the unified E authorship of Numbers 22–24.[1]

The English translation of Kuenen's *Historisch-kritisch onderzoek, Godsdienst van Israël*, and *Profeten en profeten in Israël*, together with his articles on 'Critical Method' and 'Yahweh and the "Other Gods,"' firmly established his reputation in Great Britain as a critical scholar of the first rank, leading to an invitation to deliver the Hibbert Lectures in 1882. Kuenen published these under the title, *National Religions and Universal Religions*.[2] In five lectures he endeavored to show that nationalism has been transcended by universalism in Islam, Buddhism, and Judaism-Christianity; also that the decisive factor in each instance was the creative personality of a dynamic spiritual leader. While these lectures contained much of scientific value, particularly for the study of comparative religions, it was the honest appraisal of some of his closest associates that they fell somewhat short of his usual level of achievement.[3] The lectures on Israel, Judaism, and Christianity are generally acknowledged as the best.

Kuenen broadened his critical studies to other than Hexateuchal books, treating Ezekiel, Qoheleth, and Ezra in some detail.[4] But the Hexateuch and the history of Israel depending on its analysis continued to be his

charged Kuenen with inconsistency in not applying the same critical principles to Islam that he applied to Judaism and Christianity. On the other extreme, interestingly, a Dutch humanist, Domela Nieuwenhuis, charged Kuenen with being an unscientific apologist (*Dageraad*, July 1882).

4 'Ezechiël,' *Bibliotheek van Moderne Theologie en Letterkunde*, 1881, pp. 571–601; 'Qoheleth (E. Renan),' *TT*, XVII (1883), 113–44; 'Ezekiel,' *The Modern Review*, XVIII (1884), 617–40; 'L'oeuvre d'Esdras,' *Revue de l'Histoire des Religions*, 1886, pp. 334–58.

forte. To the end of his days he kept everything of importance appearing in these areas of study under his constant scrutiny.[1] Here Kuenen was the real master, no longer, as in his younger years, seeking to strike a modest balance between conflicting opinions, but speaking out with originality and with a constant sense of the authority he had gained through long experience and study. None but Wellhausen himself was his equal.

The final work of Kuenen calling for notice here is the second, completely revised edition of his early work on Old Testament introduction, *Historisch-kritisch onderzoek*.[2] This revision was the mature book of Kuenen's advancing years. Through its English and German translations it had wide influence. Although it contained some ideas that were still peculiarly Kuenen's own, in general it demonstrated that his criticism had been so long tested and revised by discussion with other scholars that it could now represent the consensus of international critical thought, alongside the notable works of Julius Wellhausen. There is no need to review the contents of this book in detail, since the theory it presents is well known to most present-day readers. The most striking thing about it is the orderly care with which it analyzes first the various literary documents, then assesses their respective places in Israel's history. Every piece of literature is given its place in the ascending scheme of development. The postexilic origin of the priestly document is, of course, determinative for this entire reconstruction. Numerous critics who formely held their judgment in abeyance in the face of the startling new theories were now moved to assent, so clearly and powerfully was Kuenen's argumentation presented. Already since the publication of *Godsdienst*, Kuenen had pretty well convinced his fellow Dutch scholars, but now he saw the majority of critics in Germany, France, England, and even far-away America come to the side of the new criticism.

For forty years, the Graf-Kuenen-Wellhausen theory reigned supreme in Holland, being accepted, as we shall see, even by some of the mediating scholars, including the Ethicals. Kuenen's personal influence extended farther and farther as his major works came to be widely read and as students from many lands came to study at his feet. In a broad sense,

1 'De critiek van den Hexateuch en de geschiedenis van Israëls godsdienst,' *TT*, XIX (1885), 491–530 (against Baudissin, Wellhausen, König); 'De jongste phasen der critiek van den Hexateuch,' *TT*, XXII (1888), 15–57 (against Vatke, Dillmann, Vernes, Halévy); 'Drie wegen, één doel,' *idem*, 473–95, 571–88 (against Renan, Kittel, Baethgen
2 *Historisch-critisch onderzoek* (etc., different spelling), 2nd ed., 3 vols., Leiden, 1887–93 (partially completed by J. C. Matthes after Kuenen's death). English translation of vol. I by Wicksteed, *An Historico-Critical Inquiry into the Origin and Composition of the Hexateuch*, London, 1886; German trans. 1887–94.
3 *Disputatio de carmine Jacobi, Gen. xlix*

Kuenen's school was quite extensive – insofar as he received due re-cognition, as large as the school of Wellhausen itself. Certainly all progressive scholars in Holland counted themselves as his followers in a general sense, if not always strictly as his personal disciples. In a narrow sense, his school consisted only of the Leiden group of modernists, since only these held to his critical views upon his theological presuppositions. This group included, of course, Scholten. It also included Tiele, Oort, de Goeje, W. H. Kosters, and others, among them most of Kuenen's students and colleagues. It is important for us now to see in what way these men generally supported, and at times challenged, the position of Kuenen's criticism. We must also go on to observe the more radical criticism of the Amsterdam scholars.

Following the beginning of Kuenen's professorial career, the earliest person to earn a Leiden doctorate in Old Testament studies was J. P. N. Land, who wrote a dissertation in 1857 on Genesis 49;[3] the fact that he refrained from trying to date the various sources he succeeded in identify-ing reflects the relative caution of the Leiden scholars at this period. In 1864 Land was appointed to the Athenaeum in Amsterdam, but later returned to Leiden to teach philosophy, to which subject his interest definitely inclined in his later years, although he continued to produce a few works of merit in the fields of Old Testament criticism and Semitic linguistics.[4]

Other early Leiden dissertations in the field of Old Testament were a study by P. de Jong on the 'Maccabean' Psalms (1857), one by J. C. Matthes on 'false prophecy' (1859), an analysis of the Balaam stories in Numbers by Oort (1860), and I. Hooykaas's history of Israel's wisdom literature (1862).[5] A word about two of these will provide a character-istic picture of all. Matthes's book surveyed the Old Testament material relevant to his study and examined the psychology of prophetism, con-cluding that the distinction between genuine and false prophecy was unknown to the Hebrews themselves, the only distinction being the measure of a prophet's consciousness of communion with God.[6] Hooy-kaas, who was to become prominent in the modernist 'ethical' movement,

---

4 See especially his *Hebreeuwsche Grammatica*, Amsterdam, 1869, and *Anecdota Syriaca*, 4 vols., 1862–75. Biographical notice in *LAMMNL*, 1898, pp. 350ff.

5 De Jong, *Disquisitio de Psalmis Maccabaicis;* Matthes, *Dissertatio historico-critico de pseudoprophetismo Hebraeorum;* Oort, *Disputatio de pericope Num. xxii: 2-xxiv historiam bileami continenta;* Hooykaas, *Geschiedenis der beoefening van de wijsheid onder de Hebreën.* From Hooy-kaas's dissertation onward the Dutch language was regularly used; the same was true at the other universities as well.

6 Matthes refused to see any supernatural factor in prophetism, explaining it as the highest expression of human genius. Lacking presently available knowledge of ancient

employed the critical methods Kuenen had taught him to analyze the wisdom books, rejecting the traditional view of their origin and assigning each a place in a rigid framework of historical development.[1]

Already mentioned has been Dozy's controversial book, *De Israëlieten te Mekka*, which appeared in 1863. We have seen Kuenen's vehement rejection of Dozy's thesis, which nonetheless influenced him in his further development.[2] Dozy was attacked from many sides. In fanciful reconstruction, he identified the Simeonites with the Ishmaelites, positing a migration of Baal-worshippers from this tribe to Mecca in David's time to become the ancestors of the modern Moslems. Dozy had little to go on beside his vivid imagination. His Arabist interest was strongly at work, but also in evidence was his low regard for Old Testament tradition, typical of the period generally and affecting much of the work of the Leiden scholars.

The young Leiden critics were often embroiled in controversy among themselves, and many of their arguments concerned abstruse points of literary criticism. As an example, we may mention an instance in which Land and Oort found themselves disputing over the analysis of Numbers 16–17, with Kuenen eventually supporting Oort.[3]

We have mentioned Oort several times. He has been called the greatest of the second generation of the modernists. This was mainly because he managed to outlive all this colleagues, remaining active to the ripe age of ninety-one. After twelve years in the pastorate, he began a long and fruitful teaching career, first for two years at the Amsterdam Athenaeum and, after 1875, for thirty-two years as professor of Hebrew and Old

psychology and of contemporary parallels, he based these opinions mainly on the logic of rationalism. Cf. his 'Profetisme onder Israël,' *GB*, XXXV (1861), 705–87, in which he writes, 'Just like every other historical phenomenon, prophetism not only may but must be interpreted according to normal spiritual and human norms... Science is rational. It can never be satisfied with supernaturalism' (p. 784).

1 Hooykaas had, of course, no glimpse yet of extra-biblical wisdom literature, which has so radically changed critical opinions and methods. Thus his criteria were subjectivistic. He placed in the period from Solomon to 722 B. C. the more theoretical essays on wisdom, in the period from 722 to 536 the practical and earthy proverbs, in the period 536 to Sirach artificial and sceptical writings like Qoheleth. See Matthes's criticism in *GB*, XXXVI (1862), 931ff. Hooykaas remained a Hervormd minister all his life, being an important leader in the Protestanten Bond. His scientific works were few. He wrote on the Septuagint *(Iets over de Griekse Vertaling van het Oude Testament*, Rotterdam, 1888), arguing for the superiority of the Lucianic text over the Masoretic Hebrew, and was a co-translator of the 'Leidsche Vertaling.' See biographical information in *LAMMNL*, 1895, pp. 1ff.

2 See p. 64, n.5. Kuenen concluded that Dozy's fantastic hypothesis would be refuted not by traditional reaction but by scientific criticism. Among Dozy's critics were Hoekstra, Oort, de Goeje, and Land. Apparently the only German scholar taking the trouble to

Testament Literature at Leiden (this was a position in the literary faculty). He became a leading spirit in the formation of the 'Rechts-moderne' group within the modernist school, the group that took a mediating position between the Scholten-Opzoomer intellectualists and the orthodox Ethicals, seeking a more vital religious impulse on modernist presuppositions in the spirit of Hoekstra.[4]

During his early career, Oort took part in various debates in the *Theologisch Tijdschrift*, often coming to Kuenen's defense. Among his writings were to be a valuable series of studies on the Minor Prophets, but eventually his chief interest came to be centered in the intertestamental and Talmudic periods. In connection with his Talmudic studies he was to become involved in a lively controversy with Dutch Jewish scholars.[5] Oort would gain his greatest renown, however, for his role in the preparation of the 'Leidsche Vertaling,' a Bible translation embodying the principles of the Kuenen school, of which something will be said later.

His biographer explains the reason why Oort proved to be most original in his intertestamental and Talmudic studies. It was that his main activity fell in a period immediately following the first great triumphs, in a time, that is, when no further great discoveries seemed likely and when many high hopes had already been dashed .In other words, Oort worked under the psychological hazard of awe for Kuenen's growing authority. Thus he did some valuable work in elaborating details of analytical criticism, but he was at his best in popularizing critical results, and most original in areas untouched by Kuenen.[6]

Further examples, in addition to the aforementioned debate concern-

offer serious refutation was Graf (*ZDMG*, XIX, 330–51).

3 Land, *GB*, XXXIX (1865), 977–90; Oort, *GB*, XL (1866), 205–17; Land, *idem*, 416–37; Kuenen, 'De opstand van Korach (etc.),' *TT*, XII (1878), 139–62. Oort correctly saw that the Korah tradition was the latest strand. Land's reconstruction was quite arbitrary because he had no clear principle of historical criticism, cf. his dissertation.

4 Vanderlaan, *op. cit.*, pp. 98f, has the following to report regarding Oort's theological position: 'Professor H. Oort, perhaps the only survivor of the ethical group, now holds a position closer to ordinary theism. In preaching, he uses the expression, "God the Creator," in the sense that in dealing with the external world we are dealing with the activity of God. But in conversation with the writer he once outlined his tentative position about as follows: The ethicals erred in trying to distinguish sharply between nature and the moral world. The two are parts of one system of things. Of the origin of the world we know nothing; but in the existing world, both in nature and in man's spiritual life, the Spirit of God is operative. We may say, then, that Dutch modernism came out of its "ethical" controversy with theism conserved as a permanent possession. There is general agreement that a religion without theism would not be a religion, and should go by some other name.'

5 See T. Tal, *Prof. Oort en de Talmoed*, Amsterdam, 1880; cf. Nat, *op. cit.*, p. 160.

6 C.E. Hooykaas, 'Levensbericht,' *LAMMNL*, 1929, pp. 2f

ing Numbers 16–17, may be given to illustrate the peculiar hazard under which Oort worked. He would present a study, find himself engaged in debate with Land or some other scholar, see Kuenen come in with the final word. This is what happened with respect to his dissertation on the Balaam stories. Land's extensive review (1861) was mainly appreciative, but set the pattern of criticism; Kuenen later provided his magesterial analysis of this material (1884).[1] In a book on human sacrifice in Israel, written in 1865, Oort claimed that Molech worship had been accepted as an essential part of Hebrew religion from the beginning; Kuenen vigorously attacked this view in the first three studies of his *Theologisch Tijdschrift* series, 'Critische bijdragen,' mentioned above.[2] In 1866 Oort analyzed the Dinah story in Genesis 34, defending its unity but flatly denying its historicity and dating it in the period of the judges; he was at the time able to claim the support of Kuenen's *Historisch-kritisch onderzoek*, but Kuenen later, in one of his 'Bijdragen tot de critiek van Pentateuch en Jozua' articles, came to repudiate all of Oort's conclusions.[3] Again in 1869 much the same thing happened: Oort analyzed the Sinai pericope, later (1881) to be corrected by Kuenen.[4] Also in 1869, Oort made a critique of Kosters's dissertation, in this instance eventually emerging with Kuenen's approval.[5] Finally we may mention an exchange between Oort and Kuenen occurring in 1871–72; it involved the former's attempt to identify the 'Beth-ephrath' of Micah 5:1 with the dynasty of Saul; when both de Goeje and Kuenen opposed him, Oort rather meekly retracted his view.[6]

Another important leader of the Leiden group was Willem H. Kosters. He proved himself to be much more independent than Oort. He studied under Kuenen from 1861 to 1868, then served five pastorates until taking over his teacher's chair in 1892, where he worked until his own sudden

---

1 Land, *GB*, XXXV, 881–932; Kuenen, *TT*, XVIII, 497–540

2 Oort, *Het menschenoffer in Israël;* for Kuenen's contributions see p. 68. Land argued with Kuenen about the Kenite origin of the name Yahweh in *TT*, III (1869), 347ff; he appears to be one of the earliest to defend this identification.

3 Oort, 'De sage van Dina,' *GB*, XL, 983–98; Kuenen, *TT*, XIV (1880), 257ff.Oort's dictum (p. 985) concerning the criterion of historicity is symptomatic of his arbitrary approach: 'Whenever we can find a reason for fabrication and thus can give the key to a correct understanding of the story as a tribal or folk history from later times, we must consider the entire story to be fictitious and not look for any remnant of tradition in it with a historical basis.'

4 Oort, 'De legenden van de sluiting des verbonds bij den Sinai (etc.),' *TT*, III, 1–18. He arbitrarily placed the Exodus 20 Decalogue very late, calling the entire section from chap. 19 to 34 legendary. The flimsiness of his criteria did not restrain him from boldly dating his materials to precise periods. Kuenen's much more cautious and solidly-

death in 1897. Kosters's inaugural oration, indicating his view of Scripture, has previously been mentioned.[7]

Kosters was unquestionably the pupil of Kuenen who influenced him most. As a matter of fact, Kuenen himself indicated that it was he, as much as any of the established and well-known scholars to whom he gives credit for his development, that led him to his crucial contribution regarding the history of the composition of the Hexateuch. Kosters's dissertation of the year 1868, coming shortly after Kuenen's communication with Graf, was a confirmation of Kuenen's view. Entitled *De historiebeschouwing van den Deuteronomist met de berichten in Genesis-Numeri vergeleken*, it challenged Graf's theory to the effect that the *Grundschrift* narratives were to be retained for the pre-exilic period, while its laws were to be dated after the exile. Kosters carefully examined these narratives with a view to their relationship *vis à vis* Deuteronomy, discovering that they in fact presuppose Deuteronomy, hence need to be retained with the post-Deuteronomic laws. In other words, the entire *Grundschrift*, or P, constitutes the latest document in the Hexateuch, later than D. When Kuenen's contribution to the establishment of this theory became widely known, Kosters's role also gained its due measure of recognition.

One is amazed to observe the intense interest in Old Testament criticism on the part of scholars outside the biblical field. A notable example was Dozy . De Goeje, Dozy's successor, was also interested. Far less speculative than Dozy, de Goeje was devoted to a strict historical method. We may mention as typical of his work an extensive essay on the tenth chapter of Genesis, appearing in 1870, in which he revealed his broad knowledge of ancient near-eastern history. Depending for the literary analysis of this chapter on the work of Hebrew specialists, he made his contribution by attempting to place the literary materials with-

---

based analysis has been mentioned ('Israël bij den Sinai,' *TT*, XV, 164ff).

5 Kosters, *De historie-beschouwing van den Deuteronomist met de berichten in Genesis-Numeri vergeleken*, Leiden, 1868; Oort, 'Ontleding van Num. 13 en 14,' *TT*, III, 251–66; Kuenen, 'De uitzending der verspieders (etc.).' *TT*, XI, 545ff. Kosters traced three sources in these chapters; Oort and Kuenen found only two, which the latter was to identify as J and P.

6 Oort, *TT*, V, 501–11; Kuenen, *TT*, VI, 45–66; Oort, *idem*, 273–79; de Goeje, *idem*, 279–84; Kuenen, *idem*, 285–302. Oort assumed that the text had been entirely reworked to obscure its original reference. When Kuenen pointed out the flaws in this argument, Oort diffidently acknowledged his error, but protested that Micah 4 and 5 are a hopeless puzzle, whereupon Kuenen retorted that one need not despair: sound criticism is able to solve the enigma and make the text intelligible without drastic emendations.

7 See above, p. 50. For biographical details on Kosters see the obituary by H. Oort in *LAMMNL*, 1898, pp. 230–41.

in a historical pattern. He dated this chapter very late. He supported the dictum, popular among advanced critics of the period, that the biblical materials reveal nothing of the period they describe but reveal much concerning the period in which they were composed.[1]

We must also mention in this connection the interest of the Leiden *Religionsgeschichtlicher*, C. P. Tiele, in the radical criticism of the Old Testament. Tiele, Kuenen's close friend and biographer, became world-renowned as a pioneer in the field of religious phenomenology. He served as professor of theology in the Remonstrant seminary, but in addition was appointed to the new university chair of History and Philosophy of Religion in the year 1877.[2] He wrote extensively in this field, being in 1896–98 called upon to deliver the Gifford Lectures at Edinburgh.[3] Tiele characteristically treated the Old Testament and the history of Israel from the viewpoint of radical empiricism. Thus, e.g., in his *Vergelijkende geschiedenis van de Egyptische en Mesopotamische godsdiensten* (1872), he included a chapter on the history of Israel in which he treated its phenomena from a typical evolutionary and comparative point of view.

Meanwhile, another of Kuenen's associates was moving in the opposite direction from that of Tiele's radical historicism. It is Land whom we have in mind. Land's early biblical studies showed some acumen in literary analysis but already tended toward undue speculation. In 1871 he wrote an extensive essay for *De Gids* on the development of Hebrew religion, going beyond Kuenen's recent book, *De Godsdienst van Israël*, in discarding completely the Old Testament tradition. It is impossible, Land declared, to come to a historical explanation of Hebrew origins on this basis, so completely have later generations recast the early

---

1 M. J. de Goeje, 'Het tiende hoofdstuk van Genesis,' *TT*, IV, 233–68. He dated an original document during the exile, a supplementary document in the time of Nehemiah. See his similar studies in *De Gids*, XXVIII, ii (1864), 297ff; *TT*, II (1868), 176ff; *TT*, IV (1870), 176–82

2 Mackay, *op. cit.*, pp. 166f, delineates Tiele's theological position: 'Tiele's idea was to make the science of comparative religion the centre and foundation of all religious science. He maintained that theology would be destroyed if it had not the courage to become a science like all other sciences. As in every other science, we must begin with the collection of facts, the phenomena of the different religions. These must be examined, compared, and sorted, and in this way, confining ourselves to anthropology and psychology, and excluding the speculative method, which had been condemned in all other sciences, we were to rise to a true theory of the subject. In other words, theology is to be concerned only with the forms, not with the object of religion. This is obviously the end-station of radical empiricism.'

3 See *Geschiedenis van den godsdienst*, Amsterdam, 1876 (English, French, German, and Swedish translations), and the Gifford Lectures, *Elements of the Science of Religion*, Edinburgh-London, 1897–99 (Dutch, German, and Swedish translations). Tiele prepared

records. He went on, accordingly, to reconstruct Israel's history purely on the basis of his own imagination. Emulating Kuenen, he took the eighth century as the fixed point of departure for viewing Hebrew origins. He however did none of the thorough textual study that justified much of Kuenen's reconstruction. His treatment was accordingly erratic and unsystematic. He was writing what was becoming the fashionable thing to write, but his synthetic and speculative conclusions are practically worthless. It is perhaps not too harsh to say that this essay reveals Land as a parasite on such a true working critic as Kuenen.[4] Unfortunately, there were many like him. One is not surprised that Land soon turned to completely other interests.

Of quite a different sort was the work of Kosters. We have seen that his brilliant dissertation on the P narratives played a significant role in confirming Kuenen's criticism and in correcting Graf's initial hypothesis. Kosters composed a number of valuable critical studies. In 1873 he published in *Theologisch Tijdschrift* a further analysis of the P narratives. He described the priestly document's fondness for geneologies and chronological precision, using a comparison of the J and P lists of Adam's descendents as evidence. That the author of this document was a priest appears from his great interest in ritual and order, argued Kosters. He described his style as very brief and to the point, less lively and colorful than that of J or E and further from actuality, although making a lasting contribution by way of his exalted God-concept and his high ethical understanding. Hence a further argument for the conclusion that P is the youngest document in the Hexateuch. Kosters's description of the characteristics of P has become entirely familiar to subsequent genera-

---

occasional essays on biblical criticism for *De Gids* and *TT*. Biographical sketches appear in *Mannen en vrouwen van beteekenis*, XXXI, 7 (Haarlem, 1900), and in the *Jaarboek der Koninklijke Akademie van Wetenschappen* of 1902.

4 'De wording van staat en godsdienst in het oude Israël,' XXXV, iv, 1–39, 243–74. It is significant that Land recognized the tremendous importance of the recent discovery of the Moabite stone. He had little idea, however, of how to use such evidence. As a single example of Land's method we may mention his argument for the legendary character of the wilderness tradition. It was that the records do not mention camels; if the records were historical, he argued, they would have mentioned these animals. Archaeology has made quite clear, since Land's period, that the early Hebrews did not in fact have camels, and that references to these animals in the patriarchal narratives are almost certainly anachronisms. A similar example of unsound speculative method from the Leiden school of this period is Houtsma's 'Israël en Qain,' *TT*, X (1876), 83ff, which found the Kenites everywhere, in the Midianites, Kenizzites, Ishmaelites, and the modern Arabian tribe *bal-Qain*. One should note the intense interest among the Leiden scholars in the Kenite problem.

tions, but in its time it pioneered in what was still a novel and revolutionary view.[1]

Koster's exegetical work deserves our appreciate attention. Among his numerous essays that might claim attention, one on the development of angelology, written in 1876, is characteristic. In this study he rejected the speculation that Israel's doctrine of angels arose from Persian influence. Examining carefully all the relevant Old Testament passages, he came to the conclusion that angels developed as degraded gods. In true scientific spirit, Kosters acknowledged the need for more light from archaeology and the study of comparative religions, which at the time were just beginning to reveal their possibilities.[2]

Kosters continued his important contributions to the analysis of the Pentateuch in a study of the Flood story, appearing in the 1885 *Theologisch Tijdschrift*.[3] In this essay he showed the readiness of a true critic to respond to new evidence. George Smith's deluge tablet from Assyria had startled the scholarly world, challenging in many minds the foundation of the Wellhausen hypothesis. Kosters argued that this was in no wise the correct conclusion; although the J materials in Genesis do show familiarity with the tablet, the P materials do not. Thus one adjustment which historical criticism would be obliged to make – and he was willing to make it – was to down-date the J document to ca. 700 B.C. in order to account for the intrusion of Babylonian influence. Kosters, without our present historical perspective, imagined that Babylonian influence began to penetrate Israel only shortly before the exile.

During this entire period. Oort continued to produce a large volume of scholarly studies. We mention a few as representative samples. In his Leiden inaugural he declared his determination to follow a ruthlessly 'scientific' criticism, yet found most distinctive in the study of Israel its genius for religion, which of course was not the result of supernatural influence but of purely natural origin.[4] In an 1876 essay he reconstructed the rites of the Day of Atonement on the basis of the Mishnaic tract *Yoma*, with only incidental reference to the biblical material; this was a

1 'Bijdrage ter bepaling van den betrekkelijken ouderdom der historische gedeelten van het boek der Oorsprongen,' VII, 28–59
2 'Het ontstaan en de ontwikkeling der angelologie der Israëlieten,' *TT*, X, 34–69; cf. 'De Malach Jahwe,' *TT*, IX, 359ff; 'De Cherubim,' *TT*, XIII, 455ff.
3 'Bijbelsche zontvloedverhalen met de Babylonische vergeleken,' XIX, 160–79, 321–46
4 *Israël, het volk van den godsdienst*, Leiden, 1875
5 'De Groote Verzoendag,' *TT*, X, 142–65. Oort justified his procedure by positing the rule that the tradition that departs the farthest from the Torah (the Pentateuch) is to be taken as the most trustworthy respecting contemporary usages. In other words, Oort was much more willing to rely on the Mishnaic tradition than on the bibli-

portent of the future trend of his interest to postbiblical and Talmudic studies.[5] Among a variety of studies on the prophetic literature, an 1880 article strongly argued that Amos came from northern Israel, the reason being that Judahite glosses in the book bring every reference to Judah under suspicion.[6] Finally we mention an 1884 article in which Oort presented a surprisingly fanciful reconstruction of the Aaronite priesthood. Oort indicated his very low respect for the textual tradition in his willingness to substitute speculation for objective evidence. Although Kuenen reviewed this article with mixed praise, there is a glaring contrast between the method followed by Oort and the method employed in the best of Kuenen's work.[7]

Lesser luminaries of the Leiden Old Testament school were M. Th. Houtsma and Adam van Doorninck. Houtsma became professor of Hebrew at Utrecht. Both men were primarily interested in textual criticism, becoming noted for characteristically radical emendations. Their contributions in this area of study appeared in successive issues of *Theologisch Tijdschrift*.

We have noted both the growing agnosticism of Allard Pierson and some of his efforts to apply his philosophical view to biblical criticism. We may mention one other ambitious work produced by him in the area of Old Testament interpretation, the first volume of his book *Geestelijke voorouders*, appearing in 1887. With no particular scholarly command of the Hebrew language, Pierson not surprisingly produced an extremely subjectivistic and arbitrary book. It was a running synthesis of Hebrew origins based generally on the results of the most advanced criticism, with the governing principle of interpretation throughout that all the biblical traditions are legendary, and hence without the least historical value. It is reported that this book was received with considerable coolness by the Leiden modernists.

The important Old Testament scholar of the Amsterdam group was J. C. Matthes. His progress in the direction of Pierson's viewpoint was slow, accelerating after his appointment to teach at the Amsterdam

cal report in Lev. 16 – a surprisingly selective bias!

6 'De profeet Amos,' *TT*, XIV, 114–58; cf. Oort, 'Het vaderland van Amos,' *TT*, XXV (1891), 121–26. Oort admitted that there is no reference to a Tekoa outside Judah, but preferred to believe that there must be another town of the same name rather than accept the textual tradition.

7 'De Aäronieden,' *TT*, XVIII, 289–335; see Kuenen, 'De geschiedenis der priesters van Jahwe (etc.),' *TT*, XXIV (1890), 1–42. In Oort's reconstruction, Aaron was the patriarch or eponym of all 'spirituals' in northern Israel, including prophets and priests. To help Josiah's reform, the Pentateuchal stories made this Aaron the brother of Moses and the ancestor of all the priests. After the exile all priests came to be called Aaronites.

University in 1877. Growing out of the former Athenaeum, this university began to distinguish itself as the intellectual center of the most extreme
rationalism in Holland. Pierson's influence was one of the important
contributing factors; another was the fact that as a municipal university
this institution was less susceptible to popular conservatism than the
nationally controlled state universities. When Matthes came to Amsterdam, the conservative J. G. de Hoop Scheffer, professor in the Mennonite
seminary, was teaching Old Testament exegesis for the university, and
continued to do so until he retired in 1890. Meanwhile, all other subjects
in this general field of study were transferred to the literary faculty
under Matthes, and this included exegesis after 1890. This continued
to be the place assigned on the roster to biblical criticism until as late as
World War II. Thus at Amsterdam exegesis became a purely secular
subject, and the writings of Matthes and his associates give abundant
evidence that this is precisely how they handled it.

Matthes displayed unusual ability and wide interest as a biblical critic.
His studies appearing in the various journals, chiefly *Theologisch Tijdschrift*, dealt with a variety of Old Testament books, but he continued to
follow the impulse of his dissertation in showing a special interest in the
prophetic writings. In addition, he produced several books, including a
translation and critical introduction to Job and a recasting of his dissertation in the English language.[1] He participated with spirit in polemics
against conservatives of every stripe, a characteristic example being his
exchange with the Ethical scholar Gerrit Wildeboer concerning the Old
Testament teaching respecting the origin of sin.[2] After the death of
Kuenen, as we have seen, Matthes completed the publication of his
father-in-law's revised *Historisch-critisch onderzoek*.

Two later books summarizing the results of the Leiden criticism were
G. G. Chavannes's *La Religion dans la Bible* (1889) and G. J. P. J. Bolland's *De Pentateuch naar zijne wording onderzocht* (1892). Chavannes, a
pupil of Kuenen, sought to systematize the history of Israel's and the
early church's religion according to scientific principles; his book assumes
a uniform evolutionistic development and treats the biblical text with

1 *Het boek Job vertaald en verklaard, inzonderheid naar aanleiding van de jongste buitenlandsche
kommentaren*, 2 vols., Utrecht, 1866; 2nd ed., 3 vols., Groningen, 1876; *The False Prophets
of Israel*, London, 1884
2 Matthes, 'Oorsprong en gevolgen der zonde volgens het Oude Testament,' *TT*,
XXIV (1890), 225–54; 'De boom des levens,' *idem*, 365–70; Wildeboer, 'De straf der
zonde volgens Genesis 3,' *TS*, VIII (1890), 351ff. Matthes took the view that not death
but early death was the threat involved in Gen. 2–3. He expressed the fear that Wildeboer would be too stubborn to be convinced by his arguments, but perhaps the reverse
was true.

notable freedom. Bolland was a brilliant autodidact; he came to teach philosophy at Leiden from missionary service in Java, where he actually wrote his book. This was a rather poorly composed work in which he tried to present with a great show of learning the results of the Kuenen-Wellhausen Pentateuchal analysis. It presented nothing new, and its importance for us lies mainly in what it reveals of non-specialist interest in biblical criticism.[3]

After Kuenen's death in 1891, it was Kosters who was appointed to take his place at the University of Leiden. He now grew to full maturity in his own right, gaining the attention of worldwide scholarship. In 1893 he published a sensational book, *Het herstel van Israël in het Perzische tijdvak*, which was quickly given a German translation. Previously, in a dispute with J. Halévy, Kuenen had reaffirmed the importance of the book of Ezra as a keystone in his reconstruction of Israel's history, assuming the book's basic historicity.[4] Kosters now threw the whole Kuenen-Wellhausen theory into confusion by his argument that Ezra's account of the return from exile, including especially the edict of Cyrus, was purely legend, and that the Jews did not in fact come back to Palestine until the time of Ezra, ca. 450 B.C. Although Oort had high praise for Kosters's book, calling it a model of calm and nonpartisan research, it was in actuality highly speculative. Kosters was forced to defend his theory against the objections of several eminent critics, including the foreign scholars J. Wellhausen, A. van Hoonacker, and E. Meyer, beside his own countryman H. J. Elhorst.[5] Untenable as most of Kosters's conclusions ultimately proved to be, he did succeed in opening up a continuing debate regarding the work of Ezra and Nehemiah. It was in any case somewhat of a distinction for him that he was the first Dutch scholar after Kuenen to receive attention from outside the country.

We cannot leave the Leiden Old Testament scholars without saying something more in particular about their Bible translation and annotation project – the most ambitious ever attempted by Dutch scholars – the so-called 'Leidsche Vertaling.'[6] This was in fact the climax of their work, an original translation of the Old Testament entirely on the critical

---

3 Chavannes published a Dutch translation in 1906. Bolland became widely known for his leadership of the theosophist movement.   4 See p. 71, n. 4.

5 Cf. Elhorst in *TT*, XXIX (1895), 77ff; Kosters in *idem*, 353ff, 549ff; XXX (1896), 489ff; XXXI (1897), 518ff. See also J. J. P. Valeton, Jr., in *TT*, XXXIV (1900), 225f; A. Noordtzij, *TTT*, VII (1909), 33ff. Kosters's arguments are ingenious but, in the light of present understanding, over-sceptical and, in the essentials, entirely unconvincing.

6 *Het Oude Testament opnieuw uit den grondtekst overgezet en van inleidingen en aanteekeningen voorzien*, 2 vols., 1899–1901. The Psalms were separately printed in 1902; Job, Prov., Eccl. appeared separately in 1903. An edition with abbreviated notes was printed in 1906 and

principles of the modernist school. In the original edition of 1899–1901, extensive notes were printed along the margins, which, together with the introductions provided at the heads of the various books, summarized the most advanced views on the points in question. A brochure was printed listing all the textual emendations used in this translation.[1] One hundred fifty-two pages in length, it resembled the marginal notes in the third edition of Kittel's *Biblia Hebraica*, although the proposed emendations were not so copious as those of the Kittel Bible. The striking fact is that all these emendations were actually used in the translation of the text, giving the 'Leidsche Vertaling' a most individualistic character.

We are indebted to Oort for an account of the preparation of this version.[2] He tells us of an earlier abortive attempt to produce a new translation of the Old Testament. In 1854 the Hervormde Synod had commissioned Kuenen, together with Professors Juynboll, Veth, and Roorda, to this task. A companion translation of the New Testament, in which Scholten prepared the Fourth Gospel, actually came to completion in 1869, but after considerable preparatory discussion, work on the Old Testament translation had to be abandoned because of the sharp division of sentiment within the church and the committee's fear of being accused of partisanship. In truth, the committee itself was divided.

When a new plan for a translation outside church control was proposed, Kuenen was no longer able to object to its basis, but he was nonetheless reluctant to engage in the work. Oort reports that Kuenen was hesitant because his interest lay in critical studies rather than in the work of translation, but M. A. Beek adds that Kuenen was aware that the time was not so ripe for such a project as the others imagined.[3] However, Kuenen at last consented to provide leadership to the new committee and be responsible for the final editing. The work began in 1885. Kuenen did not live to see it completed, but it bears the unquestionable marks of

---

one without notes in 1914. Oort later prepared a companion translation of the New Testament.

1 *Textus Hebraici Emendationes Quibus in V.T. Neerlandice Vertendo usi sunt*, Leiden, 1901

2 'Kuenen als godgeleerde,' pp. 562–65; cf. also 'Gedenkblad bij de voltooiing der Nieuwe Vertaling van het Oude Testament,' Supplement to *De Hervorming*, March 30, 1901. 3 *op. cit.*, p. 152

4 'De begrippen rein en onrein in het Oude Testament,' *TT*, XXXIII (1899), 293–318; 'Rouw en doodenvereering bij Israël,' *TT*, XXXIV (1900), 96–128; 'De doodenvereering bij Israël.' *TT*, XXXV (1901), 32–49; 'Het matriarchaat inzonderheid bij Israël,' *TTT*, I (1903), 1–23; 'Der Sühnegedanke bei den Sündopfern,' *ZAW*, XXIII (1903), 97ff; 'Zoenoffers,' *TTT*, II (1904), 69–92; 'Rouw en doodenvereering bij Israël,' *TTT*, III (1905), 1–30 (revising his previous theory that the Hebrews actually worshiped the dead).

his guidance. J. Dyserinck and J. C. Matthes had originally been appointed to the translation committee, but soon dropped out. Before it was completed, two more members, Hooykaas and Kosters, also died, leaving Oort to present it to the public. It most faithfully represented the principles and methods of Kuenen and his closest followers, hence was rightfully designated as the 'Leidsche Vertaling.'

Meanwhile, the Amsterdam group was diverging more and more from the Leiden group, and in 1903 organized the *Teyler's Theologisch Tijdschrift* as their own party periodical. The absence of Scholten and Kuenen and the increase of ethical (Rechts-moderne) influence no doubt had much to do in stimulating this withdrawal. Matthes continued to be the leading Old Testament scholar in this left-wing group. He began to come strongly under the influence of the *religionsgeschichtliche* viewpoint, represented in Holland by Tiele and abroad by Frazer and Gunkel. A number of studies from Matthes's hand dating from 1899 to 1905 reveal his growing interest in the dynamistic element and primitive taboo.[4] In a 1902 study appearing in Germany, Matthes opposed Bernhard Duhm in taking what was then the radical new position that the Psalms were directly connected with the temple cultus.[5] He next became involved in a lengthy debate with a number of Dutch scholars regarding the date and meaning of the Decalogue, maintaining what had already by this time become the minority position. viz., that it originated in the seventh century B.C.[6] A series of his studies in *Teyler's* expanded the role of primitive myth in Israel's early development.[7] In 1907 Matthes wrote a sharp attack on Bruno Baentsch's pace-setting argument for early monotheism, insisting that Moses was a low-grade henotheist at best.[8] In still other studies Matthes emphasized dynamism in the rite of circumcision and in the idea of the Holy Spirit.[9] Finally, we mention two collections of his popular essays concerning the prophets

5 'Die Psalmen und der Tempeldienst,' *ZAW*, XXII (1902), 65–82

6 'Der Dekalog', *ZAW*, XXIV (1904), 17–41; 'De tien geboden,' *TTT*, IV (1906), 44–77. Matthes leaned heavily on the argument that the Hebrews spoke Arabic in the wilderness. The other scholars involved were Eerdmans, Wildeboer, and L. H. K. Bleeker. More details are given below in connection with Eerdmans.

7 'Israëlietische geschiedenis,' III (1905), 482–513; 'Anmerkung zur Simsonsage,' IV (1906), 224–27 (with Duhm); 'De scheppingsverhalen,' V (1907), 1–17; 'Het stilstaan der zon,' VI (1908), 471–94

8 Baentsch, *Altorientalischer und israelitischer Monotheismus*, Tübingen, 1906; Matthes, 'Jahvisme en monotheisme,' *TTT*, V (1907), 303–35. Matthes characterized Baentsch's book as pure phantasy, an aimless duel with windmills.

9 'De besnijdenis,' *TTT*, VI (1908), 163–91; 'De Heilige Geest,' *Een bundel verzamelde opstellen* (Haarlem, 1913), pp. 238–60

and wise men of Israel, presented for the humanistic Vrije Gemeente of Amsterdam, as examples of Matthes's criticism.[1] Throughout these and his other essays, Matthes consistently followed a rigidly historicistic method, avoiding the theological interpretation for which Pierson had criticized Kuenen and the Leiden scholars.

When Matthes retired in 1906, he was succeeded by his pupil H. J. Elhorst. By comparison with Matthes, the latter was conservative both in point of view and in productivity. The writings of Elhorst indicate that he may have been coming under the influence of a more cautious criticism. He was impressed by the vast flow of new data emerging from archeological research.[2]

Another representative of the Amsterdam group, but one who lacked Elhorst's caution, was Job van Gilse, who made his claim for immortality by his essays dating the book of Obadiah in A.D. 70–135 and the apocalypse of Isaiah 24–27 in A.D. 119.[3] Apparently some of this group had lost all historical sense. We observe during this same period the Amsterdam New Testament scholar, Daniel Völter, indulging in wild conjectures concerning the Egyptian identity of the Genesis patriarchs.[4]

---

1 *De Israëlietische profeten*, Amsterdam, 1905; *De Israëlietische wijzen*, Amsterdam, 1911. Both series appeared first in *Stemmen uit de Vrije Gemeente*. The closest parellel in America to this congregation is the Ethical Culture Society. Its meetings are not worship services, but gatherings for intellectual and ethical stimulation.
2 See his dissertation, *De profetie van Micha*, Arnhem, 1891; his criticism of Kosters (above) *De profetie van Amos*, Leiden, 1900; *Israël in het licht der jongste onderzoekingen*, Amsterdam, 1906; 'Die israelitischen Trauerriten,' Wellhausen Festschrift (Giessen, 1914), pp. 117ff.
3 *TT*, XXX (1896), 455ff; *TTT*, VI (1908), 71ff; *TTT*, VIII (1910), 45ff, *TTT*, IX (1911), 377ff; *NwTT*, II (1913), 293ff; *NwTT*, III (1914), 167ff
4 Cf. *Die Urgeschichte Israels im Licht der aegyptischen Mythologie*, Amsterdam, 1898; *Aegypten und die Bibel*, Leiden, 1903; 4th ed., 1909; 'Egypte en de Bijbel,' *TTT*, II (1904), 229–42; *Die Patriarchen Israels und die aegyptische Mythologie*, Leiden, 1912. Völter advocated pan-Egyptianism with a vengeance: Moses was Thot, Yahweh was Sopd or Shu, etc., etc.

Chapter Four

Old Testament Interpretation Among

Dutch Conservatives, ca. 1850-1910

Not all theologians and biblical scholars in The Netherlands were willing to make the adjustment to the new attitudes that the modernists had made. Following modernism's initial triumphs, conservatism remained strong in the churches throughout the nineteenth century. The claims of science had indeed put it on the defensive, but it had the advantage of credal authority supporting it. Not surprisingly, the tactic of the most rigid orthodoxy was to entrench itself in traditionalism and ignore as far as possible the claims of scientific criticism. It became sterile and unproductive in the field of biblical research, indulging only in negative polemics against the liberal views. It used the Bible solely for pious edification and for proof-texting points of dogma.

A strong movement developed among some theological conservatives, however, that managed to retain a relative doctrinal orthodoxy while coming to terms with scientific exegesis. This attitude was represented in Holland almost entirely by the Saussaye Ethicals, who, as we have seen, believed it was possible to study the Bible critically while maintaining a supernaturalistic belief. Some of the Ethical scholars proved to be, in contrast to the orthodox rigorists, extremely active in the work of biblical research, rivalling in productivity even the Leiden modernists themselves. Accordingly, they came to have a wide and lasting influence both on Dutch theology and Dutch biblical study, as we shall see.

It is this striking contrast between two approaches to biblical criticism within the conservative camp that concerns us for the present. Now that we have viewed both the strengths and the shortcomings of the modernist position, we have a perspective for evaluating the significance of these two conservative alternatives.

THE WORK OF ORTHODOX POLEMICISTS

It will be recalled that the three influential groups within the Hervormde Kerk before 1850 were alike supernaturalistic and biblicistic. For the Groningers and 'old liberals,' as well as for the creedal Calvinists and the adherents of the *Réveil*, the Bible was a supernaturally inspired book, with God as its author. Many of the 'old liberals' become modernists, and eventually the Groningen school died out, leaving the orthodox to defend the supernatural Bible. They attempted to do this on the principle of verbal inerrancy, which meant that for them there could be no acceptance of the relativistic and historically conditioned approach to the human element emphasized by the modernists.

Orthodox work in biblical interpretation during the early years of the modernist conflict can only be described as lamentably inadequate. It was utterly obscurantistic and impotent, insofar as it existed at all. Indeed, one looks almost in vain among the learned periodicals and in the lists of serious books for competent orthodox contributions to biblical research. Some simply tried to ignore criticism. Thus H. H. Kemink took up eighty-four pages in the 1856 issue of *Jaarboeken voor Wetenschappelijke Theologie* for his running account of Israel's history from a strictly traditional viewpoint, making no reference whatever to critical views, and— we may add – unmistakeably contributing to this journal's early demise.[1] The following year, the Utrecht linguist W. G. Brill wrote a 'history' of Egyptian-Hebrew relations from Abraham to Jeremiah which completely ignored the historical and literary criticism of the Old Testament, neither using it nor opposing it. The amazing thing about this book is that it was apparently meant not as popular-devotional but as a serious piece of scientific scholarship. It reflects the naive irenic view of Brill – apparently typical of many churchman and some scholars during this period – that theology could simply ignore the radical claims of criticism, hoping perhaps that it would go away.[2]

Other orthodox scholars took a more responsible attitude toward the claims of scientific criticism. In 1862 H. F. T. Fockens entered into a spirited defense of the traditional view over against Oort and Land in their discussion of the Balaam pericope.[3] In 1866 the Leiden Orientalist, Antonie Rutgers, argued against the critics for the authenticity of the

1 'Schets der Israëlietische staatsgeschiedenis van Mozes tot de Babylonische ballingschap,' XIII, 749–833.
2 *Israël en Egypte*, Utrecht, 1857. Apart from the Old Testament, Brill consulted only Lepsius, *Die Chronologie der Aegypter*, Berlin, 1849. Brill repeated this performance in his *Bijbelstudiën* (Leiden, 1874–81), a series of 'historical' studies along traditionalistic lines. He declared that he believed in 'positive' Bible study, testifying that 'whoever understands the Bible's contents can do nothing else than accept it.'
3 *NJWT*, V, 383–98.
4 *De echtheid van het tweede gedeelte van Jesaja aangetoond*
5 *Oratio de monotheismo Israelitarum* (etc.), Utrecht, 1867
6 'When I had decided to express my opinion in this controversy, I hesitated for a while concerning which of the rejected books I should handle. After careful consideration I chose the second half of Isaiah' (pp. vif). Modernist rejoinders to Rutgers were made by A. D. Loman in *De Gids*, IV (1866), lff; and by Land in *TT*, I (1867).

second half of Isaiah,[4] and a year later his Utrecht colleague H. C. Millies chose the defense of a primitive Hebrew monotheism as the subject of his rectoral address.[5] One needs to observe the motivation of these pieces. Rutgers, for example, began his book by expressing his annoyance with the critics and exposing their dogmatic prejudice against supernaturalism. He seemed to be especially irritated with their claims to practice the only scientific method. Yet it appears quite clearly to us that Rutgers was himself motivated by apologetic impulses rather than by an objective study of the text, inasmuch as he first decided to wage his combat against the critics, then chose the subject for treatment.[6] Such orthodox polemic made little impact. It was a sign of the times that the modernist de Jong followed Millies at Utrecht in 1868, while the modernist Oort replaced Rutgers at Leiden in 1875.

So far as one can discover, the above represents the best that orthodoxy within the Hervormde Kerk was able to produce in its attack on higher criticism until approximately three decades later. A more durable kind of orthodox resistance came to be found among the biblical scholars representing the separatistic movements. Representative of the Christelijke Gereformeerde Kerk (Afscheiding) was the Kampen Old Testament professor, M. Noordtzij, who took every opportunity, particularly in a series of rectoral orations, to attack the critics.[7] Noordtzij never wearied of calling attention to ways in which archaeological research in his time was forcing revisions in the dominant critical hypotheses. His writings were definitely not the kind of uninformed polemic characteristic of so many orthodox theologians. Nevertheless, his tactic of attacking the weak points in his opponents' positions without offering an effective answer to their essential challenge robbed his work of influence outside the circle of his own adherents.[8]

7 *De Beoefening der exegetische theologie, inzonderheid van den tekstkritiek, de geschiedenis des Bijbels en de exegese* (1875); *Egyptologie en Assyriologie in betrekking tot de geloofswaardigheid des Ouden Testaments* (1882); *De leer van Jezus en de apostelen over de Heilige Schrift des Oude Testaments* (1885); *Israëls verblijf in Egypte, bezien in 't licht der Egyptische ontdekkingen* (1892); *Oostersche lichtstralen over westersche Schrift-beschouwing* (1897); *De verhouding van Schriftgeloof en Schriftkritiek, vooral met het oog op het Oude Testament* (1907); *Babylonische Psalmen in vergelijking met die des Oude Testaments* (1911).

8 B. D. Eerdmans judged Noordtzij's polemic in the following words (*Het verband tusschen de beoefening van het Oude Testament en de Semietische studiën in het algemeen* (Leiden, 1898), p. 7): 'That Noordtzij's argument has not stopped the critics is perhaps due to the method he uses. He picks one of the most extreme critical views as an example, demonstrates its untenability, thence proclaims the absurdity of historical criticism as a whole.' Nevertheless, Noordtzij's writings often contained material of lasting worth. Several of his students, such as C. van Gelderen and his son Arie, have given a good account of themselves as Semitic and Old Testament scholars.

Kuyper's Doleantie movement, leading to the formation of the Gere-formeerde Kerk in 1892, likewise took a firm stand against higher criticism, though for the first twenty years of its existence the Doleantie group produced little that could pass as genuine biblical scholarship. As soon as the Free University of Amsterdam was organized, it made its position clear over against historical criticism. Several rectoral addresses, those of Abraham Kuyper, J. Woltjer, and H. H. Kuyper, cried the alarm that modern criticism was the most dangerous enemy of the Christian faith.[1]

Abraham Kuyper, as a matter of fact, came out for a rigid biblicism long before the Doleantie or the organization of the Free University. In the year 1869 he tried to get a group of conservative scholars to co-operate with him in writing a 'history of revelation' on the basis that the Bible *is* the Word of God. Failing to obtain the necessary collaboration, he went ahead with his own book, *De Schrift, het Woord Gods* (1870). In this book he made no distinction between moderate and radical criticism, between that of the modernists and that of the Ethicals. With him this was a matter of absolute principle. There could be no compromise, no mediating position. All kinds of criticism were illegitimate. In one of Kuyper's later works this attitude is expressed as follows: 'If the Christian theologian acknowledges in even one cardinal point the contentions of historical criticism concerning the Holy Scriptures, the entire principle by which his theology lives falls to the ground.'[2] A prominent Gerefor-meerde dogmatician of Kuyper's era, Herman Bavinck, fully supported the former's view. Emphasizing the absolute authority of the entire Scripture, Bavinck accounted for the rise of historical criticism as out-right rebellion against God's revelation, to be resisted with the same determination as rebellion against God himself.[3]

Gereformeerde theology acknowledged, it is true, a human factor in the Bible. In its doctrine of 'organic inspiration' it admitted that the writers of the several books were not deprived of their personalities, were not forced to write against their will, and were not taken out of their cultural circumstances. This does not mean, however, that the human factor is to

---

1 A. Kuyper, *De hedendaagsche Schriftkritiek in haar bedenkelijke strekking voor de gemeente des levenden Gods* (1881); Woltjer, *Overlevering en kritiek* (1886); H. H. Kuyper, *Evolutie of revelatie* (1903). The last was severely attacked by Eerdmans (*TT*, XXXVIII (1904), 293ff) and Wildeboer (*SWV*, XLI (1904), 148ff).

2 *Encyclopaedie der heilige godgeleerdheid*, 3 vols., Amsterdam, 1894; citing 2nd ed. (1909), II, 340. Kuyper was not embarrassed by the evidences of human conditioning in the Bible; for him these could not militate against an acknowledgement of God as its true primary Author. He glorified the 'mysteriousness' of the human factor, rather than

be considered independently. This is not a self-explanatory factor beside the divine factor, but was used by God as the instrument of his revelation, being exalted and purified by that revelation. In effect this means that the fallibility and imperfection of the Bible's human composers have been superseded or supplanted by the infallibility and perfection of divine inspiration. Genuine higher criticism is said therefore to have no business with the Bible, and the Christian is therefore warned not to seek any compromise with it. As Bavinck has put it, man may not dare judge the Bible since the Bible judges man. With childlike faith the Christian must simply accept the Bible's words at face-value.[4]

Out of the circles most closely associated with conservative elements in the Hervormde and Gereformeerde churches came the theologian who was to attempt a serious but utterly presumptuous refutation of Kuenen and of modern criticism in general. This person was P. J. Hoedemaker, a man of unusual gifts and of complex temperament, being under such diverse influences as Kuyper's neo-Calvinism, Chantepie de la Saussaye's Ethical theology, and Emerson's transcendentalism. A more confused and turbulent career than his could hardly be imagined. Born in The Netherlands, he grew up in America and studied for a while at New Brunswick College in New Jersey. After a fling at politics, he studied for the ministry and became a very popular preacher in Chicago in 1861. The next year, however, he left his pulpit and went to Europe, studying at Bonn, Heidelberg, and Strasbourg. Finally he obtained a doctorate at Utrecht in 1867 with van Oosterzee. He served churches in Rotterdam and Amsterdam; then, in 1880, he took a post at the Free University, which had just been organized. In 1887 he left this position out of protest against the Doleantie. But in 1890 he was back in Amsterdam, where he became the leader of the Calvinistic group within the Hervormde Kerk, seeking reformation of the church through evangelization and re-organization.

This was the man who undertook Dutch conservatism's most serious attempt at refuting the Kuenen theory. In 1895 he published a lengthy book, *De Mozaïsche oorsprong van de wetten in de boeken Exodus, Leviticus, en*

feeling any obligation to explain it in historical terms; cf. *Het werk van den Heiligen Geest* (1889–89), p. 36.

3 *Gereformeerde dogmatiek*, 4 vols., 1895–1901. The denomination's leading dogmatician of the present generation, G. C. Berkhouwer, has taken much the same position in *Het probleem der Schriftkritiek* (1938). The literature on the doctrine of Scripture in this denomination is very extensive; cf. J. Ridderbos, *Gereformeerde Schriftbeschouwing en organische opvatting*, Kampen, 1926.

4 *op. cit.*, 4th ed. (1928), I, 412f

Numeri. It typified his impulsive and superficially brilliant character. Hoedemaker realized that he was not qualified to write a serious scientific refutation of the great critics, yet the urging of friends and the gnawings of a conviction that *something* had to be done led him to it. After a busy summer of reading the works of Kuenen and Wellhausen, and with the substance of various lectures as a basis, Hoedemaker was ready to write.[1]

In fifteen 'Lezingen,' Hoedemaker tried to uphold the Mosaic origin of the Pentateuchal laws. His argumentation was largely polemic, his only positive suggestion being that the various legislative strata correspond to the three important stopping-places in the wilderness journey: Sinai, Kadesh, and Moab. This was a book of four hundred and thirty pages, long enough to represent a serious piece of research. Yet much of this space was wasted in oratory and in circumvention of the real problems. It is easy to understand the exasperation of scholars like Matthes and Valeton, who were especially annoyed at the presumptuous tone of the book.[2] Despite his appeal to Scripture, Hoedemaker did not come to grips with the real problems of the criticism of Scripture. He pointed out many of the weaker points in the Kuenen-Wellhausen theory, but even in this he was not original, simply borrowing from such writers as König and Green.

No doubt this book had considerable influence – but not in restraining historical criticism. It only succeeded in stoking the fires of anti-traditionalistic zeal among the younger members of the modernist school.

1 G. Wildeboer clearly had this in mind in his sarcastic reference to 'theologians who imagined themselves able in a few months – in a short summer vacation – to gain a mastery of and actually become capable of refuting what persons of unusual talent had discovered through long toilsome years' (*De tegenwoordige stand van het Oudtestamentische vraagstuk*, 1907, p. 9). Hoedemaker declared in his introduction that he intended to write a similar treatment of Deuteronomy and the prophetic books, but apparently the severe criticism he received discouraged him, for this never appeared.

2 Matthes exclaimed, 'All apologetic is mischief!'; cf. *TT*, XXIX (1895), 422–49, 497–518, 660; see also Valeton's more considerate criticism in *Ph. J. Hoedemaker: De Mozaïsche Oorsprong (etc.)*, Utrecht, 1895, answered in Hoedemaker's *Als verleiders en nochthans waarachtigen*, Leiden, 1896; see further Valeton, *Christus en het Oude Testament*, Nijmegen, 1895.

3 A Gereformeerde scholar of the present century, G. Ch. Aalders, exhibits considerable indebtedness to Hoedemaker's theory of legislative strata in the Pentateuch; cf. *A Short Introduction to the Pentateuch*, London, 1949 (see below).

4 *De eenheid van het scheppingsverhaal tegenover de resultaten der kritiek verdedigd en gehandhaafd.* Its publisher, D. A. Daamen of Leiden, had published Hoedemaker's book the year before. A. van der Flier, G. Jzn., undertook a refutation in *De eerste twee hoofdstukken van Genesis*, Leiden, 1897. The unity of Gen. 1–2 has continued to be a rallying -point for traditionalists in Holland; cf. Aalders, *De goddelijke openbaring in de eerste drie hoofdstukken van Genesis*, Kampen, 1932.

5 The author summed up the 'results' of his study in twelve propositions at the end.

Where it did have influence – among the uninformed laity and orthodox theologians – it had the effect of hardening them in their bias against any wholesome criticism, thus perpetuating the separations in the church occasioned by this vital issue.[3]

In 1896 a Hervormde minister, H. van Eyck van Heslinga, attempted a serious and scholarly defense of the unity of the two creation stories in Gen. 1 and 2.[4] His essay, a brochure of eighty pages, was significant because it, together with Hoedemaker's book, represented the best that adherents of the traditional view were able to produce in this period. It also demonstrated the preconceptions and emotions which determined much of their resistance to historical criticism. Van Eyck van Heslinga was courteous and tried to be fair to his opponents. He seemed to be well trained in Hebrew and in exegesis, having studied with Valeton at Utrecht, and was able to point out some real flaws in current critical theories, but he plainly showed his strong emotional bias. He cried, 'They take our Bible away from us and hand it back, after their critical revision, torn and tattered, and, what is worse, as nothing but a collection of sagas and myths!' What he composed was essentially a running polemic which scarcely dealt with the real issues involved in the analysis of these crucial chapters. Like the Gereformeerde theologians, he made no distinction between various types of criticism; 'de critiek' as such was condemned.[5]

During this period, Dutch Roman Catholic theologians virtually

Because these were not so much results as presuppositions, and because they reveal so much of the mentality of the author and his circle, we translate them in full: '(1) The study of Scripture must take account of the revelation given us therein and therewith, as also of its organic unity as a vehicle of the divine thought and thoughts. (2) Once this factor is taken into account, a divisive criticism becomes impossible, such as with unrestrained arbitrariness tears, divides, and relocates the form and content of Scripture. (3) The method actually employed by criticism contradicts the method which it calls the only valid one, i.e., positing a hypothesis without any *a priori* presuppositions... (4) With respect to Gen. 1 and 2, criticism attempts to prove its interpretation by an *a priori* assumption that that interpretation (a mere hypothesis) has already been demonstrated. (5) If one actually follows such an objective method, it is impossible to come to the results of criticism. (6) Only if the results of criticism are assigned their proper hypothetical value can they be considered to represent objective scientific inquiry. (7) The results of criticism, together with its consequences, can be reconciled only with a naturalistic standpoint hostile to the Scriptures. (8) The results of criticism are in conflict with Scriptural hamartiology, Christology, soteriology, and pneumatology, viewed as a whole. (9) In Gen. 1 and 2 no basis for the disruptive analysis of the Pentateuch can be found. (10) In Gen. 1 and 2 no reason for denying Mosaic authorship can be found. (11) The text of Gen. 1 and 2 teaches [sic!] the unity of that which is being narrated, and contains no more than a single creation story. (12) The unity of the creation story, taught by the text of Gen. 1 and 2, is supported and confirmed by the Word of the Lord in Matt. 19:4–5.'

ignored the scientific study of the Bible, using Scripture purely for traditional purposes. Only very occasionally did a polemical piece appear in their journals. Thus P. L. Dessens, professor at the Grootseminarie at Warmond, attacked Kuenen's Pentateuchal criticism in a feeble article appearing in the 1886 *Katholiek*. He attempted to defend Mosaic authorship from a dogmatic point of view, with frequent appeal to the church fathers.[1] J. Schets, professor at Hoeven, went so far as to write a book attacking Kuenen; this book, published in 1891, demonstrated considerable skill and learning but displayed enormous irritation with what was viewed as a preposterous unbelief.[2] In the Catholic periodical *Maasbode* of Dec. 12, 1891, Schets reported Kuenen's death, disdainfully declaring that the Leiden professor had not been truly learned and that his criticism did not truly deserve to be called scientific.

Meanwhile, Dutch Jewish scholars paid little attention to scientific biblical criticism. Sizeable as the Jewish community was, it produced only an occasional philological study in the journal, *Israëlietische Letterbode*, together with a book or two on Hebrew grammar. M. Monasch, *corrector* at the Jewish seminary in Amsterdam, did write a three-volume history of the Israelite people, but this was essentially popular, glorifying the Jewish people and based entirely on the traditional biblicistic viewpoint.[3]

THE WORK OF THE ORTHODOX ETHICALS

The followers of Chantepie de la Saussaye, retaining the essentials of orthodox belief, accepted historical criticism as a method and devoted themselves with great energy to the scientific study of Scripture. This meant that they relinquished biblicism, based on the theory of absolute inerrancy and verbal inspiration. It also meant, however, that they were in a position to acknowledge both the claims of religion and those of science.

The Ethicals did much to encourage the popular acceptance of a reverent higher criticism, an example being an address by J. H. Gunning, J. Hzn., delivered to a gathering of ministers in 1885 under the title, *De critische beschouwing van Israëls geschiedenis;* in this he argued

---

1 'Pentateuch-critiek,' *De Katholiek*, LXXXIX, n.r. I, 22–44
2 This book had a mocking and presumptuous title, *Prof. Kuenen's Pentateuch-critiek historisch-critisch onderzocht* (a review of *Historisch-critisch onderzoek* (etc.), 2nd ed.).
3 *Geschiedenis van het volk Israël*, Amsterdam, 1891–95. Cf. J. D. Wijnkoop, *Handleiding tot*

that the Kuenen analysis of the Old Testament literature did not come out of unbelief as such, and was not necessarily in conflict with faith in Christ, or even with belief in the revelatory character of Israel's religion. In addition, Ethical scholars like Gunning were constantly at work at exegetical study, attempting to put their principle to good effect in solid productivity. Not surprisingly, they were bitterly attacked both from the right and from the left. The modernists denounced them with something of shocked surprise, as they saw them 'stealing' their criticism and using it without their theological presuppositions. The orthodox rigorists condemned them as hypocrites and apostates, as betrayers of the faith, as guilty of a sin even worse than that of the modernists.

It is best to illustrate the principles and methods of the Ethical school from the actual writings of some of its leading adherents, and once again we pass by the work of the New Testament scholars, notably Doedes, and view only that of the Old Testament specialists. One of the most prolific of these was J. J. P. Valeton, Jr., professor at Utrecht from 1877 to 1912. He was widely influential. His father, of the same theological viewpoint, had been professor of Old Testament at Groningen. The younger Valeton studied at Utrecht and wrote his dissertation there in 1871.[4] The method he followed in this composition is indicative of his whole approach. He attempted to define the character, historical appearance, and preaching of the prophet Isaiah, assuming the results of modern criticism but not attempting to enter into questions of literary analysis. As he stated it, the latter would take him too far from his purpose; he preferred to engage in a sympathetic and positive study rather than to do something in the at the time more fashionable field of 'negative' criticism.

Valeton (hereafter we refer only to the younger), together with the modernist de Jong, took over the teaching duties of the strictly orthodox Millies. Valeton's piety was as vital and as biblical as that of his predecessor, but his method of criticism was entirely that of Kuenen. G. Ch. Aalders has said of Valeton and another Ethical *Oudtestamenticus* Gerrit Wildeboer: 'These scholars may have sought to instill greater religious warmth in their expressions (particularly Valeton), and practised greater scientific moderation and caution, but in principle they stood in regard to the Old Testament precisely upon the same standpoint as did the Leiden

de kennis der Hebreeuwsche taal, 1888 (English trans. London, 1898); also A. S. Onderwijzer's ambitious translation of the Hebrew Pentateuch, combined with translation of the Onkelos Targum and Rashi's commentary (Amsterdam, 1894–1900).
4 *Jesaja volgens zijne algemeen als echt erkende schriften*

100

school.'[1] Aalders meant this as a criticism, but his estimate is correct.

Valeton had an early opportunity to express his view of revelation in an address made to the 1876 meeting of the Hervormde Predikanten Vereeningen in Utrecht. The title of this address expresses the author's point of view: 'Het openbaringskarakter van de boeken des Ouden Verbonds (The revelatory character of the Old Testament books).'[2] Valeton set aside the traditional doctrine of verbal inspiration, yet declared his full conviction that the Bible is truly God's authoritative and objective word to man. We may call his understanding of inspiration dynamic, i.e., he held that the Bible is an effective revelation insomuch as God has worked in and through its writers by way of his sovereign providence. 'Providence' is the key to Valeton's concept. Rather than speaking of revelation as a supernatural irruption into the course of nature, Valeton viewed it as God's work in and through all the world's ordinary processes, which through his providence have become the vehicles of his divine purpose.

During the later seventies, Valeton could be seen busy producing the first of an impressive array of biblical studies on a variety of technical problems. He generally used the Ethical periodical *Studiën*, and later its successor, *Theologische Studiën*, as the vehicle of his writing. His work ere long came to the approving attention of leading scholars outside Holland. In 1877 he produced, with Albert Ritschl's theory of justification in mind, a solid study of the terminology of atonement in the Old Testament.[3] The following year he became one of the first to argue for the historicity of Hosea's marriage, and soon received the support of the great Wellhausen in the latter's revised fourth edition of Bleek's *Einleitung in das Alte Testament*.[4]

Such approval of the work of a supernaturalist by one of the giants of their own camp apparently annoyed the Dutch modernists. They were deeply puzzled about Valeton's position as a respectable critic. He felt it necessary to respond to this in a short essay, 'Pro domo,' appearing in the 1879 *Studiën*, which constituted in effect a manifesto for Ethical criticism. Valeton here stressed the fact that he maintained both his-

1 *op. cit.*, p. 8
2 *Studiën*, II, 175–99
3 'Schulddelging voor God in het Oude Testament,' *Studiën*, III, 159–77; cf. Ritschl, *Die christliche Lehre von der Rechtfertigung und Versöhnung*, 1870–74.
4 'Hosea 1 en 3,' *Studiën*, IV (1878), 143–64; Valeton expressed pleasure at Wellhausen's independent corroboration of his views. Studies in Obadiah and Joel preceded and followed this study; cf. *Studiën*, I (1875), 1–38; 122–45; III (1877), 92–107; VII (1880), 50–75, 243–70.
5 V, 207–16

torical criticism and belief in the Bible as God's transcendent revelation. He let Oort, Kuenen, and the rest know that their prejudice against supernaturalism, as he called it, could not deny him the right to claim scholarly respectability.[5]

Valeton began to receive support from other Ethical Old Testament scholars. A student of Doedes, F. J. van den Ham, chose as the subject of his Utrecht dissertation the 'historical' superscriptions in the Psalms, concluding that only a few are authentic, the others involving mistaken guesses.[6] Though relatively conservative, this study did employ the techniques of objective criticism. In 1888 van den Ham was appointed to the Groningen faculty. His inaugural address approvingly summarized the Kuenen Pentateuchal criticism, indicating the ways in which biblical science had gained by the purging of traditional interpretations.[7]

In 1880 J. Th. de Visser wrote a dissertation on demonology in the Old Testament. This was a worthwhile historical study with theological evaluation. De Visser was Valeton's pupil. Another was J. H. Gunning, J. Hzn., whose dissertation, completed in 1881, was a careful study of divine retribution in important Old Testament passages. He acknowledged Kuenen's influence, having first studied at Leiden, but gave greatest tribute to Valeton, whose warm piety he shared and whose more conservative criticism he preferred.[8]

Valeton had now apparently found his full stride. He dared enter areas of research heretofore dominated by such authoritative scholars as Kuenen himself. The most important of these areas was the Pentateuch. Valeton subjected Deuteronomy to a painstaking analysis in an extensive series of articles appearing in *Studiën* from 1879 to 1881. One hundred thirty-nine pages in length, this series actually comprises the most extensive study of this Bible book ever produced by a Dutch scholar in modern times. Proceeding verse by verse, Valeton worked without rationalistic and evolutionary interpretations. Denying that Deuteronomy was a deliberate attempt at deception, as Kuenen claimed, he concluded that it was originally a collection of early laws by various writers, compiled and provided with a historical introduction by a redactor in the time of

6 *De Psalmen met historische opschriften*, Utrecht, 1871
7 *De Israëlietische oudheid en de Pentateuchkritiek*, Groningen, 1888. Van den Ham did little further writing. He assisted his colleague Wildeboer in his magnum opus, *Letterkunde des Ouden Verbonds*, 1893 (see below).
8 De Visser, *De daemonologie van het Oude Testament*; Gunning, *De goddelijke vergelding, hoofdzakelijk volgens Exodus 20:5, 6 en Ezechiël 18:20*. Both de Visser and Gunning did some minor writing on biblical problems, cf. Gunning's justifications of historical criticism mentioned above.

Manasseh.[1] It is interesting to note that this was close to Kuenen's original view of Deuteronomy, as stated in *Historisch-Kritisch onderzoek* (1861) and approaches the consensus of the present day.

We must make a selection from Valeton's numerous writings during the years that followed to illustrate the principles of this developing criticism. He presented a synthetic picture of his understanding of Hebrew origins in a lengthy 1881 article entitled, 'Bijdrage tot de kennis en waardeering van den israëlietischen godsdienst,' stating that Yahwism was a supernaturally revealed religion, monotheistic in principle at its very beginning, though only partially such in practice until the eighth century B.C. Valeton emphasized that monotheism was no intellectual dogma but the true and vital religion of Israel coming into its full right in the midst of a heathen environment.[2] In another article of the same year, Valeton studied the Garden of Eden tradition in Gen. 2–3, arguing that it was not meant as allegory, as some were claiming, but as a poetical construction of actual historical origins; he favored Friedrich Delitzsch's recently published view that Eden was located in Babylonia, and expressed an awareness of the growing importance of Assyriology for Old Testament exegesis in general.[3] In an 1886 semidevotional treatment of Isaiah 53, Valeton came out for a messianic interpretation, bolstering his view, however, with careful linguistic exposition.[4]

New voices were being heard in the Ethical journal, *Theologische Studiën*, in support of this type of biblical exposition. Professor J. J. van Toorenenbergen of Amsterdam summarized Franz Delitzsch's approach to the tradition of Mosaic authorship for the Pentateuch, stating, in agreement with Delitzsch, his acceptance of higher criticism alongside a cautious respect for the tradition; it was not 'all or nothing,' as the modernists were claiming; van Toorenenbergen insisted that each passage has a right to be weighed on its own merits for its level of historicity.[5] At this time H. Zeydner began his valuable series of text-critical studies

1 'Deuteronomium,' V, 69–206, 291–313; VI, 133–74; VII, 39–56, 205–27
2 *Studiën*, VII, 1–27, 81–120
3 'De hof van Eden,' *idem*, 363–88; cf. Delitzsch , *Wo lag der Paradis?*, Leipzig, 1881.
4 'Jesaja 53, een bijbelstudie,' *SWV*, XXIII, 429–73
5 'Het oorspronkelijk Mozaïsche in den Pentateuch,' IV (1886), 13–31, 92–108, 365–82
6 IV, 196–207, 249–64; VI (1888), 247–64; XVIII (1900), 417–19
7 'Micha Studiën,' VI, 235–46; VII (1889), 436–53; X (1892), 239–60. Pont wrote an Amsterdam dissertation on Psalm 68 (1887).
8 'Uit de geschiedenis en de opteekening der priesterliche Thorah,' V (1887), 236–50, 328–55. Wildeboer criticized Wellhausen's views concerning the centralization of the cultus, the work of Moses, and the composition of the priestly laws. He wrote: 'Onesidedness has necessarily been the characteristic of the newer criticism in its early development

on the Psalms and Minor Prophets.[6] A leading Lutheran minister, J. W. Pont, published an extensive study of Micah, sharply criticizing those who denied the authenticity of this book, in particular Kuenen and Stade.[7] But the most influential voice was that of Gerrit Wildeboer, who reviewed the Pentateuchal analysis of Wellhausen, admitting the points he had proved but announcing that the time had come for scientific criticism to go beyond Wellhausen (and by implication Kuenen) to a more secure and in many ways less negative position.[8]

Wildeboer had entered the university at Leiden in 1874, where he studied Hebrew and Old Testament criticism with Kuenen and Oort.[9] In his early student years he had still been an antagonist of historical criticism, but before he finished his academic work in 1880 he had learned to employ most of its methods within the framework of his supernaturalistic thought.[10] He wrote his dissertation in the area of New Testament textual criticism,[11] but was appointed in 1884 to teach Old Testament criticism at Groningen. In 1907 he returned to Leiden to become Oort's successor. He became well-known abroad by way of several of his important books.

Wildeboer, like Valeton, repudiated the theory of evolution as applied to Israel's religion, claiming that this was based on unacceptable dogmatic presuppositions rather than on scientific data. Kuenen's school consequently could never quite bring itself to acknowledge that he was completely scientific, even though he reproduced its biblical criticism almost to the point of slavish imitation, far more so than Valeton. Here was Wildeboer's definition:

Criticism is a serving and not a ruling science, as popular speech puts it. It is actually nothing else than a strictly scientific, historical exposition of the scriptures. It desires to allow the Bible to bear testimony to itself, and therefore repudiates all interpretations of later collectors, scribes, and scholars who would demand of us that we read the Scriptures through their spectacles.[12]

and particularly in its brilliant triumph under Wellhausen's leadership... But the time has come to correct, modify, or substantiate better many of the new concepts.'

9 See biographical notices by L. H. K. Bleeker in *TS*, XXX (1912), 81–96, and by J. Domela Nieuwenhuis in *Levensberichten van Nederlandsche Letterkunden*, 1916–17.

10 Wildeboer was one of the few critical scholars to speak kindly of his teacher, the old conservative Rutgers; cf. 'Het verhaal van den zonnenstilstand,' *TS*, IX (1891), 249–57.

11 *De Waarde der Syrische Evangelieën door Curston ontdekt en uitgegeven*, Leiden, 1880

12 *De Letterkunde des Ouden Verbonds* (Groningen, 1893), p. vi. For further description of critical method by Wildeboer cf. 'Iets over karakter en beginselen van het historisch-kritisch onderzoek des Ouden Verbonds,' *SWV*, XXX (1893), 1003ff, and 'Iets over de methode der O.T.'ische kritiek,' *TS*, XVI (1898), 291–305.

Kuenen could not have objected to this statement in itself; what he and his school disliked was Wildeboer's and Valeton's 'spiritual' interpretation, going beyond the reach of historical criticism itself.

In his inaugural address at Groningen, Wildeboer made very clear how the ethical-mystical principle enunciated by Chantepie de la Saussaye influenced biblical interpretation, and vice-versa. His subject was the significance of Hebrew prophecy for Christian theology.[1] For Wildeboer, the uniqueness and genius of Israel lay solely in its relationship to the only true God in a vital, personal fellowship. He declared that accordingly an appropriation of the ethical and religious values in Israel's religion must be of infinitely greater concern to Christian theologians than any barren empirical evaluation. Moreover, metaphysical concepts are of little importance. We need to see, in addition to the human factor, the divine reality of a genuine and objective revelation.

Before long, Wildeboer wrote an important book, *Het ontstaan van den kanon des Ouden Verbonds* (1889) which came to be widely used and gained him an international standing.[2] He also became interested at this time in popularizing current criticism of the Pentateuchal laws. In one instance, he found it necessary to defend his presentations to Dutch jurists on this subject against attacks from the orthodox right.[3] Shortly thereafter, Wildeboer wrote the book for which he is best known in Holland, *De letterkunde des Ouden Verbonds naar de tijdsorde van haar ontstaan* (1893).[4]

This last was a comprehensive book attempting to set in strict chronological order, according to the results of modern criticism, all the various literary materials in the Old Testament, from the Decalogue at the beginning to Esther at the end. It is somewhat amazing to the present-day reader to note the bland assurance of Wildeboer's arrangement. The very idea of putting all the Old Testament materials

---

1 *De profetie onder Israël in hare grondbeteekenis voor Christendom en theologie*, Leiden, 1884. Wildeboer revealed his considerable indebtedness to W. Robertson Smith. He also paid tribute to his predecessor, Valeton Sr., expressing substantial agreement with the latter's point of view .

2 This book went through four editions and was translated into English (1895).

3 See his articles in *Tijdschrift voor Strafrecht*, IV (1890), 205–30; V (1891), 251–69; VIII (1893), 169ff. D. P. D. Fabius, law professor at the Free University, bitterly took him to task, accusing him of superficiality. Wildeboer retorted that, easy as it would be to forgive Fabius for his ignorance, since he was a non-specialist, the latter's arrogant and condescending tone was completely inexcusable. Later studies in Pentateuchal law were Wildeboer's treatment of the Decalogue in *TS*, XXI (1903), 109–18, and his evaluation of the Hammurabi Code in *Tijdschrift voor Strafrecht*, XVI (1904), 70ff.

4 This work went through three editions. It was translated into English, French, and German.

5 'De Israëlietische Godsnaam,' *TS*, VII (1889), 173–221; 'Beteekenis en gebruik van

in strict chronological order seems rash today. While admitting that some very old documents are incorporated in these materials, Wildeboer emphasized that absolutely all parts of the Old Testament are post-exilic in their present form. Nevertheless, he upheld the general reliability, originality, and independence of these writings. This book had chiefly ministerial students and non-specialists in view. In it Wildeboer appears more as a synthesizing popularizer than as an original and analytic critic. It cannot be compared in scientific value with the best writings of Kuenen. Yet Wildeboer seemed to have been widely known and appreciated, within and outside Holland, as the numerous editions of this and other of his major writings testify.

Valeton was at this time producing a number of careful exegetical and linguistic studies. He was particularly interested in garnering empirical data regarding key terminology involved in the controversy over the Wellhausen-Kuenen Hexateuchal reconstruction.[5] In 1894 he published a book on *Amos en Hosea*, containing an extensive critical introduction, which was translated into German and received favorable notice from foreign critics like Budde and G. A. Smith.[6] Further examples of Ethical criticism in this period were the doctoral dissertations of two of Valeton's pupils, L. H. K. Bleeker's study of sections of Jeremiah and A. van der Flier's examination of Deuteronomy 33; both represented a cautious but thoroughly competent literary and historical criticism.[7] Bleeker was to become Wildeboer's successor at Groningen.

Wildeboer, like Valeton, began to demonstrate his competence as a linguistic technician, writing a number of detailed exegetical studies.[8] International recognition of his skill came when he was engaged to write the commentaries on Proverbs, Esther, and Ecclesiastes for Karl Marti's *Kurzer Handkommentar* (1897–98). He gained a distinction almost equal to

het woord Thora in het Oude Testament,' *idem*, IX (1891), 101–56; also three studies on the word *berith* (covenant) written in German and appearing in *ZAW*, XII (1892), 1ff, 224ff; XIII (1893), 245ff; cf. his earlier study of the root KP R (see p. 96, n. 3).

6 *Amos en Hosea. Een hoofdstuk uit de geschiedenis van Israëls godsdienst*, Nijmegen, 1894. German trans. Giessen, 1898.

7 Bleeker, *Jeremia's profetieën tegen de volkeren*, Groningen, 1894; van der Flier, *Deuteronomium 33, een exegetisch-historische studie*, Leiden, 1895 (cf. Bleeker's critique in *TS*, XIV (1896), 359–81).

8 'De eerste vier verzen van den zestienden Psalm,' *Feestbundel aan Prof. M. J de Goeje* (Leiden, 1891), pp. 47ff; 'De vier en tachtigste Psalm', *SWV*, XXIX (1892), 775ff; 'Nog eens de vier verzen van Ps. 16,' *TT*, XXVII (1893), 610 ff (in answer to Zeydner and van Gilse); 'Zu Ps. 17:11, 12,' *ZAW*, XVII (1897), 180; 'Zu Prov. 8:31,' *ZAW*, XVIII (1898), 255; 'Die älteste Bedeutung des Stammes ṢDQ,' *ZAW*, XXII (1902), 167ff; 'Nahum 3:7,' *idem*, 318ff; 'MṢR', *ZAW*, XXIX (1909), 73, 219f.

Kuenen's in being asked to deliver as many as four addresses to the Koninklijke Akademie van Wetenschappen.[1] The subject to which he most frequently returned during the years around the turn of the century was the nature of God's revelation to Israel.[2] Thus in his 1898 rectoral address, *Jahwedienst en volksreligie in Israël*,[3] he again attempted to clarify his understanding of the relationship between, on the one hand, the divine grace and providence which produced a revelation of absolute and continuing validity and, on the other hand, the natural life and development of the Hebrew people. Wildeboer described the distinctive practices of naturalistic lay-religion in early Israel. Yahwism, according to him, emerged already in the patriarchal period in opposition to this lay-religion, being strengthened and clarified by Moses and the great prophets. He particularly emphasized that prophetic religion did not evolve out of lay-religion, but came as a decisive break with it. Thus Israel possessed both a natural 'developed' religion and a supernatural 'established' religion, alongside each other. The latter came to a high point in the preaching of Second Isaiah, but – Wildeboer went on to add – even this was not complete until God fully revealed himself in his Son Jesus Christ.

Wildeboer's last sizeable composition was his book, *Het Oude Testament van historisch standpunt toegelicht*, which was published in Groningen in 1908. This was a kind of supplement to his *Letterkunde des Ouden Verbonds*, but apparently did not receive the wide acceptance that the latter had enjoyed. It too was primarily intended for ministers and theological students rather than for specialists, offering them a thorough integration of the most up-to-date criticism with belief in a supernatural revelation. Of special interest is Wildeboer's treatment of pre-Mosaic religion. He admitted freely that the patriarchs had been nomads, that they worshiped stones, trees, and stars; indeed, that they even worshiped their own ancestors. At the same time, he claimed, they acknowledged the true deity under the various El-forms (El-Shaddai, El-Bethel, El-Elyon, etc.). The polydaemonism and polytheism were the point of contact for God's true self-revelation, which transformed and purified them into something worthy.

Here was Wildeboer's last attempt to synthesize faith and science. Whether his theories had much influence on the modernist critics is

1 'De tijdsbepaling van het boek der Spreuken, *Verslagen en Mededeelingen der Koninklijke Akademie van Wetenschappen, Afd. Letterkunde*, 1899; 'De kerkvader Origenes en de kanon des Ouden Verbonds,' *idem*, 1902; 'De patriarchen des Ouden Verbonds en de wetgeving van Hammoerabi,' *idem*, 1904; 'Iets over "ziel" en "geest" in het Oude Testament,' *idem*, 1911

doubtful, but there can be no question that he strongly influenced more conservative ministers and theologians, who eagerly welcomed such a grand harmonization as he was able to offer them.

Valeton continued active as long as Wildeboer did (the latter died in 1911, the former in 1912). In 1902–05 Valeton's important commentary on the Psalms appeared.[4] He was requested to write the essay on 'Die Israeliten' for the younger Chantepie de la Saussaye's *Lehrbuch der Religionsgeschichte*, published in Tübingen in 1905. An essay clearly prophetic of emerging trends was his 1909 lecture before the Koninklijke Akademie van Wetenschappen, 'Karakter en literairische opzet van het Sinaï-verhaal.' It was transitional to present methods, plainly showing the influence of rising German form- and tradition-criticism. Valeton declared that in this essay he was not interested in literary analysis as such; though admitting the composite origin of the Sinai material, he insisted that it still comprised a unity in its present form – the unity of a mosaic. In his summary he explained his viewpoint:

We all admit that in the Sinai narrative we have no literary unit written *aus einem Gusse;* on the other hand, it is not, as generally represented, a story compiled from originally separate, parallel narratives. It is *torah,* i.e., teaching. It is a compilation, with all sorts of targumic additions, explications, and emendations, of different and originally independent laws and lawbooks... which each reveal their own special character, come from various periods, and even have undergone their own peculiar history, but now have been formed, according to a definite plan, together with several old tales, into the constitutive elements of the composite Sinai-story.[5]

Thus Valeton admitted that the Sinai material contains many diverse elements, but his main interest lay in describing literary types, not in documentary analysis as such. In this he may be described as a true forerunner of current biblical criticism.

We take as a final statement of Valeton's attitude toward the Bible – representative of the Ethical school as a whole – these words from a 1909 essay:

I for myself have had the experience that if one lives according to Scripture – and its scientific investigation is, thank God, no hindrance to this – then one involuntarily comes more and more under its 'authority.' This is not to say that I swear by the letter of it, or that I find no errors in it, or that I subscribe directly to

2 Cf. 'De openbaring in Israël,' *SWV,* XLI (1904), 148–83; 'De profeten als organen van Gods openbaring,' *idem,* pp. 672ff (German trans. 1904).
3 German trans. 1899
4 *De Psalmen,* 3 vols., Nijmegen, 1902–05; 2nd rev. ed. 1912
5 p.112

every word of it; what I mean is that I neither can nor will seek to extricate myself from the overpowering influence which Scripture as a whole increasingly exerts upon me, in spite of the human failings and peculiarities which it possesses in common with every other book.[1]

1 *TS*, XXVII (1909), 10. In this particular article, Valeton had been arguing in support of Wildeboer against Matthes's interpretation of Josh. 10:12-14, which records the sun's standing still. Matthes insisted that this was literally intended, being, of course, a primitive legend without historical foundation. Valeton argued that it is rather an imaginative, poetic description of an actual historical occurrence. See Wildeboer in *TS*, IX (1891), 249-57; Matthes in *TTT*, VI (1908), 471-94; Valeton here and in *TS*, XXV (1907), 363-74.

Chapter Five

New Beginnings in Dutch

Old Testament Scholarship

Because the Hervormde Kerk aspires to be a people's church for the whole nation, it includes many groups within itself, even while remaining officially Calvinistic.[1] The result of this inclusiveness has been the development of parties or 'richtingen' within the church, ranging from pietism on the right to extreme liberalism on the left.[2] Despite this variety, there began a strong resurgence of conservatism in the church around the turn of the century, with the result that the Hervormde Kerk became quite a different thing than the modernists of Kuenen's generation tried to make of it. An important effect has been the strengthening of conservative representation among the professors of theology at the universities,[3] while these in turn supported the movement toward greater conservatism in the churches. Utrecht's theological faculty came early to consist largely of adherents of the Ethical school, as we have seen. In 1912 Valeton was succeeded by Arie Noordtzij, the son of the old Kampen professor. The younger Noordtzij was himself strongly attached to an orthodox theology, including a belief in verbal inspiration.[4] The situation was much the same in the New Testament department, where the chair was occupied after 1908 by J. A. C. van Leeuwen, who moved rightward from the Ethical position to the Gereformeerde camp. Thus Utrecht took on a pronouncedly orthodox complexion, in the biblical field as well as in other departments of theological study. Through the appointment of Wildeboer in 1884 and of Bleeker in 1907, the theological faculty at Groningen meanwhile remained moderately conservative in the Old Testament field, with similar orientation in the New Testament chair.

Leiden, on the other hand, continued to have mainly liberal scholars

1 Cf. Lindeboom, *op. cit.*, III, 198ff, for details about the Dutch denominations.
2 Cf. Knappert, *Godsdienstig Nederland* (Huis ter Heide, 1928), pp. 98–101, for a description of these *richtingen*. See also Haitjema, *De richtingen in de Nederlandse Hervormde Kerk*, 2nd ed., 1953.
3 Although the theological faculties of the state universities are not under church control, conservative influence in the church has at times been able to make itself felt in the appointment of faculty members through political pressure.
4 Aalders, 'De studie van het Oude Testament', p. 9, reports that young Noordtzij was seriously considered at the time to succeed Wildeboer at Leiden; but cf. what Reitsma, p. 541, says about this matter. Apparently, opposing parties in the church took serious concern in this appointment. Noordtzij's successor was a moderate conservative, A. H. Edelkoort.

of various stripes in its New Testament, Old Testament, and Semitic chairs, though even here the conservative shift began to appear. A break in modernist dominance came in 1889, when a leading Ethical, J. H. Gunning, Sr., succeeded L. W. E. Rauwenhoff. Gunning was in turn followed by another Ethical in 1899. In 1903 the modernist van Manen was succeeded in the New Testament chair by the English scholar Kirsopp Lake, also a modernist but a high-church Anglican. Three years previously, Tiele's place had been filled by the Norwegian W. Brede Kristensen, and in 1907 Wildeboer took Oort's chair in Semitic studies. Kristensen's appointment was especially significant because of the striking difference between his methods and Tiele's. Tiele had been fond of broad speculations concerning the universal evolutions of religion – comparable to Kuenen's theorizing in respect to the evolution of Israel's religion – but his successor concerned himself solely with simple scientific description.[1]

The municipal university of Amsterdam remained markedly liberal throughout the early years of the present century; it is noteworthy that not until the end of the second World War did Old Testament exegesis again come under the control of its theological faculty. The Free University of Amsterdam and the Kampen Theological School, on the other hand, have meanwhile remained as bulwarks of Protestant orthodoxy, while the University of Nijmegen, established in 1923, later became an influential center of Catholic scholarship.

Dutch scholars continued to differ concerning the nature of the Bible. Generally, there were four distinct ways of looking at the problem. First, ultra-conservatives admitted a human factor in the composition of the Bible but assumed an essentially docetic view in which the factors of this humanness were superseded; they emphasized that the Bible *is* the Word of God, verbally and totally. Next, a significant and influential group has come to believe that God's transcendent Word is in the Bible, making the Bible the reliable record of or witness to that Word. Third, the modernists continued to call the Bible God's Word only in the sense that every religious writing is a revelation of God. And finally, there have been those who would not acknowledge God's existence, and who consequently could not find anything 'divine' in Scripture whatever. Only among the ultra-conservatives can the doctrine of Scripture be said to have dominated the choice of exegetical methods. Among the other

1 Cf. K. H. Roessingh, 'De Leidsche Theologische Faculteit 1875–1925,' *Verzamelde werken* II, 393–406.
2 *TT*, XLIII, 56off; XLIV, 173ff, 289ff, 437ff, 443ff. For a similar, more recent ex-

groups the methods of historical criticism were unhesitatingly employed, although always results have to some degree depended on the underlying commitment regarding the nature of the Bible.

Early in the century, in 1909 and 1910, B. D. Eerdmans became involved in a three-cornered debate with Valeton and Wildeboer on this vital question. Their discussion concerned in particular the legitimacy of 'spiritual' exegesis alongside a strict historical interpretation. In a final exchange, Wildeboer, who defended this 'spiritual' exegesis, compared Eerdmans to a man who can see in one of Rembrandt's masterpieces nothing but the texture of the canvas and the technique of the brushwork, while likening himself to another viewer who is able to look beyond the rude externals to an appreciation of the genius and beauty in a great work of art. The point seemed well taken, but Eerdmans, who, as editor of the *Theologisch Tijdschrift* in which this debate appeared, had the last word, repudiated the comparison. He countered by likening Wildeboer to a man who imagines that he sees mystical meanings in a painting that were never put there by the artist at all.[2] This debate typifies the continuing cleavage separating Dutch scholars and theologians on the doctrine of Scripture.

We turn now to a consideration of ways in which new scientific discoveries were forcing revisions in critical theory in a period when the trend was toward disillusionment both with the theology and the biblical criticism of the modernist school. Our attention will be claimed, first and most intensively, by the jarring challenge of one of the new breed of modernists, B. D. Eerdmans of Leiden, and will next be focused upon continuing efforts on various sides to explore new avenues of discovery.

EERDMANS'S REVISION OF THE KUENEN THEORIES

We have seen that the period between 1870 and 1910 was a time of unchecked confidence among the adherents of the Graf-Kuenen-Wellhausen hypothesis. Many of them seemed to believe that ultimate truth had been attained. In the Netherlands, the Leiden and Amsterdam scholars treated conservatism with the disdain of a vaunted superiority, despising even the beliefs of able critics like Valeton and Wildeboer.

change between P. A. H. de Boer and Th. C. Vriezen, see *Nederlands Theologisch Tijdschrift*, VI (1951– 52), 1ff, 90ff, 109ff.

Kuenen and his followers did much, together with their colleagues in other lands, to establish modern biblical criticism on a scientific basis, and the present generation of scholars will not easily forget its debt to them. However, later developments in this science have demonstrated the weaknesses of some of their methods, the error of many of their conclusions, and the vulnerability of their over-confident attitude. In the days of their ascendency, these scholars were in no mood for self-criticism – making it necessary for another generation to correct their excesses. Their victory had been too easy for their own good. Their opponents either remained silent, busied themselves with polemics, or attacked only a few minor points in their critical position. Because of this, the Kuenen school allowed themselves in more than one respect to go much too far, and particularly in their lack of modesty and simple Christian charity.

Nonetheless, a remarkable difference may be observed in the spirit of Kuenen's school at the beginning and at the end of this period. At the time when Kuenen was writing his *Godsdienst van Israël,* he and his school were glowing in the freshness of a tremendous discovery: the riddle of the ages had been unlocked, and their eyes had gone open. By the turn of the century, however, many of the best critics in Holland and elsewhere were beginning to see that their work had only begun, and that some of their steps would have to be retraced.

For one thing, a reaction had set in against the excessive atomization of the Hexateuchal documents by some of Kuenen's and Wellhausen's disciples, who had come to act as if literary analysis were an end in itself. In his inaugural address at Leiden, Wildeboer pointed out the weaknesses of this imbalance:

With all the respect that we owe to the men of the second half of the nineteenth century, it must nevertheless be admitted that their group was often too one-sidely literary-critical. It seemed to them that our science has scarcely anything else to do than arrange the various traditions in their proper chronological order. It seemed to them often as if the various concepts originated at the same time that they appeared in written form. Accompanying this misunderstanding, there were other one -sided emphases. The truth of the oral traditions, both before and after composition in written form, was not highly enough respected; it was not kept in mind sufficiently that very contrary or even contradictory ideas... could have existed at the same time; from the perilous *argumentum e silentio* they all too often were ready to make unwarranted conclusions; from passages sounding alike they all too quickly concluded interdependence; also, difficulties in a document were simply eliminated by the supposition that they were interpolations.[1]

1 *De tegenwoordige stand van het Oudtestamentische vraagstuk,* pp. 15f; cf. also Rowley, ed., *The Old Testament and Modern Study,* pp. 55ff; H. F. Hahn, *Old Testament in Modern*

But now, what had formerly been tremendously significant and fruitful was appearing to be increasingly sterile, leading some scholars to wonder whether the very principle of documentary analysis was after all mistaken. Johannes Dahse's text-critical studies attempted to capitalize on this feeling of surfeit with excessively acute literary analysis. Although Dahse's efforts to destroy the divine-names criterion were not altogether successful, they did stimulate a wider reaction, both outside the Kuenen-Wellhausen school and within it, as specifically in the case of Eerdmans, as we shall see.

In the second place, a great number of archeological discoveries from Mesopotamia, Egypt, Palestine, and elsewhere, were having their effect in clearing up dark spots in Israel's history. Probably the most influential early discoveries were those of the Amarna tablets in 1887–88, which shed light on the activities of the Hebrews in the blank period before Joshua; of the Hammurabi Code in 1901–02, which showed that the Pentateuch-al laws had a very ancient Babylonian model; and of the Elephantine letters in 1906, which illuminated certain aspects of the later periods of Israel's history. The scholarly world was constantly on edge in those days for the light of new discoveries. A whole new world was being opened up by archaeology, and now it seemed that everything must be re-examined. Many rites of Israel's religion formerly held to be very young were now seen to be very old. If scholars could be so far wrong in such points, who of them could claim certainty for his views in any other point? One important principle that was demonstrated very clearly through these discoveries was that the relatively late date of a particular document is no reason to suppose that its content may not have originated centuries earlier.

The Kuenen school in Holland professed to be receptive to this new light, but in general it may be said that they were altogether too slow in making necessary revisions. Their orthodox opponents were much more eager to point out the consequences. Professor Noordtzij at Kampen was so happy about the Amarna tablets, for instance, that he urged his students to make a close study of them.[2] A writer in Kuyper's paper, *De Heraut*, went so far as to claim that if Kuenen had only known of the Amarna letters before he wrote his *Historisch-critisch onderzoek* (2nd ed.), he would have come to entirely different results. But established Assyriologists were making similar claims. Particularly Hammurabi's Code kept Dutch scholars of all persuasions busy trying to make necessary adjust-

Research (Philadelphia, 1954), p. 22.
2 *Oostersche lichtstralen over westersche Schriftbeschouwing*, Kampen, 1897

ments in their theories.[1] Literary criticism had found a powerful agent of control in these monuments of ancient cultures.

A third influence of significance in this period was the rise of the *religionsgeschichtliche* school and form-criticism, both of which were associated particularly with the name of Hermann Gunkel and were inspired to a great extent by the new discoveries in the Near East. In 1895 Gunkel published his *Schöpfung und Chaos in Urzeit und Endzeit*, exploring the rich mythological background of some of the oldest Old Testament motifs in connection with the traditions of ancient Babylon. This and other writings of Gunkel and his school forced students of the Old Testament to re-examine their view of Israel's historical development in the light of her cultural environment. Closely related to this research was Gunkel's method of form-criticism, which examined the various types of Old Testament literature in the light of their particular *Sitz im Leben*. One of Gunkel's best-known writings illustrating this method was his commentary on Genesis, published in 1901. His method has come to be widely accepted by modern scholars everywhere. We have seen that Valeton was influenced by it. Eerdmans appears to have had little feeling for form-criticism, but he was deeply interested in the *religionsgeschichtliche* insights that Gunkel and his school were bringing into prominence.

It was, as a matter of fact, Eerdmans, more than any other scholar, who turned Dutch biblical criticism into new channels. In the year of Kuenen's death, 1891, Leiden University graduated this young doctor; he was to occupy the great master's chair for forty years, and would lead the first serious revolt against his teacher's views.[2] Eerdmans studied at Strasbourg, Leipzig, Heidelberg, and Oxford, in addition to Leiden, and was appointed to be Kosters's successor in 1898. In his early years he accepted as a matter of course Kuenen's Hexateuchal criticism. But he

1 See Valeton, *Een oud-Babylonische wet in verband met de Mozaïsche wet* (1903); Eerdmans, 'Assyriology and Old Testament Studies,' *Museum*, X (1903); Noordtzij, *De onjuistheid van de hypothese van Prof. Friedrich Delitzsch over Babel en Bijbel* (1903); Wildeboer, 'De patriarchen des Ouden Verbonds en de wetgeving van Hammoerabi' (1904); *idem*, 'Iets over Babel en Bijbel,' *Onze Eeuw* (1904), pp. 67ff; Th. L. W. van Ravesteijn, 'God en mensch in Babel en Bijbel,' *TS*, XXXIV (1916), 1–38. The excesses of the extreme pan-Babylonian school found no favor in the Netherlands, though Eerdmans was the most friendly toward it.

2 Eerdmans's dissertation, *Melekdienst en vereering van hemellichamen in Israëls Assyrische periode* (Leiden, 1891), indicates his interest not only in Israel's sacred literature but in Assyriology and the history of religions. He studied parallels for Hebrew Melek (Moloch) and star worship in Phoenician, Egyptian, and Babylonian religion, claiming that the worship of stellar deities in Israel was an Assyrian-Babylonian import, with close affinities to the rites of Ishtar. He claimed that Melek worship had no clear parallels to Babylonian religion, but that originally Yahweh and Melek were the same deity, the

was all the while being profoundly affected by the new developments described above, particularly by Assyriological research and by the rise of *Religionsgeschichte*. This in itself is little wonder, for Eerdmans was actually more directly under the influence of C. P. Tiele, his *promotor*, than under the influence of Kuenen – and Tiele was, it will be remembered, one of the founders of *Religionsgeschichte* as a modern science.[3]

Although some of Eerdmans's early writings gave little indication of the direction his thought was to take, already in the first decade-and-a-half since he completed his studies at Leiden there were hints of a coming radical change. It will be worthwhile to mention briefly a few of these writings. Eerdmans composed them as a consciously loyal member of the Kuenen school, yet in a spirit sufficiently independent to forebode the revolutionary revision he was soon to demand.

In 1894 Eerdmans wrote a short study for *Theologisch Tijdschrift* in which he argued that *elohim* in the Book of the Covenant refers to the Hebrew household gods in distinction from Yahweh, the national god.[4] As we shall see, this insight, applied more widely, became the keystone of his Pentateuchal criticism.

In 1903 he stirred up a spirited and protracted debate among his fellow scholars in Holland by his defense of a mosaic origin for the Exodus 20 Decalogue. All the commandments had been defended as Mosaic, though on different grounds, in the Utrecht dissertation of P. G. Datema, published in 1876.[5] This book had made little impact; the times and the writer's methods were against him. But Eerdmans now forced the Kuenen-Wellhausen school to take seriously his defense of a Mosaic Decalogue because he wrote as one of them. It was his contention that all except the second, fourth, and fifth commandments formed a necessary part of the covenant that the Hebrew tribes contracted at Sinai.[6]

former gradually suppressing the latter. Eerdmans specifically rejected Kuenen's often-defended view that Melek worship was always illegitimate after the Mosaic era. This remained Eerdmans's view as late as 1947 (*Religion of Israel*, pp. 82f).

3 Tiele's affinities with Gunkel's point of view are indicated with special clarity in the dissertation of another of his disciples, A. Rutgers van der Loeff, *Bijdrage tot de kennis van Semietische kosmogonieën* (1895), which argued for the dependence of the Genesis creation stories upon Enuma Elish. This scholar continued his analysis in *TT*, XLVI (1912), 314ff; XLVII (1913), 208ff; *NwTT*, II (1913), 411ff.

4 'De beteekenis van Elohim in het Bondsboek,' XXVIII, 272–87

5 *De dekaloog*. Datema claimed that Moses was an absolute monotheist.

6 'Oorsprong en beteekenis der tien woorden,' *TT*, XXXVI, 19–35. He took essentially what had been Kuenen's own position in the first edition of *Historisch-kritisch onderzoek*. He continued to defend his position in *TT*, XXXIX (1905), 307ff, *The Expositor*, 7th ser., VIII (1909), 21ff, 58ff, 223ff; *Alttestamentliche Studien*, III, 121–46.

Matthes, Wildeboer, and Bleeker began arguing with him and with each other on this point, the first claiming that the complete Decalogue dates from the eighth century, and the latter two defending, with Datema, a complete Decalogue given by Moses. It is significant that Eerdmans supported his position mainly on the basis of *religionsgeschichtliche* insights, rejecting both a rigid, unbroken evolutionism and a traditionalistic supernaturalism. The date he here assigned to the Decalogue was vital to his entire reconstruction of the development of the Pentateuchal laws.[1]

In the following year, 1904, Eerdmans gave a further indication of the way his biblical criticism was developing in a *Theologisch Tijdschrift* article, 'De groote verzoendag.' In this he attempted to refute the accepted theory to the effect that the Day of Atonement must have originated in post-exilic times because it is mentioned only in the late priestly source, Leviticus 16. Admitting that this chapter in its present form is post-exilic, Eerdmans argued notwithstanding that the ritual of this day originated in connection with the pre-exilic New Year's festival, and that the passage in question merely records the ritual as it came to exist after a development of several centuries.[2] When he wrote on this topic again – in 1911 – Eerdmans no longer defended Leviticus 16 as post-exilic, either in form or in substance.[3] Such argumentation constituted a serious challenge to the reigning documentary hypothesis.

Finally, it is instructive to take notice of his article, 'De beteekenis van het Paradijsverhaal,' written for *Theologisch Tijdschrift* in 1905. While acknowledging the presence of J and E documents in the Paradise story, Eerdmans was here chiefly concerned with the primitive religious conceptions underlying it. He traced a basic old Semitic story, in which the Tree of Life was forbidden, and whose central theme was God's fear that man should become immortal like himself, supplemented by a secondary tradition deriving the knowledge of good and evil from sexual awakening. This article reveals Eerdmans as giving mere lip-service to the Kuenen-Wellhausen documentary theory and coming more and more under the dominance of *Religionsgeschichte*.[4]

---

1 Wildeboer, *TS*, XXI (1903), 109–18; Bleeker, *idem*, 310–15; Matthes, *ZAW*, XXIV (1904), 17–41; Wildeboer, *idem*, pp. 296ff; Matthes, *TTT*, IV (1906), 93–110; Bleeker, *De zonde der gezindheid*, Groningen, 1907. In respect to the tenth commandment – against coveting – Wildeboer and Bleeker held to its high spirituality but adduced this as evidence for a high monotheism in the time of Moses, while Matthes, also interpreting it as highly spiritual, took this as evidence for a late period of evolutionary development. Eerdmans, meanwhile, took it as Mosaic but gave it a dynamistic interpretation. The differences between these three approaches is quite revealing of the methodologies and presuppositions employed.

2 *TT*, XXXVIII, 17–41; Eerdmans rejected Wellhausen's view that the Day of Atone-

Thus it was quite clear that the occupant of the Old Testament chair at Leiden was moving away from the theory of interpretation that had long been dominant there. It must not be thought, however, that Eerdmans's changing viewpoint was influenced solely by the previously mentioned developments in exegetical methodology. As much as anything, it was disillusionment with the theology of modernism that encouraged him to move his tent to new ground.

Eerdmans was little understood by others. He was too conservative for many modernists and too liberal for the conservatives. He was known to his intimates as a deeply devout man, having never lost the religiosity of the orthodox tradition in which he was reared. Yet his open and often fierce antagonism against what he considered a pious superficiality on the part of the Gereformeerden and many other orthodox churchmen estranged him from them. He attacked Abraham Kuyper, and was a bitter enemy of biblicism and clericalism.[5] Yet he seemed to be even more contemptuous of what he considered to be the vacillating indefiniteness of the Ethical position. As a modernist of the right wing he carried on in the spirit of Hoekstra, Hooykaas, and Oort. As Dutch modernism shifted more and more from the intellectual determinism of its early period, it was Eerdmans who gave voice to the criticisms of the dissatisfied and who pointed the movement to new fields for development.

In 1909, after forty years of strong advocacy for the modernist viewpoint, *Theologisch Tijdschrift* entered a new phase under the editorship of Eerdmans.[6] We have seen that the Amsterdam modernists had established their own journal, leaving *Theologisch Tijdschrift* completely in the control of the Leiden group. In an opening article, Eerdmans announced the change that had affected him and a large segment of Dutch modernism. Writing under the pseudonym 'Agnotos,' he posed the vital question whether the new departure sponsored by his group was 'Reactie of vooruitgang' – 'reaction or progress' – the title of his article. He explained and defended his revolt against the old modernism, trying to

---

ment was originally a fast commemorating the exile and Houtsma's view that it was originally a harvest fast designed for warding off rain.
3 'The Day of Atonement,' *The Expositor*, 8th ser., I, 493–504; cf. 'Ezra and the Priestly Code,' *idem*, 7th ser., X (1910), 306–26; *Alttestamentliche Studien*, IV, 73–82.
4 XXXIX, 481–511
5 Cf. *Het recht der Vrijzinnigen in de Nederlandsche Hervormde Kerk en de zoogenaamde Orthodoxie*, Leiden, 1901; 'De theologie van Dr. A. Kuyper,' *TT*, XLIII (1909), 209ff.
6 This new series continued under Eerdmans's editorship until 1919, when it was abandoned.

show that this was not motivated by defeatist reaction, but was a necessary and wholesome step forward.

The die-hards of the old modernist school had been looking angrily at the younger generation, who were beginning to talk again of 'Christ,' of sin and salvation, and – worst of all – of a revolt against Kuenen's Bible criticism. Eerdmans recollected that the old school detested the very name 'Christian,' which to some of them was like a red flag waved in front of a bull. They did not even want to be called 'liberal,' but solely 'modernistic.' But, wrote Eerdmans, it was impossible for the younger generation simply to stand upon the shoulders of the older modernists. They had come to a point where they realized that they must begin afresh with the problems which the older generation had vainly imagined to have solved once for all.

Eerdmans tried to explain the dissatisfaction of the young generation. The old modernism had been characterized by its unlimited optimism based on Hegelian evolutionism, and by its violent antagonism to orthodox dogmatics and church authority. But it had sadly misjudged the religious needs of man, and disillusionment was bound to come. It had also miscalculated the effect of its teachings on the loyalty of its converts. The practical effect of accepting modernist doctrine had commonly been to kill off spiritual life, encouraging laxity and lukewarmness, often leading to complete abandonment of the church and its causes.

Even the Protestanten Bond had disappointed those who had pinned such high hopes upon it, continued Eerdmans. It had been organized to give opportunity for a free development of religious life among those who had broken with traditional religious forms. It was to have been both the means and the center of a reorganized and revitalized Christianity. But it turned out otherwise, and the ideas of the founders proved not to be the ideals of those who joined the movement. These either turned completely against religion, toward an outright humanism, or sought a meaningful religious impulse precisely in the institutional church, which the Bond's founders had rejected along with orthodoxy.

The old modernists could not bring themselves to acknowledge that it was perhaps their basic principles that were at fault in all this, but the new generation saw it plainly enough. They were beginning to question seriously whether modernism had actually said the last word:

Either religion is a gigantic error, nothing but the consequence of the stunted insight of earlier generations, and thus can say nothing more to us and can have no place any longer among us people of the twentieth century; or else modernist theology has not had the correct view of mankind and religion, and has missed the very essence of religion.

Eerdmans also felt it necessary to criticize the old modernists' superficial use of historical criticism as a basis for their denial of a genuine Christology and of the possibility of miracles. Historical criticism was almost worshiped by them; yet, wrote Eerdmans, this was mostly lip-service. Very few modernists actually took the trouble to master its demanding techniques. 'Historical criticism has become something like what the Confession is for the orthodox: honored, but no longer actually understood.' On this superficial basis the modernists had boasted that 'science' had made Christology impossible. To them Jesus was what Eerdmans bitingly called 'nothing but an earlier representative of the current modernist way of thinking.' The young modernists were now searching for a genuine Christology and a realistic doctrine of sin and salvation. Eerdmans for himself denied the historicity of the virgin birth and resurrection, and yet he acknowledged that as a sinner he needed light and redemption from some higher being. These, he wrote, were to be found only in Jesus Christ.

Another very basic point was what Eerdmans had to say about miracles. The older modernists had claimed that 'science' had proved the unhistoricity of miracles, as if science could ever *prove* such a thing. This all depended upon their prejudgment that miracles are impossible, said Eerdmans. Kuenen, for instance, had based the case against miracles on the point of probability in his well-known essay on 'Critical Method,'[1] yet all the old modernists believed that any unbiased investigator was bound to conclude the unhistoricity of the *Heilsfeiten*, simply because of their prejudgment against the possibility of miracles. Eerdmans explained:

There are various miracle stories in the Old and New Testament in which *e mente auctoris* a miracle has undoubtedly occurred. Nonetheless, 'the' historical criticism, as the old modernism conceived of it, rejected such stories out of hand as unhistorical, not on the ground of the documents themselves, but simply because they did not believe in miracles. If they had believed in them, they would have accepted, on the ground of those same documents, the view that they now reject professedly on the basis of the documents.

Eerdmans did not believe in miracles himself; what he was criticizing was lack of candor. Since Kuenen wrote his essay on 'Critical Method,' he continued, scholarship has learned to appreciate much more the world-

[1] See above, Ch. 3.

view of the Bible and 'thereby many eyes have gone open to the fact that a lack of presuppositions is pure illusion.'[1]

It was at this time, while Eerdmans was defending the new tack taken by *Theologisch Tijdschrift* under his editorship, that he was also busy presenting to the world his revolutionary critique of the Kuenen-Wellhausen Pentateuchal analysis. Between 1908 and 1912 he published four volumes in a series entitled *Alttestamentliche Studien*. He chose to write in German in hope of finding a wide readership – realizing, as few of his immediate predecessors had, the disadvantage of writing in the relatively unfamiliar Dutch language. Three volumes of this series dealt directly with the literary criticism of the Pentateuch, while the second concerned the history of the patriarchal period as reconstructed on the basis of this literary criticism. Eerdmans in effect returned to a fragmentary-supplementary hypothesis, based on *religionsgeschichtliche* insights. He began the first of the series, *Die Komposition der Genesis*, with the announcement: 'In this work I declare my independence from the critical school of Graf-Kuenen-Wellhausen, refuting in its essentials the so-called new documentary theory.' It was his purpose to overthrow this theory, not through a return to tradition but through what he considered a more rigorous and advanced criticism than that of this predecessors.

Eerdmans believed that the emphasis of the critics on such items as the divine names in Genesis was a colossal error. It committed the grave mistake of ignoring the polytheistic origin of the Genesis sagas. Recalling the article he had written in 1894 concerning the polytheistic import of the name *elohim* in the Book of the Covenant, Eerdmans remarked that this insight had forced the change in his entire outlook toward Pentateuchal criticism.

He proceeded to examine in detail the P, J, and E materials in Genesis, demonstrating what he considered to be numerous errors in the accepted analysis. He showed the unevenness in style of P, as also the fact that P does not really make a connected narrative, as Kuenen *cum suis* claimed, concluding that P is no distinct document but merely a series of old traditions incorporated by the scribes into an already existing corpus. He emphasized that the characteristics generally ascribed to J and E often fail to appear in them, particularly their supposedly distinctive use of the divine names and J's alleged fondness for anthropomorphisms, concluding that J and E too needed to be discarded. In the place of these

1 For a further defense of Eerdmans's point of view see Roessingh, *Rechtsmodernisme*, Haarlem, 1918. See also a sharp attack in Bruining, 'Godsdienst en verlossingsbehoefte,' *TTT*, VIII (1910), 1–23, 214–48.

documents, Eerdmans recognized the existence of a series of originally separate sagas, grouped together according to their concept of the deity, with the completely polytheistic stories earliest and the purely Yahwistic stories at the end. He proposed a new theory of literary development based on a 'Jacob' and an 'Israel' recension.

If Eerdmans could have proven the case he was attempting to make, he would have brought about a virtual revolution in Pentateuchal criticism, completely upsetting the triumphant achievements of his predecessors. Few scholars, however, were ready to accept either his negation of the documentary hypothesis or his attempted reconstruction. Both inside The Netherlands[2] and abroad, Old Testament scholars undertook refutations, the most effective of which was Walther Eichrodt's study written in 1916.[3] Since then, few scholars have considered Eerdmans's criticism as posing a serious threat to the established criticism.

Undoubtedly the basic error of *Die Komposition der Genesis* was Eerdmans's polytheism theory. He claimed that *elohim* means 'gods' everywhere in Genesis, 'Yahweh' having been sporadically substituted for it by a late redactor. He believed, furthermore, that Israel's religion was polytheistic up to the time of the Deuteronomic reform. In other words, a high monotheism emerged in Israel even later than Kuenen had taught. There was no gradual progression from Mosaic henotheism to prophetic monotheism, but dark paganism emerging abruptly into orthodoxy. Eerdmans's had no strong sense of historical development, but was completely fascinated by the primitive religious elements that he tended to see everywhere in the early writings of the Old Testament. This shortsightedness is what repelled most biblical scholars at a time when criticism needed a fresh appreciation of the individual narratives such as Eerdmans was offering them.

Eerdmans next published as a companion volume to the preceding a study of historical problems connected with the patriarchal period, *Die Vorgeschichte Israels*. Two of his most striking theories in this book were that the patriarchs were not pure nomads, but engaged in rudimentary agriculture, and that the Kenites – the original Yahwists – were not a nomadic tribe but a guild of smiths. These theories were of importance for establishing the dating of the legal codes in the Pentateuch, in particular the Book of the Covenant, which, Eerdmans claimed, reflected the agricultural situation of the patriarchs and hence need not be later than Moses.

2 Cf. Elhorst, *TTT*, VI (1908), 323ff; van der Flier, *TS*, XXVII (1909), 387ff.
3 *Die Quellen der Genesis* (*BZAW* XXXI). Cf. also H. Holzinger in *ZAW*, XXX (1910), 245ff, XXXI (1911), 44ff.

Eerdmans soon continued his literary criticism in an even more ambitious study, *Das Buch Exodus*. Here again he offered no trifling refinement of the Wellhausen theory, but a radical and thorough criticism based on a completely different conception of Israel's political and religious development. Where *Die Komposition der Genesis* had in certain points badly failed, this book succeeded in offering a compelling challenge to the documentary analysis. Eerdmans showed that many P sections are actually derived from pre-exilic materials. He also demonstrated the precariousness of trying to isolate J and E throughout Exodus, pleading instead for a complex fragmentary-supplementary theory of literary development. He did impressive work on the law-codes, arguing that they are pre-exilic, that the Decalogue is Mosaic in its original form, and that the Book of the Covenant was the very code inscribed on Moses' tablets. The most basic fault of *Das Buch Exodus* was, as in the volume on Genesis, Eerdmans's polytheism theory, which once again assumed what needed to be proved, viz., that *elohim* refers to many gods rather than to one. Here again, *religionsgeschichtliche* interests prevailed over accepted canons of literary criticism.

Das Buch Leviticus was the last volume of the series, *Alttestamentliche Studien*. Here Eerdmans dealt with the very heart of the priestly material. He produced a searching analysis that raised some serious questions regarding the Kuenen-Wellhausen criticism. According to the latter, virtually all of Leviticus is postexilic. Eerdmans may have seemed deliberately contrary in arguing that the entire book is pre-exilic except for the few sections held to be pre-exilic by the critics. He would not admit that the so-called Holiness Code, chaps. 17–26, possesses the characteristics of a distinct document. His reconstruction placed the origin of most of the book prior to the eighth century B.C., with supplements dating from the reigns of the last kings of Judah and only a few minor postexilic additions. Once again, *religionsgeschichtliche* insights had great influence in forming Eerdmans's opinions. His polytheism theory shaped this work to the same degree that it had the previous volumes. Nevertheless, Eerdmans succeeding in pointing to what has since become the

---

1 7th ser., X, 306–26; cf. 'Have the Hebrews been Nomads?' 7th ser., VI (1908), 118–31; 'The Passover and the Days of Unleavened Bread,' *idem*, VIII (1909), 448–62; 'The Book of the Covenant and the Decalogue,' *idem*, 21–33, 58–67, 223–30; 'The Day of Atonement,' 8th ser., I (1911), 493–504 (see above); 'The Ark of the Covenant,' *idem*, III (1912), 408–20; 'The Hebrew Feasts in Leviticus 23', *idem*, IV (1912), 43–56; 'Primitive Religious Thought in the Old Testament,' *idem*, VI (1913), 385–405 (translated from a rectoral address, *De beteekenis van het Oude Testament voor onze kennis van de ge-*

prevailing tendency in Pentateuchal analysis, viz., a tracing-back into the pre-exilic period of many priestly traditions.

As one compares Eerdmans's book on Genesis with his book of Leviticus, one is impressed with the increasingly greater weight of his argumentation. He was evidently learning by experience. His presuppositions and methods remain basically the same, but his skill in anticipating objections is much greater. There is, indeed, so much of real value in Eerdmans's total presentation that it seems quite unfortunate that his work has been judged largely on the basis of the Genesis book, in which his most serious shortcomings were plain to see. The Wellhausen critics could point to them and feel safe in drawing back into their shell for another decade or two, until the new methods of Gunkel and others forced them to concede many of the revisions that Eerdmans was here pleading for.

In 1910 Eerdmans wrote an important essay in English supporting his theory of Pentateuchal origins. This was his article, 'Ezra and the Priestly Code,' appearing in *The Expositor*, which carried several of his compositions during this period.[1] His argument was to the effect that Ezra's lawbook was not P, as held by the Wellhausen school, but a work that paralleled much of the material in the present Pentateuch and was subsequently lost.

Eerdmans planned to extend the *Alttestamentliche Studien* to cover at least the rest of the Pentateuch, but nothing came of it. The reason was unquestionably the cool reception his views were receiving, plus the inhibiting effects of the World War that began in 1914. Although The Netherlands did not become directly involved in that disastrous war, it felt its cultural effects no less than other European countries. Eerdmans entered politics in 1914, as a matter of fact, and did not resume his regular work at Leiden until 1927. Between 1913 and 1925 he published nothing whatever in the area of serious biblical criticism, but the period between 1925 and the date of his death (1948) was marked by two important surveys on the religion of Israel, literary analyses of Numbers, Deuteronomy, Job, and Psalms, and other significant writings.[2] All of

dachtenwereld der oudheid, Leiden, 1913).

2 'Der Sabbath,' *Festschrift für Karl Marti* (*BZAW*, XLI, 1925), pp. 79–83; 'Deuteronomy,' *Old Testament Essays* (London, 1927), pp. 77–85; *De godsdienst van Israël*, 2 vols., Huis ter Heide, 1930; *Studies in Job*, Leiden, 1939; 'Essays on Masoretic Psalms,' *Oud-Testamentische Studiën*, I (1941), 105–300; 'The Hebrew Book of Psalms' *idem*, IV (1947); *The Religion of Israel*, Leiden, 1947; 'The Composition of Numbers,' *Oud-Testamentische Studiën*, VI (1949), 101–216; etc.

these later writings supported and developed the viewpoint of the *Alttestamentliche Studien*. To the end, Eerdmans allowed his *religionsgeschichtliche* interest to color his reconstruction of Israel's history and literature.

It is interesting to compare Eerdmans with his colleague Wildeboer, for whom he often expressed open scorn. Wildeboer, it will be recalled, closely reproduced the literary reconstruction of Kuenen; yet, with all his deviation from Kuenen's theory, it was Eerdmans who inherited his liberal spirit. Wildeboer's variegated writings seemed to be inspired by no unified scientific principle, their only common feature being their attempt to integrate criticism with supernaturalism. (Much the same was true of Valeton.) Eerdmans's writings, on the other hand, fitted together and supported one another like spars in a bridge. Though his basic orientation was toward insights from outside Israel as a unifying principle of interpretation, while Kuenen largely followed the evidence of internal development, Eerdmans consciously attempted, like Kuenen, to allow his criticism rather than his faith to dominate his results.[1]

It can be readily understood that Eerdmans felt badly about his lack of acceptance among liberal scholars. What undoubtedly irritated him even more, however, was the use orthodox apologetes tried to make of his criticism. He was often cited by such persons with approval. They were, of course, interested only in his attack upon Wellhausenianism, not in his methods as such or his scientific presuppositions. Abraham Kuyper went so far on one occasion, while making a tirade against biblical criticism in Parliament, as to claim that because of Eerdmans's work, Kuenen's theories were completely negated. The historian who mentions this incident remarks about Eerdmans's keen annoyance, adding that it did not cost him much difficulty to refute such an absurdity.[2]

Unfortunately, Eerdmans's manner did not attract his students to him, and this fact further added to his isolation. In the forty years of his pro-

1 An instructive comparison of Kuenen and Eerdmans appears in Otto Eissfeldt's critique, 'Zwei Leidnischer Darstellungen der israelitischen Religionsgeschichte,' *ZDMG*, LXXXV, n.F. X (1931), 172–95. Eissfeldt evaluated Eerdmans as following a 'geschichtliche' method, resisting the lately emerging theological method of German criticism. Of special interest is the point that Eissfeldt made concerning Kuenen's versus Eerdmans's preconditioning. He pointed out that Kuenen, like Wellhausen (cf. the latter's 'Reste arabischen Heidentums,' 1887), was predisposed toward connecting the early Hebrews with the nomadic Arabs, as appears in his dissertation and in his Hibbert Lectures; in the latter he showed a profound acquaintance with and sympathy for things Islamic and Arabian. Eerdmans, on the other hand, was influenced in his formative years by the spectacular discoveries in Mesopotamia and hence shows strong affinities toward the 'pan-Babylonian school.' Eissfeldt judges Eerdmans as falling short in many respects, and prefers the method of Kuenen and Wellhausen, though of course without their biases and shortcomings. It is nonetheless striking, as one reads Eissfeldt's critique,

fessorate at Leiden, very few students obtained degrees under him. It was probably awe more than dislike that kept his students at a distance, however. Some of them have borne testimony to a deep respect for his character and methods.[3] In his later years, Eerdmans was honored as nestor of a Dutch Old Testament *gezelschap* which he helped organize. Rejected by the Germans, he found continuing high regard among the British.

Eerdman's influence can still be traced in The Netherlands, not only in concrete ideas directly borrowed from him, but more generally in the widespread caution of many present Dutch scholars toward the documentary hypothesis. It appears also in the keen interest of some of his pupils in textual criticism, which his own work indirectly inspired.[4]

THE WORK OF CRITICAL SCHOLARS IN EERDMANS'S GENERATION

As we have seen, both modernists and Ethicals had accepted the principle of historical criticism. It is now our interest to view the work of both these groups up to approximately the first World War, indicating ways in which they adhered to the Kuenen-Wellhausen theories and ways in which they responded to the new scientific impulses of the twentieth century. We shall not be surprised to see that the Amsterdam scholars on the extreme left and the Ethical scholars in the middle were the most wary of Eerdmans's proposals, while the Leiden scholars were influenced by him the most.

We begin with the modernists, and mention first Th. W. Juynboll, who became a member of the Utrecht faculty in 1917 as Houtsma's successor. He wrote little in the field of biblical exegesis, but showed Eerdmans's influence in an analysis of Exodus written in 1911.[5] Another

that present research is substantiating many of Eerdmans's arguments over against the Wellhausen viewpoint.

2 Lindeboom, *op. cit.*, III, 62

3 Cf. P. A. H. de Boer, *Het koningschap in oud-Israël* (Amsterdam, 1938), p. 27.

4 Cf. M. A. Beek, *Das Danielbuch*, Leiden, 1935; F. Dijkema, 'Het boek Jona,' *NwTT*, XXV (1936), 338–47; A. J. Wensinck, 'De oorsprongen van het Jahwisme,' *Semietische Studiën* (Leiden, 1941), pp. 23ff; P. A. H. de Boer, *Genesis 2 en 3: het verhaal van den hof in Eden*, Leiden, 1941; and 'De voorbede in het Oude Testament,' *Oud-Testamentische Studiën*, III (1943); A. R. Hulst, *Belijden en loven in het Oude Testament*, Nijkerk, 1948.

5 'De verschillende bestanddeelen der traditie betreffende Mozes en den uittocht uit Egypte in Exodus 1–11,' *TT*, XLV, n.r. III (1911), 299–311. Completely ignoring the classical division into J, E, and P, the writer found no less than six different sources in these chapters. This is a sample of the endless variety of analyses which the fragmentary theory tends to produce.

scholar, F. Dijkema, seemed more in step with current trends of scholarship. Thus in a 1905 study he effectively argued that neither the prophets nor the psalmists were opposed to the Hebrew cultus in principle – an almost heretical position at the time in the eyes of many Wellhausenians.[1] In the period after World War I, Dijkema wrote important studies on the form of Hebrew poetry and the role of prayer in Hebrew religion, subjects largely neglected by the Wellhausen school.[2]

W. Brede Kristensen took Tiele's place at Leiden in 1900. We have described his method, as compared with Tiele's, in a previous paragraph. Although the entire field of comparative religions was his responsibility, he showed a strong predilection for the insights of Egyptology, which he brought to bear on points of biblical exegesis in a number of weighty essays. Kristensen was strongly opposed to the speculative methods employed by Völter,[3] yet he himself felt free to identify a number of phenomena in Hebrew religion with parallel phenomena in the religion of Egypt.[4]

When Wildeboer died, he was succeeded at Leiden by A. J. Wensinck. Wensinck had written a Leiden dissertation entitled *Mohammed en de Joden te Medina* in 1908, and became known chiefly as an expert in Arabic and Aramaic,[5] but was made responsible upon his appointment chiefly for the teaching of Hebrew. As a matter of fact, from 1914 until 1927, while Eerdmans was active in politics, Wensinck took over most of Eerdmans's lectures in addition to his own. Like Eerdmans and Kristensen, Wensinck was strongly inclined to interpret early Hebraism in terms of primitive religions; in distinction from the former, who emphasized Babylonian religion as a source of inspiration, and from the latter, who emphasized Egyptian religion, he stressed the role of the early Arabs in in-

1 'Profeten en psalmen in hunne verhouding tot de offers,' *TT*, XXXIX, 18–39
2 'De vorm der Hebreeuwsche poëzie,' *NwTT*, XVII (1928), 97–117; 'Een vergeten hoofdstuk,' *idem*, XVIII (1929), 348–59; see also his studies on Hosea and Song of Solomon in *idem*, XIII, 324ff; XVI, 223ff. Dijkema continued active until World War II. An article on Jonah showed Eerdmans's influence (*NwTT*, XXV, 338ff.)
3 See his criticism of Völter's *Aegypten und die Bibel* (1903) in *TT*, XXXVIII (1904), 53ff.
4 E.g., the two trees of Paradise and the spirit of God; cf. *TT*, XLII (1908), 215–33; XLIII (1909), 398ff; see also his studies on the ark and Moses' staff in the Minutes of the Royal Academy for 1933 and 1953. Kristensen employed a far more rigid scientific method than did Völter, but emphasized the role of primitive dynamism in Hebrew religion.
5 Cf. *Het oudste Arameesch*, Utrecht, 1909. P. Kahle, *The Cairo Geniza* 2nd ed. (New York, 1960), pp. 203ff, assesses the importance of Wensinck's Aramaic studies.
6 'Psalm 91,' *TT*, XLVII, n.r. V (1913), 258–67
7 'De oorsprongen van het Jahwisme,' *Semietische Studiën* (ed. P. A. H. de Boer, Leiden,

fluencing the Hebrews. Thus, for example, he tried to explain Psalm 91 as a series of magical formulae on the basis of analogies in Arabian and present-day Jewish superstition.[6] He explained the patriarchal faith as belief in an impersonal divine force and Yahweh as a god of storm, mainly on the basis of Arabian parallels.[7] He laid great stress on ritual as a dynamistic force employed by the Hebrews for obtaining Yahweh's attention and favor.[8]

Turning now to the Ethicals, we observe that they were able to continue the work of their most eminent predecessors, both in quantity and in quality. In general, the Ethicals were less inclined than the modernists to allow their exegesis to be colored by insights from any particular field of antique research, though they were eager to accept the impact of all these fields upon the literary criticism of the Bible. We have previously mentioned the early work of Valeton's pupils, Bleeker and van der Flier. The latter continued to contribute to biblical research, largely in the pages of *Theologische Studiën*. We may mention a very thorough exegetical study of his, published in 1910, concerning the much-discussed Paradise story in Genesis. While he agreed that the story must be interpreted in the light of ancient culture, he insisted that it is not at all out of order to look for something genuinely original in it. An important methodological issue involved in van der Flier's study was Eerdmans's contention that the Paradise story must be very late because the rest of the Old Testament shows little acquaintance with it; on the contrary, argued van der Flier, the whole Old Testament depends on the patent meaning of the story, even while making no express reference to it, and Eerdmans is wrong in assigning a primitive dynamistic meaning to it.[9]

Among Bleeker's critical studies we may mention his important con-

1941), pp. 23–50 (originally published in 1917). Wensinck held that patriarchal religion was little more than animism. The *elohim* were not a plurality of gods but the collective ancestors which the Hebrews worshiped. Yahweh is HAWA, the hurricane (Arabian god Kozaḥ). Moses' conversion was like Mohammed's conversion to Allah. One notes that Wensinck did not accept Eerdmans's dictum respecting an early origin for the Decalogue, dating it in the seventh century B. C.

8 'The Significance of Ritual in the Religion of Israel,' *TT*, LII, n.r. IX (1919), 95–105; *Some Semitic Rites of Mourning and Religion*, Amsterdam, 1917; *Liturgie in het Oude Testament*, Baarn, 1938. Cf. also *De beteekenis van het Jodendom voor de andere Semietische volken van Voor-Azië*, Leiden, 1912; *The Second Commandment*, Amsterdam, 1925; *Hoofdvormen van Oostersch monotheisme*, Leiden, 1928.

9 'Het Paradijsverhaal,' *TS*, XXVIII (1910), 300–48; van der Flier had rebutted van Eyck van Heslinga (see above); cf. also 'Enkele opmerkingen over het Paradijsverhaal,' *NTS*, XX (1937), 306–15. He took a position against Kosters in 'Het getuigenis van Zacharja en Haggai over Juda's herstel,' *TS*, XXIV (1906), 1–66.

tribution to the discussion of the Paradise story. This was a pamphlet with the title, *Genesis 1 en 2*, written in 1918 in answer to Herman Bavinck's treatment of the doctrine of creation in his *Gereformeerde Dogmatiek* (2nd ed., 1906). Bleeker dealt respectfully with Bavinck, far less harshly than the typical liberal of his time, yet he challenged his treatment clearly and boldly. Bavinck, typical of even the most advanced Gereformeerden, had tried to show exegetically that Genesis 1 and 2 are from the same hand (cf. van Eyck van Heslinga). Their differences, he claimed, were to be explained as mere shifts of emphasis. Bleeker argued that this was exegetical nonsense, that the differences in the divine names, style, and chronological order of events clearly points to dual authorship.[1] In summation, he emphasized that Genesis 1 recalls a Babylonian background while Genesis 2 depends upon the geography of Palestine.

The remainder of this pamphlet applied the results of Bleeker's exegesis to an analysis of Bavinck's theological and apologetic arguments. He pointed out the folly of protesting against scientific claims regarding the world's origin on the basis of the Bible, inasmuch as the Bible writers themselves do not agree on the order of events. As to the attempt of conservatives like Bavinck to interpret the 'days' of Genesis 1 as geological periods, Bleeker emphasized that the writer of this chapter himself certainly had no such idea in mind.[2] Finally, Bleeker challenged Bavinck's view of revelation, which he thought had clearly predetermined his exegesis. Bavinck, claimed Bleeker, had adopted a position which unavoidably led to distortion in Bible study by way of its violent harmonizing. Bavinck was hence one 'who hears but does not hear, who sees but does not see.'

The last pupil of Valeton to receive his doctorate in Old Testament studies was Th. L. W. van Ravesteijn, who wrote his dissertation in 1910 on the eschatology of Isaiah. On various grounds he rejected the common division of this book into three sections (1–39, 40–55, 56–66), remarking, 'Even Old Testament criticism has a tradition that impedes free investigation.' He then proceeded to argue for the essential harmony of the eschatological imagery of the three sections of the book.[3] Van Ravesteijn's further writings, many of which were concerned with problems in the exegesis of Jeremiah, followed a competent but cautious criticism.[4]

1 Bavinck had naively relied on the seventeenth-century *Staten Vertaling's* rendering of imperfect consecutives as pluperfects.
2 'It is not a question of what we want it to mean, but of what the writer intended' (p. 17) – a point obvious to most interpreters, but ignored by many orthodox.
3 *De eenheid der eschatologische voorstellingen in het boek Jesaja*, Utrecht, 1910
4 Cf. 'Historie en profetie, inleiding tot het optreden van Jeremia in 626,' *TS*, XXXI

Another important Ethical scholar who contributed to Old Testament criticism in Holland was, like Kristensen and Wensinck, a specialist in another field. This was H. Th. Obbink, professor of comparative religions at Amsterdam from 1910 and from 1913 in Utrecht. Obbink studied with Eerdmans but wrote his dissertation at Utrecht in 1901 *(De heilige oorlog volgens de Koran)*. He became the author of numerous works in the fields of Egyptian, Assyrian, and Hebrew religion. Obbink was renowned as a teacher, writer, and speaker, and from 1929 to 1946 he served as court-preacher to the Queen. He edited several periodicals, the best-known of which was the *Algemeen Weekblad voor Christendom en Cultuur*, to which he himself contributed a long series of semi-popular biblical studies. His book, *De godsdienst van Israël*, which went through three editions from 1912 to 1927, popularized a moderately critical viewpoint regarding Hebrew origins. Among Obbink's more serious scholarly studies was his book, *Het Bijbelsch paradijsverhaal en de Babylonische bronnen*, published in 1917, in which he compared Genesis 2–3 with parallel Babylonian myths. He argued that while J was familiar with these myths, this writer freely adapted them to his monotheistic point of view. He pointed to two striking differences between the biblical and the Babylonian stories: (1) in the Babylonian stories man had divine knowledge but could not obtain immortality, while in Genesis man had divine life but was denied divine knowledge; (2) the biblical story involves ethical issues which are completely absent in the Babylonian myths. Later, Obbink defended this presentation in *Die Zeitschrift für die alttestamentliche Wissenschaft*, coming under attack by Karl Budde.[5] This willingness to welcome the data of scientific investigation, while emphasizing theological significance, was typical of the Ethical approach.

Another extremely prolific scholar has been F. M. Th. de Liagre Böhl, the youngest son of Eduard Böhl, the well-known scholar of Basel and Vienna. The son studied at Erlangen, Vienna, Bonn, and Leipzig, and, after a year of teaching at Berlin was appointed to teach Hebrew at the University of Groningen in 1913. In 1927 he went on to Leiden to become professor of Akkadian. Böhl has written many books and articles on Assyriology, the history of the ancient Near East – including the history of Israel – and archaeology. He served as editor of the commentary

(1913), 165ff; 'Jeremia's eerste prediking,' *idem*, 241ff; 'Jeremia 4:5–6:30,' *TS*, XXXII (1914), lff; 'Jeremia en Deuteronomium,' *NTS*, I (1918), 97ff; *Jeremia, Tekst en Uitleg*, 2 vols., Groningen, 1925–27.

5 'The Tree of Life in Eden,' n.F., V (1928), 105–12; Budde, *idem*, VI 54–62. An anthology of Obbink's writings appears in *Keur uit de verspreide geschriften*, Amsterdam, 1939.

series, *Tekst en Uitleg*, and helped organize 'Ex Oriente Lux' and the 'Nederlands Archaeologisch-Philologisch Instituut voor het Nabije Oosten,' both with headquarters at Leiden.

Böhl brought the insights of wide learning in the cultures of the ancient Near East to his studies of Hebrew origins,[1] using these in turn in his unusually fruitful exegetical studies of the Old Testament. As an example, we may choose his commentary on Genesis for the new series, *Tekst en Uitleg*.[2] Although this was published after the first World War and was semi-popular in orientation, it represents clearly the foundations of Böhl's scholarship. He indicated the documentary sources, which he proclaimed to be the assured result of three generations of dedicated study, giving special praise to Kuenen. He argued that the patriarchal stories originated as family idylls and grew up around the ancient sanctuaries, but gave four reasons for believing that actual persons and events lay behind them. These were: (1) the deviating reports; (2) the uniqueness of the patriarchal names; (3) the very tradition of a period before Moses, who was the founder of Yahwism; and (4) the fact that the patriarchs are not glorified. Genesis 1 to 11 he declared to be built upon mythical and legendary materials, but he insisted upon the high religious and moral value of these materials. This commentary, once again, exemplified the principles of the Ethical scholars, combining successfully scientific and theological values. It set a worthy precedent for the remaining books in the series, and pointed, with minor modifications, to the current basis of the critical interpretation of Genesis.

A fitting way of concluding this survey of critical study of the Bible in Holland before World War I will be to summarize H. Th. Obbink's excellent vindication of reverent criticism appearing under the title, 'Een en ander over de studie van het Oude Testament.'[3] Obbink began this essay by characterizing his time (1915) as peculiar. The Kuenen-Wellhausen school no longer dominated the scene, as it did twenty-five years before, when it had the field virtually to itself. In that period, Obbink said, critics imagined that everything was solved; scholars like Oort began to turn their attention to other fields of study because there seemed to be nothing more to do in Old Testament criticism. But now all had changed; there was no longer unanimity among the critics, not even on major points. The old assurance was gone: 'If they at that time

---

1 Böhl has been strongly influenced by Gunkel and Mowinckel. Some of his earlier studies in patriarchal history are: *Kanaanaër und Hebraër, BWAT*, 9, Leipzig, 1911; *Kanaän vóór den intocht der Israëlieten volgens Egyptische en Babylonische bronnen*, Groningen, 1913; 'Die Könige von Genesis 14', *ZAW*, XXXVI (1916), 65–73; *Het tijdperk der*

thought they had arrived at the end, we now know that we are just at the beginning!'

Obbink continued: In theory the Kuenen-Wellhausen school dealt only with literary criticism, but actually the currently popular doctrine of evolution determined for them what was young and what was old. Thus Hebrew religion had to be forced into the straight-jacket of a primitive animism developing gradually to a prophetic monotheism. Likewise, the Darwinian principle of ontogony repeating itself in phylogony was applied rigidly to Hebrew religion, requiring that it be interpreted as undergoing a cycle of development identical to that of every other religion.

It was Obbink's judgment that a limited historical knowledge had been basically at fault in the deficiencies of the Wellhausen theory. At that time anyone previous to the seventh century B.C. came under the judgment of being prehistorical and hence mythical, whether he be Menes, Sargon, or Moses. Hence Israel before the prophets *had* to be a primitive, polytheistic people. Yahweh was a mountain-god, a fire-god, a pestilence-god, a smith-god, or what have you? In the Mosaic era Israel was devoted to fetishism. The Wellhausen school was fascinated with 'survivals,' i.e., animistic and fetishistic practices, and naturally found them everywhere. Their mistake was in calling these normative, with the result that the prophets had to be viewed as founders rather than as reformers of Yahwistic monotheism. Moses himself was scarcely historical, let alone the true founder of Yahwism.

What were the reasons for Wellhausen's triumph, Obbink went on to ask. The answer was that no true scholar could be satisfied any longer with sterile traditionalism. A better viewpoint was bound to emerge; that it went to such extremes when it did come was largely due to the behavior of the traditionalists, who either remained silent or busied themselves with attacking motives. At very best, they attacked only the most minor weak-spots in the critical position. What were the results of this triumph? The critical school gained too easy a victory. With no scientifically grounded refutation to contend with, there were no bounds to its feeling of self-assurance, no occasion for penetrating self-criticism.

But now, Obbink went on to say, whole new vistas had opened up in biblical study. Archeological explorations in particular were forcing

aartsvaders, Groningen, 1925 etc.

2 Groningen, 1923–25

3 *SWV*, LII, 195–213

everything to be re-examined. Many practices formerly held to be young were now seen to be a thousand years older than Moses. Even though certain biblical documents must assuredly be late in their final redaction, this was really of very minor significance since final redaction has little to do with ultimate origin. The Old Testament as a whole was no longer isolated, an erratic block in the midst of an uncomprehended world. It was now seen in clear relation to contemporary cultures.

Obbink turned next to the problem of theological preconceptions influencing critical results. He emphasized that biblical criticism had always been and always would be conditioned to some extent by a particular scholar's religious standpoint. The unfortunate thing is that a scholar was prejudged by this standpoint; in other words, he was either applauded or condemned, depending on whether his conclusions supported liberalism or conservatism. Obbink underscored: 'The liberals are just as guilty of this as the orthodox!' In fact, he added, the liberals had done much harm by their premature attempts to popularize the results of their criticism. They all but killed off spiritual life in the congregations (a point stressed also by Eerdmans in his 'Agnostos' essay). The present generation of scholars was doing its best to review the old viewpoints, 'but the damage to the spiritual life of many persons is not easily restored; it wasn't meant to be so, but so it is.'

And what about rising *Religionsgeschichte?* Did this threaten religion? Obbink noted the apprehension of many theologians in this regard, but did not share it. He emphasized that always and everywhere the facts must be faced – from whatever source they might come. Interpretation of these facts is another matter, and much interpretation among practitioners of this kind of research is not necessarily in conformity with the facts.

It is of course bad, Obbink continued, that these new insights were being used as propaganda for antisupernaturalism. 'The thing that makes biblical criticism dangerous is not the method but the standpoint of the researcher. If he is an unbeliever, he necessarily arrives, by whatever method, at anti-religious or irreligious results... A person who does not believe in revelation will never find it.'

Was it right to speak of a conservative reaction, asked Obbink. Were present scholars less critical than the Wellhausenians? No, for 'the apparently conservative results are the consequence not of a less rigid but of a more rigid criticism.' Scholars had not drawn back for fright of the consequences of their criticism, but had only applied those consequences more logically. Now various lines of reserach were correcting and stimulating one another, preventing the extremes of the recent past, and for this true scholars could only be grateful.

Some of Obbink's contemporaries might have judged this essay as partisan and one-sided, but the vast majority of present scholars – fifty years later – would agree with the general tenor of his remarks. Obbink stood close to the Wellhausenians in time; we already stand far off from them. Yet his perspectives seemed clear enough, in light of our own, to validate his conclusions. He and the men of his generation surely stood at the beginning of new, and in many instances better, things.

THE WORK OF PROTESTANT AND CATHOLIC CONSERVATIVES

Our survey cannot be complete until we have also glanced at Old Testament study among Dutch conservatives. Such study has been insignificant in the minor groups. Only among the strictly Calvinistic Gereformeerden and among the Roman Catholics after World War I has there been serious scholarly study of the Bible.[1] As we view the development of these two important church groups during the early part of the present century, a striking similarity in their attitude toward Scripture presents itself. We see the Gereformeerden producing a large outpouring of Scriptural research even while adhering rigidly to their biblicistic commitment. We also see the Catholics remaining steadfast in their devotion to a biblicistic dogma. A contrast appears in the relative sterility of the latter in the field of biblical research so long as they held fast to this dogma; only in the period beyond the limit of our survey did they break free and blossom out into an era of growing fruitfulness in this field.

The acceptance of a reverent higher criticism of the Bible has not yet, even at this late date, appeared in the Gereformeerde Kerken of The Netherlands. The Gereformeerden have held fast to their biblicistic basis despite their growth in scholarly attainment, simply because they believe that their whole theology depends upon a belief in the Bible as the infallible and directly authoritative Word of God.

In spite of this biblicistic commitment, there has always been a healthy cultural interest in this group. As a matter of fact, Kuyper

[1] A Hervormd scholar who took a rigidly conservative position in Old Testament studies was A. Troelstra; cf. his book, *De Naam Gods in den Pentateuch,* Utrecht, 1912 (English trans. London, 1912), and 'Deuteronomy' *Bibliotheca Sacra,* LXXXI (1924), 393–409.

accentuated the intellectual side of religion in his neo-Calvinistic revival, more than the spiritual side that Chantepie de la Saussaye thought so important. The result has been a ponderous rationalistic supernaturalism, carrying on the spirit of eighteenth-century Protestant scholasticism. The Gereformeerde Kerk has not, in any case, remained out of touch with the world and with culture; it is not essentially ascetic or separatistic. The result is that many of its theologians and spiritual leaders have seen the need of doing fuller justice to the human factor in Scripture, resulting in controversy coming into this church on the issue of accepting historical criticism.

In 1917 a church trial began against the Rev. J. B. Netelenbos which ended, after three years, in his condemnation. Netelenbos had tried to develop a more scientific doctrine of Scripture upon the basis of his church's dogma, but ran afoul of the official interpretation of that dogma. His views would seem extremely conservative to many scholars. In regard to Scripture, he explained that he accepted the doctrine of organic inspiration, that he only wanted to bring this into its full right. He wrote:

We must reckon with the human imperfection of the Holy Scriptures and therefore distinguish between its essence and its external appearance, between the truth that God has revealed and the figures and forms in which the writers of the Bible have expressed that truth.[1]

He explained that he conceived of this human form as willed by God and standing under God's providential guidance, but denied that the form as such was inspired and infallible. Netelenbos also pleaded for historical criticism, saying that it was illegitimate only when it challenged Christian faith. The Synod declared, however, that the form as well as the content of Scripture was inspired, and that all criticism must be repudiated.

A few years later another heresy trial arose in the Gereformeerde churches which received a great deal of unfavorable publicity. It created, as a matter of fact, a popular uproar, and became the talk of the day throughout Holland. This was the case of Dr. J. G. Geelkerken, who was condemned by the Synod of 1926 for allegedly heterodox views in connection with Scripture. Here again, the defendant stoutly averred his

1 From the report of the *ad hoc* committee, cited by Berkouwer, *op. cit.*, p. 259.
2 This 'Schlangenprozesz' became notorious abroad, being compared with the 'Affenprozesz' in America (the Scopes trial); cf. M. Rade, *Glaubenslehre*, 1927, II, 170, 256.
3 Cf. Berkouwer, *op. cit.*, pp. 265ff; Knappert, *Godsdienstig Nederland*, pp. 163ff.
4 The Gereformeerden were not yet done with heresy trials. In 1933 Dr. J. G. Ubbink was condemned as Netelenbos and Geelkerken had been because of his essentially identical views. Ubbink very plainly stated that Scripture is a human, fallible report of the

complete loyalty to the church's doctrines of verbal inspiration and the divine authority of the Bible. He had pleaded, however, for more justice for the human factor, laying stress on the role of the cultural environment of the writers. The case at the Synod was ostensibily centered about charges that Geelkerken did not believe in the historicity of the serpent and other features of the Paradise story,[2] but it was actually resolved upon his vague plea for giving science a role in interpreting the Bible. For implicit errors in this plea the Synod condemned him, thus indicating its extreme vigilance in guarding Scripture's independence from scientific investigation. The Geelkerken case infuriated many within and without the Gereformeerde denomination because of the flimsiness of the charges upon which Geelkerken was condemned.[3] A number of young ministers and six congregations left the denomination together with Dr. Geelkerken and organized a separate group, which, at the end of World War II, united with the Hervormde Kerk.[4]

There are many who might think that scholarly interest in biblical exegesis could scarcely flourish in a group which has so sharply repudiated the historical criticism of the Bible, but this has not been the case. It is true, as would be expected, that devotional and dogmatic treatments of biblical themes have been popular, but various scholars among the Gereformeerden have shown both proficiency and industry in the philological and exegetical study of the Bible.

During the early years of this denomination's existence, very little of importance was produced in the biblical field. Between 1885 and 1905, Old Testament subjects at the Free University had to be taught by the church-historian Rutgers, but when C. Van Gelderen came to that institution in 1905, and after him, in 1920, G. Ch. Aalders, considerable study began to be carried out. It would indeed be difficult to find a more prolific scholar in Holland than Aalders, who has, moreover, sponsored the writing of a greater number of dissertations relating to the Old Testament than any other Dutch professor. Today, even upon its narrow, anti-critical basis, Gereformeerde biblical scholarship is lively and productive.

We may briefly mention the point of view of several important early

---

actual Word of God, admitting however that there had been a guidance of the Holy Spirit which had kept the writers of the Bible from making any errors in declaring the revelation of God's will. At any rate, he distinguished between an infallible divine factor and a fallible human factor in the Bible, and this the church could not tolerate. Since his condemnation, no further serious attempt has been made to challenge the church's dogma, even though sympathy still lingers with certain more scientifically-orientated theologians for acknowledging the legitimacy of criticism.

biblical scholars belonging to this denomination. Arie Noordtzij belongs to the first half of this century, and, as a matter of fact, wrote his dissertation at Leiden in the year 1896. We have seen that he taught at Utrecht after 1912. In 1905 he wrote a valuable historical study on the Philistines.[1] He evidently felt free to move about in various theological camps. Thus his early writings appeared in the Ethical *Theologische Studiën*, in *Die Zeitschrift für die alttestamentliche Wissenschaft*, and in *Teyler's Theologisch Tijdschrift*.[2] His Utrecht inaugural represented his most constant theme, viz., that God's revelation appears infallibly and authoritatively in the various forms of ancient Near-Eastern culture.[3] He never wearied of insisting that a recognition of the Bible's human conditioning does not militate against belief in inerrancy. Though this insistence undoubtedly restricted the breadth of his argument, it did put him in a mediating position with respect to his denomination and more liberal groups.[4]

C. van Gelderen was another of the older Gereformeerde scholars who showed a relatively greater degree of willingness to acknowledge the claim of extrabiblical data. He studied at Berlin and Leipzig, and was appointed to teach Semitic literature at the Free University in 1905. His inaugural address, *Israëlietische oudheidskunde en archaeologia sacra*, expressed the main interest of his life work, which was to relate the Bible to its antique environment in a way compatible with his church's doctrine.

One of the great stalwarts of Gereformeerde Old Testament study was M. Noordtzij's successor at the Kampen Theological School, Jan Ridderbos. He graduated from the Free University in 1907 with a dissertation on Jonathan Edwards, but since then wrote extensively on various aspects of Old Testament exegesis. His inaugural address, once again, defined the basic commitment determining his work in this field. In it he dealt with the doctrine of Scripture in the history of the church, judged from the norm of Reformed doctrine. He had much to say about the modern critical view, but all this had the one aim of identifying it with rationalism and evolutionism. He elaborated three principles which in his opinion

1 *De Filistijnen: hun afkomst en geschiedenis*
2 See especially 'De jongste Arameesche papyri,' *TTT*, VII (1909), 33–58, in which he entered as Daniel into the lion's den of ultra-liberalism, armed with the mortal weapon of the Elephantine letters. He claimed that these refuted Wellhausen and Kosters in respect to the historicity of Ezra.
3 *De Oudtestamentische Godsopenbaring en het Oud-Oostersche leven*. English trans. in *Bibliotheca Sacra*, LXX (1913), 622ff. See also *Gods Woord en der eeuwen getuigenis, het Oude Testament in het licht der Oostersche opgravingen*, Kampen, 1924.
4 Noordtzij was a constant antagonist against the Kuenen-Wellhausen criticism, cf. *Het probleem van het Oude Testament*, Kampen, 1927 (English trans. in *Bibliotheca Sacra* of 1940). Nevertheless, his position at a state university allowed him more freedom than most

govern the Reformed view of Scripture: (1) the Bible is, in all its parts, the Word of God; (2) however, it was limited by the historical circumstances of its origin and thus contains certain features which are not necessarily normative for the Christian church; (3) the Old Testament gains its true value for the Christian church in the light of the New Testament.[5]

Ridderbos remained active into the second half of this century, composing his articles particularly for the journal, *Gereformeerde Theologisch Tijdschrift*, which was begun in 1900. He has been most constantly occupied with the prophets. It is not our purpose to survey these writings, hence we mention only two of his compositions which appeared before the end of World War I. In *Israël en de Baäls*, his rectoral address of 1915, he insisted on an absolute cleavage between heathenism and revealed religion; not evolution, but human sin and divine revelation account for the history of Israel. In 'De boom der kennis van goed en kwaad,' appearing in 1918, he added his contribution to the debate concerning the Paradise story, interpreting it from a highly theological (i.e., scholastic-Calvinistic, biblicistic) point of view, much in the manner of Bavinck's previously-mentioned treatment.[6]

Finally we mention G. Ch. Aalders, who received his doctorate from the Free University in 1911 and was appointed to the post of Old Testament exegesis there in 1920. Aalders has become widely known outside his denomination and The Netherlands as an able spokesman for ultra-conservative biblical scholarship. His writings have been even more extensive than those of Ridderbos. In his dissertation on *De valsche profetie in Israël*, he took the position that there is a true, inspired prophecy, that this is opposed by false prophecy, whose origin lies in the sinful 'mantic' inclination of the human spirit, which continually rebels against God's true revelation. In the years previous to World War I, Aalders took occasion to attack the views of Eerdmans,[7] and before the end of that war published a series of articles assailing the Wellhausen criticism as well.[8] Aalders, together with Ridderbos, was highly influen-

Gereformeerde scholars enjoyed, as one may witness, e.g., in his introductions to Leviticus and Numbers in the *Korte Verklaring* commentary series (1940, 1941).

5 *De beteekenis van het Oude Testament voor de Christelijke religie*, Kampen, 1913

6 *GTT*, XVIII (1917/18), 403–22, 433–51. Ridderbos's two sons, Nicolaas and Herman, have lately become noted for their relatively progressive positions regarding Old and New Testament criticism, respectively.

7 'De boom des levens,' *GTT*, XII (1911), 241–49; *Sporen van animisme in het Oude Testament?* Kampen, 1914

8 'De Wellhausensche Pentateuchtheorie en de tekstkritiek,' *GTT*, XIV (1914), 4–17; *Iets over bronnenscheiding in den Pentateuch*, Amsterdam, 1916; 'Geeft de Heilige Schrift zelf in Ex. 6:2 een getuigenis ten gunste van de moderne Pentateuchkritiek?' *GTT*, XVIII

tial in maintaining the church's rigid front in the Geelkerken controversy. Constantly he has argued for the strictly literal interpretation, with only minor modifications in the traditional scheme.

The method of Aalders has been all too typical of Gereformeerde scholarship, and certainly enjoys the favor of the church's official declarations. There are an increasing number of scholars and theologians in the church, however, who see the evils of what they call a 'geweldige harmonistiek,' and some are no longer inclined to defend to the last ditch the literal historicity of every detail of Scripture, admitting at least that literary license may lie behind many of them. The condemnation of Netelenbos and the others has stifled for the time any outright expressions in favor of a more historical view of Scripture, but many believe that the time is coming when either a new conflict will break out or the church will peacefully adapt itself to a more scientific view.

The Gereformeerden and other orthodox may perhaps learn from the experience of the Roman Catholics, who discovered at long last that there is nothing to be feared from the right kind of historical criticism.

The Roman Catholic church has been on the increase in The Netherlands and is now the largest religious body in the land. Previous to 1957, it was organized under an archbishopric in Utrecht, together with four suffragan bishoprics, but since then two more bishoprics have been added.[1] In the days of the Reformation and the religious struggles, Catholicism came to be identified with Spanish tyranny. The natural reaction was that the Roman church was put under the ban once the revolution succeeded. Catholics were denied freedom of worship, so that during most of the seventeenth and eighteenth centuries they could assemble only in clandestine sanctuaries. Because the provinces of Brabant and Limburg were predominantly Catholic, they were kept in a status of political subjugation. Gradually, however, tolerance for Catholics increased, and after the uprising of 1795 they received official sanction for their religion. However, when the Pope issued an apostolic brief in 1853 setting up a new administrative organization for The Netherlands,

---

(1917/18), 49–56; 'Ex. 6:2v. en de Pentateuchkritiek,' idem, 154–56; 'De getuigenis des Nieuwen Testaments in betrekking tot het litterair auteurschap van den Pentateuch,' idem, 305–26

1 Cf. Delleman, op. cit., pp. 108ff; Knappert, Godsdienstig Nederland, pp. 47ff.

2 Cf. Reitsma, pp. 493f

3 Cf. H. J. van Vorst, Het aardsche Paradijs, hoe het was en waar het lag, Tilburg, 1903, in which, with considerable scholarship, a non-literal interpretation was advocated. The author nervously claimed full ecclesiastical permission for his view. He was plainly on

feeling was still so strong that the nation became convulsed in an anti-Catholic outburst, the so-called 'April-beweging' that resulted in the downfall of the prime minister. According to historians, this violent reaction was largely due to the belligerent tone of the Pope's brief.[2] Ultramontanism was still very strong among Dutch Catholics at the time, owing to Protestant oppression and antipathy; but during the past century this attitude has gradually decreased as tolerance has grown, and the opposite feeling seems to characterize Dutch Catholics today in their relationship to the Roman hierarchy.

As has been suggested, the most notable thing about the development of biblical studies among Dutch Catholics has been their gradual acceptance of historical criticism after a long period of rigid traditionalism. In this they have proved to be in the vanguard of advancing Catholic liberalism. The biblicistic and polemic attitude of nineteenth-century Catholic scholarship has been mentioned. J. Schets's sharp criticism of Kuenen was altogether typical of the Dutch Catholics in this period, as also in the early decades of the present century. As one scans the issues of *De Katholiek, Studiën,* and *Nederlandsche Katholieke Stemmen* from this period, one is indeed impressed by the utter dearth of scientific biblical study. This vacuum was due largely to Catholic preoccupation with dogma and ritual, but partly also to a rigid biblicism.

In other lands, a few Catholic scholars were working in the early part of this century to obtain a place within the chruch for the methods and results of higher criticism. Apparently little of their spirit filtered through to Dutch Catholics, however. Although there were a few Catholic scholars in The Netherlands who tried to employ an enlightened criticism of the Bible,[3] most Dutch Catholics continued to resist what they considered an unavoidable concomitant of rationalism. In this they had the early decrees of the papal commission for the study of the Bible on their side, as churchmen like H. Wilbers and J. Kroon did not hesitate to point out.[4]

The church of Rome had been long in the forefront in the battle against higher criticism.[5] In 1878 an Institut Catholique for combat-

---

the defensive, but was reaching out for the newer scientific insights.

4 See Wilbers, 'De studie van den Pentateuch,' *Studiën,* LXXXIV (1910), 357ff; LXXV (1910/11), 1ff, 204ff, 561ff; 'De historiciteit van Gen. 1–3,' *idem,* LXXXI (1914), 388ff, 476ff; LXXXII (1914), 67ff, 211ff; *Schepping, Paradijs en zondeval,* 1918. Cf. also Kroon, 'Enkele opmerkingen over het scheppingsverhaal,' *Studiën,* LX (1928), 330–40.

5 See *The Catholic Encyclopedia,* New York, 1907; *De Katholieke Encyclopaedie,* 2nd ed., Amsterdam-Antwerp, 1950; *Encyclopaedie van het Katholicisme,* Bussum, 1955; J. Levie, *The Bible, Word of God in the Words of Men,* New York, 1964.

ting this 'heresy' was organized in France, but it had to make various concessions to it during the following years. In 1890 Pope Leo XIII issued his famous encyclical against modernism, *Providentissimus Deus*, in which he spoke, among other things, of the limits of biblical criticism. This encyclical sharply defined a 'vera critica' over against the rationalistic criticism which, it claimed, proceeded from idle philosophy and judged the Bible on purely internal grounds.

A sharp conflict developed over this encyclical, so that by 1900 the biblical question was more rather than less agitated in the Catholic church. In order to settle this dispute, Leo issued his apostolic letter, *Vigilantiae*, in 1902, setting up a 'Commissio Pontificio de re Biblica.' This commission was to become simply the instrument of retrenchment for traditional versus critical views on the Bible. The influence of Pius X, who succeeded Leo in 1903, was determinative for the decrees of the Commission in its early period. Pius was a strong antagonist of modernism,[1] and made no distinction between legitimate and illegitimate biblical criticism, as his predecessor had done. It was during his pontificate that many of the commission's decrees were promulgated, and all of the early ones were entirely traditionalistic.[2] Pius made it plain that the decisions of the Biblical Commission were to be regarded upon the same footing with other doctrinal declarations of the Roman Congregations. Thus, although they were not regarded as infallible or unchangeable, they were defined as an official norm for faithful Catholics, from which they were not to depart. Changes could not be made in them except by appeal to the commission with further evidence.

Such changes have eventually come, and have been due no doubt to a subsiding of the threat of rationalistic modernism, to the increasing impact of critical scholarship, and to a more favorable attitude on the part of the pontificate. Thus the encyclical of Pius XII of 1943, *Divino Afflante Spiritu*, has actually encouraged a scientific biblical research in a moderate yet free spirit. The Biblical Commission, on its part, has come to acknowledge the legitimacy of historical criticism within the bounds of belief in the infallibility of Scripture and in God as its primary author, leaving criticism free to judge the literary aspects and scientific value of God's human instrument. A golden mean has been found in a criticism which tries to do justice both to the human origin and the divine

---

1 Cf. the encyclicals *Lamentabili* and *Pascendi Domini Gregis*.
2 Cf. *Institutiones Biblicae*, Rome, 1933. These decrees were printed in *Revue Biblique*; see also N. Grietemann, *De Kerk en de Bijbel*, Hilversum, 1938.

authority of the Bible. Happily, the recently concluded Vatican II Council has strongly endorsed this new approach.

Some non-Catholics will be inclined to believe that Catholic scholars cannot be really free in their investigation of the Bible, even with the modifications they have made. However, the latter have expressed themselves as being quite content with the measure of freedom they have obtained. This is the way, at any rate, in which one Dutch Catholic scholar has described the aims and methods of Catholic biblical research:

With great satisfaction we may bear witness to the fact that modern Bible criticism, even unbelieving and independent criticism... has accomplished useful and important work, and that the task of Catholic exegesis must remain that of understanding this terrain even better and with a still deeper scientific method. But in all of this the Catholic critic will have to separate himself in principle from independent Bible criticism... Modern Catholic Bible criticism...will, with every means and with all her energy and industry, contribute to textual, literary, and higher criticism, in order to get behind the human factor in the Bible and explain it; but it must remain deeply convinced of the fact that alongside of and above this human factor there is a divine element in the Holy Scripture, and that this must be the final goal in all its scientific investigation... All else is the means; but this alone is the goal.[3]

This is the theory that Dutch Catholics have begun to put into practice, with impressive results. It makes a story beyond the range of our study. A Thomistic dualism, together with the dependence of Catholic faith on the authority of the church more than on the infallibility of the Bible, has made acceptance of a reverent biblical criticism possible. Traditionalism held it back as long as it could, but Catholics have at last accepted it because no principle vital to their system was at stake, and have been enriched accordingly.

3 R. L. Jansen, *Gezag en kritiek*, Nijmegen, 1931. He was professor of New Testament at Nijmegen. See also J. van der Ploeg, *Enkele beschouwingen over de theologische aard en de methode der wetenschap van het Oude Testament*, Nijmegen-Utrecht, 1951.

Chapter Six

Conclusions Concerning the Mutual

Relationship of Theology and Exegesis

Here this story must end, and we must try to draw together the lessons it has taught us. We feel that we have made a good choice in selecting this country and this period for study. The factors of intense productivity on the one hand, and of maximum isolation on the other, created an ideal situation in which to observe the interplay of theology and biblical exegesis. The devastating conflict that resulted from the combination of these two factors in nineteenth-century Holland has had few parallels in other lands or in other periods. Here was concentrated the intensest antagonism between those two inseparably connected but perpetually irreconcilable forces, a creative progressivism and a conservative traditionalism. Holland had been the cradle of intellectual freedom, one of the last and best hopes of the heirs of Renaissance enlightenment, but in the post-Reformation era it subsided more and more into the grip of a dogmatic orthodoxy. The prophets of progress and the guardians of tradition lived in constant tension with each other. The former had their brief moment of opportunity under the auspices of the French Revolution, but when this allowed its excesses to discredit itself, liberalism was repressed once again in The Netherlands in a resurgence of nationalistic conservatism. This made the trauma of the modernist conflict inevitable. Orthodox rigidity provoked the excesses of modernist invective against it, which grew all the more intense because more than mere theory, i.e., control of church life and of national institutions, was at stake. Meanwhile, modernist extremes frightened the orthodox into even more stubborn resistance.

It was within this situation of intense conflict that modernist exegesis developed, together with the fierce conservative polemic against it. This we need to understand clearly. A poisoned environment inescapably affected the Bible study carried on by the respective warring parties. An ulterior polemic motivation distorted, consciously or unconsciously, even the most objective exegesis. Its most immediate purpose was, all too often, to bolster one's own dogma and refute that of one's opponents – and this is true of the modernists as well as of the orthodox.

As we look back we must indeed judge modernism as a failure. It failed to produce the final solution it claimed to offer. It deceived itself in its imagination that a grand synthesis was within its grasp. Many forces seemed at the time to be leading to such a synthesis: modern man had come of age; he had learned to trust his own reason rather than rely on church tradition; discoveries in the realm of the natural sciences seemed to be making God and the supernatural unnecessary and undesirable. And now it appeared that even the church's book of sacred texts, the Bible, could be turned against its teaching, for that book was also proving to be a product of human culture. Now, for the first time since biblicistic theism had cut itself free, under Protestant auspices, from the restraints of medieval tradition, the weaknesses and the contradictions remaining in that system seemed capable of being resolved. Catholic and Protestant scholasticism were losing the long, stubborn battle to exclude antipathetic elements that had emerged with Renaissance humanism, its defeat seemingly certain in the face of the formidable forces arrayed against it.

In this day of ultimate optimism, the Dutch modernists, like their fellow free-thinkers elsewhere, were in no mood for compromise. There was only one course for them: to substitute their new synthesis for the old tradition, without regard for consequences. This was an attitude of totalitarianism or positivism that was actually the basic weakness of modernism and turned out to be the source of its inevitable downfall.

The modernists in The Netherlands took a positivistic stance in respect to theology, in respect to scientific method, and in respect to their own position in the church. In its theology, modernism repudiated the supernatural God of the Bible. It saw no possibility, as do we in our time, of discriminating between the mythological coloration of the biblical image and the reality itself. The result was that the modernists were left with no real God, and tried in vain to validate religion without him. The truly transcendent was gone. Many adherents of the modernist cause, including Kuenen, saw the dangers and struggled to find a valid substitute for the God of the Bible, but all in vain. When they sacrificed the biblical God, they gave up the biblical faith and the biblical message as well.

In their scientific methodology, modernist biblical critics claimed to allow the facts, and the facts alone, to determine their results. Indeed, their devotion to scientific objectivity is most impressive, particularly as compared with what was commonly being carried on at the time in the name of biblicistic traditionalism. Nevertheless this too was deceiving, as we have emphasized. The modernists, some more, some less, allowed theological and scientific dogma (one is scarcely better than the other!) to play a dominant role. Thus their evolutionistic view of history, itself largely shaped by their theological commitment, dominated their study of the biblical text. The resulting image of Bible history and religion was, to say the least, a distortion. It was only their openness to new light that saved them.

In their tactics to gain domination of the church, the Dutch modernists likewise displayed this positivistic and intolerant attitude. For them it was to be all or nothing. They gambled, and lost, but only after doing severe damage within the church and creating enduring hostilities.

Despite all this, candor demands that we pay tribute to these men of devotion and integrity, who dared fight for the truth as they saw it. Those who stand for intellectual freedom, who are willing to strike out on new paths, provoking perhaps a conflict with tradition, deserve more admiration than do those who only defend the ramparts. This must be said, even though we acknowledge a debt of gratitude to those who saw that there was something ineffibly precious in the church's heritage, to be defended at whatever cost.

Aware as we are of the weaknesses of Dutch modernism, we see with equal clarity the failure of the unyielding orthodoxy of this period. Orthodoxy's claim to base its dogma on the teaching of the Bible was a sham and delusion. It was using the Bible only to bolster that dogma, often ignoring or suppressing whatever seemed to threaten it. Some may praise this single-mindedness, this unswerving reverence for the God of Scripture – the highest of motivations! – that drove it to ignore the claims of human reason. But we must see that this has been at the expense of refusing to allow the Bible to speak its true and complete message. A dogma praising the Bible as a divine book has obscured its real nature and its real message. What is this but a distortion and an imposition?

A praiseworthy exception to this severe judgment is the attempt of the orthodox Ethicals to preserve both theological meaning and scientific integrity, i.e., to acknowledge both God and man. Chantepie de la Saussaye, like the Groningers before him, was following a true instinct when he sought the ground of religion in life and worship, rather than in intellectual concept and in dogma. In this he was indeed bringing to expression, as he claimed, a side of the Calvinistic reformation, and of biblical religion as a whole, that was ignored equally by the early modernists and by their orthodox opponents. Because he knew this, Chantepie could endure living with the contradictions of his age. He was not free from theological uncertainty, but he was at any rate walking on a path to the truth. So likewise the Ethical doctrine of Scripture, rough hewn and unsophisticated as it may have been. If some of the Ethical biblical scholars compared unfavorably with the leading modernists as scientific exegetes – and we have seen that this was the case – they were at least holding the door open to further scientific insight while grasping firmly that transcendent quality which gives the Bible its true and eternal authority.

The great majority of the present generation of Dutch theologians and biblical scholars, like their colleagues in other lands, are walking this pathway, and to this extent the stance of the Ethicals has been vindicated. They have been proven to have been the true prophets of the future and the genuine upholders of tradition. Twentieth-century Catholicism is learning to follow a biblical criticism that is basically similar to theirs, however much this present generation may be able to benefit from advances in scientific learning since their time. A question that remains is whether twentieth-century neo-Calvinism in The Netherlands can make the same essential adjustment. Our study has seemed to indicate that it may gain the same benefits for its theology and for its Bible study, if and when this adjustment is made.[1]

As we cast our eyes about for examples in which, during the period under study, scientific exegesis was clearly allowed to shape theological opinion, we find ourselves at a virtual loss. As we compare Kuenen's Old Testament criticism with the writing of, for instance, Pierson, Kuenen of course comes out far ahead. Respect for the text was clearly a moderating factor in the Leiden exegesis over against the arbitrariness of the Amsterdam school. But even the most objective of scholars, even Kuenen himself, were more affected by their theological precommitment than they imagined. Obbink's remarks, summarized *in extenso* in the last chapter, are very much to the point in this respect.

The Dutch Old Testament scholar of this period who perhaps came closest to the ideal was, in our opinion, B. D. Eerdmans. Some may dispute this. Plainly enough, Eerdmans's criticism had deep roots in his theology, and doubtless this is the case with every biblical scholar. Nevertheless, it is clear that Eerdmans's drastic challenge to the accepted modernist criticism was motivated basically by scientific rather than by theological considerations. It was new light concerning the Bible's environment that led him to revise the Kuenen-Wellhausen theories of Israel's origins. If he failed to establish a new scheme to take its place, this was partly because he in turn allowed a scientific dogma to lead him astray in his search for a better understanding of the sacred text.

1 See now G. C. Berkouwer's new book on the doctrine of Scripture, *De Heilige Schrift* (Kampen: J. H. Kok, 1966—).

As was stated at the beginning, it would have been ideal to have been able to give as much detailed and concentrated attention to New Testament criticism in Holland as we have given to Old Testament criticism. For the portrait to be complete, this is really needed. Within the limits of the present study it has not been feasible to attempt it, although we may perhaps hope to see someone else dig into the fascinating story of Dutch New Testament interpretation with sufficient thoroughness to produce the balanced and complete picture that we are looking for.

Since a choice has had to be made, we do not regret our concentration on Dutch Old Testament study. We have learned much from it. For pointing up the mutual influence of theology and exegesis on each other in this difficult but immensely creative period, our account of Old Testament criticism has been the more significant, we feel, because the factors in Old Testament criticism are more numerous and complex than those affecting New Testament criticism, and because the problem of the theological relevance of the Old Testament is far more difficult than that of the New Testament. In other words, we have attempted to learn the most where the difficulties have been the greatest.

We have said enough, at any rate, about radical New Testament criticism in The Netherlands to suggest some of the reason why it was less successful than its Old Testament counterpart. The theories of Loman and van Manen had little lasting effect, while the theories of Kuenen had an influence that was widespread and enduring. There can be little question but that Kuenen had a superior genius and power of persuasion, but there is something more to this difference. His success shows the importance of constant dialogue within the scholarly world at large. This Kuenen, for one, never lost sight of. For, while Dutch New Testament criticism went its own way, following its scientific fads while taking leave of any balanced sense of historical actuality, Kuenen and his better associates continued to work in close collaboration with the foremost Old Testament critics abroad, overcoming as much as possible the barrier of language that locked so much of their productivity within their own little circle.

The greatest lesson that should have emerged from our study is that the integrity of the biblical text is the supreme prerequisite to theological progress – and to scientific progress as well (for the two go hand in hand). Scholars and theologians must learn to allow the biblical text to speak for itself, to understand it on its own terms. This is not to say that the Bible may be the only factor in shaping our theology, far from it. As men of the twentieth century, we cannot remain simply with the Bible; not even the ancient Hebrews or the early Christians did that, for the Bible represented only one facet of the religion they practised. Another factor therefore, equally though perhaps not so ultimately important, is what we can learn about the nature of human existence and about the natural world in which we live through scientific study and philosophical reflection. Each must play its proper role, yet we must emphasize and re-emphasize the need to understand the Bible independently from church tradition and independently from every scientific fad and dogma. If we are to understand it truly, it must be in accordance with all that it shows and claims itself to be: a book emerging out of a living historical situation, expressed in antique terms and figures, yet bearing witness to eternal realities and bringing a transcendent message to enlighten mankind in its earthly journey.

Appendix

I.   Professors of Hebrew and Old Testament
            in the Dutch universities since
         1850

THE STATE UNIVERSITY OF LEIDEN (FOUNDED 1575)

Faculty of Theology

Abraham KUENEN, 1852–91.   Extraordinary prof. in NT exegesis, history of the books of the OT; 1855 ordinary prof., with same subjects plus others; after 1877 also OT exegesis

Willem Hendrik KOSTERS, 1892–97. History of Israel's religion, Israel's literature, OT exegesis

Bernardus Dirk EERDMANS, 1898–1938. Same as predecessor

Pieter Arie Hendrik DE BOER, 1938–1978. Same as predecessor

Faculty of Letters and Philosophy

Antonie RUTGERS, 1837–75. Extraordinary prof. in Hebrew, Hebrew antiquities, OT exegesis, Sanskrit

Theodor Willem Johannes JUYNBOLL, 1845–61. Oriental languages

Henricus OORT, 1875–1907.   Hebrew, Israelite antiquities, OT exegesis. After 1877 the last was transferred to the theological faculty under Kuenen.

Gerrit WILDEBOER, 1907–12. Hebrew, Israelite antiquities

Arent Jan WENSINCK, 1912–39. Originally same subjects as predecessor; 1914–27 temporarily appointed to theological faculty to teach Israelite literature and OT exegesis during Prof. Eerdmans' inactivity; after 1927, only Arabic

Gerard Jacob THIERRY, 1913–50.   Extraordinary prof. in Akkadian 1913; ordinary prof. 1918; since 1927 Hebrew, Hebrew literature, Israelite antiquities

THE STATE UNIVERSITY OF GRONINGEN (FOUNDED 1615)

Faculty of Theology

Pieter HOFSTEDE DE GROOT, 1829-72. Among many other subjects he taught OT exegesis.

Daniel CHANTEPIE DE LA SAUSSAYE, 1872-73. Same as predecessor

Jozua Johannes Philippus VALETON (Sr.), 1845-84. Hebrew antiquities, Hebrew grammar, comparative Semitics, Old Testament; after 1877 he taught Israelite literature, OT exegesis, history of Israel's religion.

Gerrit WILDEBOER, 1884-1907. Same as Valeton after 1877; departed for Leiden 1907

Louis Hendrik Karel BLEEKER, 1907-41. Same as predecessor

Theodorus Christiaan VRIEZEN, 1941-56. Same as predecessor; departed for Utrecht 1956

Faculty of Letters and Philosophy

Frederik Jacob VAN DEN HAM, 1877-1912. Hebrew language and literature, Israelite antiquities

Franz Marius Theodor DE LIAGRE BÖHL, 1913-27. Same as predecessor; departed for Leiden in 1927 to teach Akkadian

Johannes DE GROOT, 1928-36. Same as predecessor; departed for Utrecht 1936; his chair discontinued by law until 1948

Johannes Hendrik HOSPERS, 1948- . Semitic languages and literature, archaeology of the Near East

THE STATE UNIVERSITY OF UTRECHT (FOUNDED 1636)

Faculty of Theology

Jozua Jan Philippus VALETON, Jr., 1877-1912. Israel's literature, OT exegesis, history of Israel's religion

Arie NOORDTZIJ, 1912-36. Same as predecessor

Johannes DE GROOT, 1936-42. Hebrew language and literature, OT exegesis, history of Israel's religion, Israelite antiquities

Albertus Hendrik EDELKOORT, 1936–42. Same as predecessor; after 1947 Hebrew language and Israelite antiquities transferred to Letters and Philosophy

Theodorus Christiaan VRIEZEN, 1956– . Same as predecessor

Faculty of Letters and Philosophy

Hendrik Christiaan MILLIES, 1856–68. Oriental languages and other subjects

Pieter DE JONG, 1868–90. Same as predecessor; after 1876, Hebrew language and Israelite antiquities

Martinus Theodorus HOUTSMA, 1890–1917. Same as predecessor

Theodor Willem JUYNBOLL, 1917–36. Same as predecessor; after retirement in 1936 his chair was discontinued by law and the subjects were handled by the Faculty of Theology until 1947.

Alexander Reinard HULST, 1947– . Hebrew language and Israelite antiquities; Babylonian/Assyrian

ATHENAEUM ILLUSTRE (FOUNDED 1632), IN 1877 THE (MUNICIPAL) UNIVERSITY OF AMSTERDAM

Pieter Johannes VETH, 1842–64. Oriental languages, philosophy, and other subjects; departed to Indische Richting at Leiden 1864

Jan Pieter Nicolaas LAND, 1864–72. Same as predecessor; departed for Leiden 1872

Henricus OORT, 1872–75. Same as predecessor; departed for Leiden 1875

Faculty of Theology

Jacob Gijsbert DE HOOP SCHEPPER, 1876–90. Temporary appointment 1876; permanent appointment 1877. Old Christian literature and OT exegesis; after 1890 all OT subjects transferred to Faculty of Letters and Philosophy until 1914

Juda Lion PALACHE, 1925–41 (both faculties). Same as predecessor

156

Albertus Willem GROENMAN, 1942–45 (temporary appointment). Same as predecessor

Martinus Adrianus BEEK, 1950– . Same as predecessor

Faculty of Letters and Philosophy

Jan Carel MATTHES, 1877–1906. Hebrew language and literature, Semitics, Israelite antiquities, history of Israel's religion

Hendrik Jan ELHORST, 1906–24. Same as predecessor; after 1914, also member of Faculty of Theology

FREE (CALVINISTIC) UNIVERSITY OF AMSTERDAM (FOUNDED 1880)

Faculty of Theology

Phillipus Jacobus HOEDEMAKER, 1885–87

Frederik Lodewijk RUTGERS, 1887–1907

Gerhard Charles AALDERS, 1920–50. OT exegesis and canonics; history of the revelation of the OT; OT hermeneutics

Nicolaas Herman RIDDERBOS, 1950– . Same as predecessor

Faculty of Letters and Philosophy

F. W. J. DILLOO, 1880–85

Cornelis VAN GELDEREN, 1905–45. Lector in Semitics 1904; prof. 1905; also OT subjects 1907–20

Willem Hendrik GISPEN, 1945– . Same as predecessor; extraordinary prof. Faculty of Theology

ROMAN CATHOLIC UNIVERSITY OF NIJMEGEN (FOUNDED 1923)

Paul HEINISCH, 1923–45

Bernardus Johannes ALFRINK, 1945–51

Johannes VAN DER PLOEG, 1951–

II. Doctoral dissertations in subjects relating to the Old Testament following 1850

Leiden

Abraham KUENEN, Specimin theologicum continens Geneseos libri capita xxxiv priora ex Arab. Pentateuchi Samaritani versione nunc prius edita cum prolegomenis, 1851 (Juynboll)

Pieter DE JONG, Disquisatio de Psalmis Maccabaicis, 1857

Jan Pieter Nicolaas LAND, Disputatio de carmine Jacobi, Gen.xlix, 1857

Jan Carel MATTHES, Dissertatio historico-critico de pseudoprophetismo Hebraeorum, 1959 (Scholten)

Hendrik OORT, Disputatio de pericope Num. xxii:2-xxiv historiam bileami continenta, 1860 (Scholten, Kuenen)

Isaac HOOYKAAS, Geschiedenis der beoefening van de wijsheid onder de Hebreën, 1862 (Kuenen)

Willem Hendrik KOSTERS, De historie beschouwing van de Deuteronomist met de berichten in Genesis-Numeri vergeleken, 1868 Kuenen)

Adam VAN DOORNINCK, Bijdrage tot de tekstkritiek van Richteren 1-16, 1879

Bernardus Dirk EERDMANS, Melekdienst en vereering van hemellichamen in Israëls Assyrische periode, 1891 (Tiele)

Arie NOORDTZIJ, Het Hebreeuwsche voorsetsel 'el, 1896

Kors Frederik SPARNAAIJ, De toekomstverwachtingen van Jeremia, 1902 (Eerdmans)

Albertus Willem GROENMAN, Het vasten vij Israël. Een vergelijkende onderzoek, 1906

Willem Dirk VAN WYNGAARDEN, De sociale positie van de vrouw bij Israël in den vóór en na-exilischen tijd, 1919 (Eerdmans)

Martinus Adrianus BEEK, Das Danielbuch. Sein historischer Hintergrund und seine literarische Entwicklung. Versuch eines Beitrage zur Lösung des Problems, 1935 (Eerdmans)

Pieter Arie Hendrik DE BOER, Research into the Text of I Samuel

1-16. A Contribution to the Study of the Books of Samuel, 1938
(Eerdmans)

Jacobus SCHONEVELD, De oorsprong van het Bijbelsche zondvloedverhaal, 1938 (Eerdmans)

Hendrik Antonie BRONGERS, De scheppingstradities bij de profeten, 1945 (de Boer)

Taeke JANSMA, Inquiry into the Hebrew Text and the Ancient Ver-
sions of Zecharia 9-14, 1947

Isaac Leo SEELIGMANN, The Septuagintal Version of Isaiah. A
Discussion of its Problems, 1948

Lambertus Arie SNIJDERS, The Meaning of zar in the Old Testament, 1953

Hendricus Jacobus FRANKEN, The mystical Communion with Jhwh in
the Book of Psalms, 1954 (de Boer)

Jacob HOFTIJZER, Die Verheissungen an die drei Erzväter, 1956
(de Boer)

Groningen

Jan Lambert DE BOER, Dissertatio theologico de libri II Samuelis
caput vii, vaticiniorum Messianorum fonte, 1858 (de Groot, Valeton Sr.)

J. Z. SCHUURMANS STEKHOVEN, De Alexandrijnsche vertaling van het
Dodekapropheton, 1887 (Wildeboer, van den Ham)

Louis Adriën BÄHLER, De Messiaansche heilsverwachting en het
Israëlietische koningschap, 1893 (Wildeboer)

Louis Hendrik Karel BLEEKER, Jeremia's profetieën tegen de volkeren, 1894 (Wildeboer)

Willem SWART, De invloed van den Griekschen geest op de boeken
Spreuken, Prediker, Job, 1908 (Wildeboer)

Jelte SWART, De theologie van Kronieken. Een bijdrage tot de
studie der Bijbelsche godgeleerdheid, 1911 (Bleeker, van den
Ham)

Johannes DE GROOT, Palestijnsche masseben (opgerichte stenen),
1913 (Bleeker, van den Ham)

Dirk KLEIN WASSINK, Persoonlijke religie in Israël (tot op

Jeremia), 1918 (Bleeker)

Alexander Reinard HULST, Het karakter van den cultus in Deuter-onomium, 1938 (Bleeker)

Cornelis Theodorus NIEMEYER, Het probleem van de rangschikking der Psalmen, 1950 (Vriezen, Hospers)

Egge Simon MULDER, Die teologie van die Jesaja-Apokalipse Jesaja 24-27, 1954

Barend Jacobus VAN DER MERWE, Pentateuch-tradities in de prediking van Deuterojesaja, 1956 (Vriezen)

Utrecht

Louis DE GEER, De oraculo in Moabitis, quod occurit Jesaiae caput xv et xvi, 1855

Frederik Jacob VAN DEN HAM, De Psalmen met historische opschriften, 1871 (Doedes)

Jozua Jan Philippus VALETON, Jr., Jesaja volgens zijne algemeen als echt erkende schriften, 1871

Pieter Gerrit DATEMA, De Dekaloog, 1876 (van Oosterzee)

Johannes Theodorus DE VISSER, De daemonologie van het Oude Testament, 1880 (Valeton)

Johannes Hermanus GUNNING, JHzn, De goddelijke vergelding, hoofdzakelijk volgens Exodus 20:5, 6, en Ezechiël 18:20, 1881 (Valeton)

Hendrik Huibert MUELENBELT, De prediking van den profeet Eze-chiël, 1888

Abraham VAN DER FLIER GJzn, Deuteronomium 33. Een exegetisch-historische studie, 1895 (Valeton)

Gerard SMIT, De profetie van Habakuk, 1900 (Valeton)

Hendrik Evert Gijsbert VAN DER MEENE, Eene bijbelsch-theologische studie over barmhartigheid, 1903

Theodore Leopold Willem VAN RAVESTEIJN, De eenheid der eschatologische voorstellingen in het boek Jesaja, 1910 (Valeton)

Theodurus Christiaan VRIEZEN, Onderzoek naar de paradijsvoorstellingen bij de oude Semietische volken, 1937 (Obbink)

Johannes Hendrik HOSPERS, De numeruswisseling in het boek Deuteonomium, 1947 (Edelkoort)

Cornelis BROUWER, Wachter en herder, 1949

Hendrik BOUT, Het zondebesef in het Boek der Psalmen, 1952

Klarinus ROUBOS, Profetie en cultus in Israël. Achtergrond en betekenis van enige profetische uitspraken inzake de cultus. Een exegetische studie, 1956

Antonie Aart KOOLHAAS, Theocratie en monarchie bij Israël, 1957 (Edelkoort, Hulst)

Louis Alexis Frederic LE MAT, Textual Criticism and Exegesis of Psalm 36. A Contribution to the Study of the Hebrew Book of Psalms, 1957 (Hulst)

(Municipal) University, Amsterdam

Johannes Wilhelm PONT, Psalm 68. Een exegetisch-kritische studie, 1887

Jan Willem VAN LENNEP, De zeventig jaarweken van Daniël (hoofd-stuk 9:24-27): exegetisch-chronologische studie, 1888

Hendrik Jan ELHORST, De profetie van Micha, 1891 (Matthes)

Abraham Kornelis KUIPER, Zacharja 9-14. Eene exegetisch-criti-sche studie, 1894 (Matthes)

Harm BOUWMAN, Het begrip gerechtigheid in het Oude Testament, 1899

Tietse Pieter SEVENSMA, De ark Gods, het oud-israëlietische heiligdom, 1908 (Elhorst)

Free University, Amsterdam

Johannes Cornelis DE MOOR, De profeet Maleachi. Bijzondere canoniek en exegese, 1903 (Rutgers, van Gelderen)

Willem Albertus VAN ES, De eigendom in den Pentateuch, 1909 (Rutgers, van Gelderen)

Gerhard Charles AALDERS, De valsche profetie in Israël, 1911 (Rutgers, van Gelderen)

Hendrik JANSEN, Het verband van zonde en dood in het Oude Testament, 1911 (Bavinck, van Gelderen)

Dirk Jan VAN KATWIJK, De prophetie van Habakkuk, 1912 (van

Gelderen)

Phillipus Christoforus SNIJMAN, De profetie van Zefanja, 1913

Nicolaas Dirk VAN LEEUWEN, Het Bijbelsch-Akkadisch-Schumerisch zondvloedverhaal, 1920 (van Gelderen)

Cornelis Jakobus GOSLINGA, Nahums godssprak tegen Nineve, 1923

Willem Hendrik GISPEN, Indirecte gegevens voor het bestaan van den Pentateuch in de Psalmen?, 1928

Jan SCHELHAAS Hzn, De Messiaansche profetie in de tijd vóór Israëls volksbestaan, 1931 (Aalders)

Hendrik BERGEMA, De Boom des Levens in Schrift en historie. Bijdrage tot een onderzoek naar de verhouding van Schrifopenbaring en traditie betreffende den Boom des Levens, binnen het kader der Oud-Testamentische wetenschap, 1938 (Aalders)

Aart DE BONDT, Wat leert het Oude Testament aangaande het leven na dit leven?, 1938 (Aalders)

Jan Leunis KOOLE, De overname van het Oude Testament door de Christelijke kerk, 1938

Jan Hendrik KROEZE, Genesis veertien. Een exegetisch-historische studie, 1938 (van Gelderen)

Nicolaas Herman RIDDERBOS, De "werkers der ongerechtigheid" in de individuele Psalmen. Een beoordeling van Mowinckels opvatting, 1939 (Aalders)

Jakobus DE KONING, Studiën over de El-Amarnabrieven en het Oude Testament inzonderheid uit historisch oogpunt, 1940 (Aalders)

Johannes Hendrik BECKER, Het begrip "nefesj" in het Oude Testament, 1942 (van Gelderen)

Berend Jakob OOSTERHOFF, De vreze des Heren in het Oude Testament, 1949

Johannes BLAUW, Goden en mensen: plaats en betekenis van de heidenen in de Heilige Schrift, 1950 (Bavinck)

Frederik Hendrik VON MEYENFELDT, Het hart (LEB, LEBAB) in het Oude Testament, 1950 (Gispen)

Jan Gerrit AALDERS, Gog en Magog in Ezechiël, 1951

Jan Christiaan Cornelis VAN DORSSEN, De derivata van de stam 'aman in het Hebreeuwsch van het Oude Testament, 1951 (Gispen)

Karel DRONKERT, De Molochdienst in het Oude Testament, 1953

Nijmegen

Adrianus VAN DEN BORN, De symbolische handelingen der Oud-Testamentische profeten, 1935

Kampen Theologische Hogeschool

Lambert ZIELHUIS, Het offermaal in het heidendom en in de Heilige Schrift, 1951

Index

168

Anthony J. Blasi

MORAL CONFLICT AND CHRISTIAN RELIGION

American University Studies: Series VII (Theology and Religion). Vol. 35
ISBN 0-8204-0497-7   190 pages   hardback US $ 33.50*

*Recommended price – alterations reserved

This work takes up the problem of moral conflict, wherein a person must choose between two or more evils. The problem lies behind such issues as the defensive war, therapeutic abortion, and contraception. It becomes a religious question because, as the author argues, religion elicits the same kind of openness to values as is needed for addressing moral dilemmas. After culling insights out of the history of Christian ethics, Blasi presents phenomenologies of both moral decision making and religion, and uses the results to address the variety of moral dilemmas.

«This is an original and enlightening study of a timely and important subject.» (Leslie Dewart, St. Michael's College, University of Toronto)

«Conflict situations will always exist. And therefore so will the need for thoughtful precision in dealing with them. Blasi's book is a significant contribution to that precision.» (Richard A. McCormick, S. J., University of Notre Dame)

«. . . the work represents a very original and inspiring contribution to moral inquiry . . .» (Béla Somfai, Regis College).

PETER LANG PUBLISHING, INC.
62 West 45th Street
USA – New York, NY 10036

James J. McCartney

UNBORN PERSONS
Pope John Paul II and the Abortion Debate

American University Studies: Series VII (Theology and Religion). Vol. 21
ISBN 0-8204-0349-0   176 pages   hardback US $ 28.95*

*Recommended price – alterations reserved

Karol Wojtyla (Pope John Paul II) was a professor of anthropology and ethics at the Catholic University of Lublin, Poland long before he was elected Pope. During this time, his interests centered around the concept of personhood and its many implications in the epistemological, metaphysical and ethical spheres. In this book, after considering the many philosophical and theological influences that helped to form his tought, his notion of personhood is discussed with reference to the status of unborn persons, that is of embryological and fetal life. His approach to personhood is then contrasted and compared with other contemporary notions in an effort to understand more clearly the status of life before birth.

Contents: Theological and Philosophical Influences on Wojtyla's Notion of «Person» – A Dialogue between Wojtyla and Others on Whether or Not the Living Human Embryo is a Person.

«To relate Wojtyla's (Pope John Paul II's) more general philosophical and theological thought to his notion of personhood (its beginning, constitutive elements, etc.) is a valuable piece of research. It is what James J. McCartney has done in this careful and well-crafted study.»
(Reverend Richard A. McCormick, S. J.)

PETER LANG PUBLISHING, INC.
62 West 45th Street
USA – New York, NY 10036

PHILIP MELANCHTHON
A MELANCHTHON READER

American University Studies: Series VII (Theology and Religion). Vol. 41
ISBN 0-8204-0563-9   304 pages   hardback US $ 45.00*

*Recommended price – alterations reserved

This volume contains nineteen texts by the reformer Philip Melanchthon (1497–1560), most of them translated for the first time in English. Melanchthon's career as humanist and educator is illustrated by six academic lectures. The *Augsburg Confession* of 1530 and occasional works on various topics reveal his efforts as a formulator and apologist for Lutheranism. His humanistic and theological interests combine in three works on ethics theological anthropology. An introduction outlines his life and the place of his thought in the reformation.

Contents: Introduction – On Correcting the Studies of Youth – In Praise of the New School – On Philosophy – Two Orations on Aristotle – Eulogy for Luther – the Augsburg Confession – Three Statements on the Eucharist – Three Prefaces – Letter to Henry VIII – Thoughts on the Interim – Refutation of Servetus and the Anabaptists – Commentary on Aristotle's Ethics, Bk. 1 – Summary of Ethics – On the Soul.

«This substantial collection of translated texts from Melanchthon, reformer and humanist, fills several real scholarly needs. Without slighting the work of Melanchthon the modest and masterly reformulator of dogma or Melanchthon the skilful aoplogist, Keen's collection includes an especially rich sampling of noteworthy, little-known works by Melanchthon the humanist and moralist. Keen's expansive and richly detailed introduction helps to show how Melanchthon the brilliant Erasmian could go on to distinguish himself as a judicious champion of Lutheran Reform; Northern Renaissance scholars as well as historians of Protestant thought should find in this book to provoke and instuct them for some years to come.» (Daniel Kinney, University of Virginia)

PETER LANG PUBLISHING, INC.
62 West 45th Street
USA – New York, NY 10036